WHEN TO RETIRE: ISSUES IN WORKING AND SAVING FOR A SECURE RETIREMENT

RETIREMENT ISSUES, PLANS AND LIFESTYLES

Additional books in this series can be found on Nova's website at:

https://www.novapublishers.com/catalog/index.php?cPath=23_29&seriesp =Retirement+Issues%2C+Plans+and+Lifestyles

Additional E books in this series can be found on Nova's website at:

https://www.novapublishers.com/catalog/index.php?cPath=23_29&seriespe =Retirement+Issues%2C+Plans+and+Lifestyles

RETIREMENT ISSUES, PLANS AND LIFESTYLES

WHEN TO RETIRE: ISSUES IN WORKING AND SAVING FOR A SECURE RETIREMENT

MAURICE R. DAVENWORTH
EDITOR

Nova Science Publishers, Inc.

New York

NOTICE TO THE READER

The Publisher has taken reasonable care in the preparation of this book, but makes no expressed or implied warranty of any kind and assumes no responsibility for any errors or omissions. No liability is assumed for incidental or consequential damages in connection with or arising out of information contained in this book. The Publisher shall not be liable for any special, consequential, or exemplary damages resulting, in whole or in part, from the readers' use of, or reliance upon, this material. Any parts of this book based on government reports are so indicated and copyright is claimed for those parts to the extent applicable to compilations of such works.

Independent verification should be sought for any data, advice or recommendations contained in this book. In addition, no responsibility is assumed by the publisher for any injury and/or damage to persons or property arising from any methods, products, instructions, ideas or otherwise contained in this publication.

This publication is designed to provide accurate and authoritative information with regard to the subject matter covered herein. It is sold with the clear understanding that the Publisher is not engaged in rendering legal or any other professional services. If legal or any other expert assistance is required, the services of a competent person should be sought. FROM A DECLARATION OF PARTICIPANTS JOINTLY ADOPTED BY A COMMITTEE OF THE AMERICAN BAR ASSOCIATION AND A COMMITTEE OF PUBLISHERS.

LIBRARY OF CONGRESS CATALOGING-IN-PUBLICATION DATA

Available Upon Request

ISBN : 978-1-60876-982-7

Published by Nova Science Publishers, Inc. ✦ *New York*

CONTENTS

PREFACE

Retirement in America is still possible but becoming less a widespread reality given the economic crisis strangling the country.This new book looks at the factors which can come into play if retirement is contemplated.

Chapter 1 - Over the past 25 years, defined contribution (DC) plans—including 401(k) plans—have become the most prevalent form of employer-sponsored retirement plan in the United States. The majority of assets held in these plans are invested in stocks and stock mutual funds, and the decline in the major stock market indices in 2008 greatly reduced the value of many families' retirement savings. The effect of stock market volatility on families' retirement savings is just one issue of concern to Congress with respect to defined contribution retirement plans.

This report describes seven major policy issues with respect to defined contribution plans:

1. *Access to employer-sponsored retirement plans.* In 2007, only 61% of employees in the private sector were offered a retirement plan of any kind at work. Fifty-five percent were offered a DC plan. Only 45% of workers at establishments with fewer than 100 employees were offered a retirement plan of any kind in 2007. Forty-two percent were offered a defined contribution plan.

2. *Participation in employer-sponsored plans.* Between 20% and 25% of workers whose employer offers a DC plan do not participate. Workers under age 35 are less likely than older workers to participate.

3. *Contribution rates.* On average, participants in DC plans contributed 6% of pay to the plan in 2007. The median contribution by household heads who participated in a DC plan in 2007 was $3,360. This was just 22% of the maximum allowable contribution of $15,500 in that year.

4. *Investment choices.* At year-end 2007, 78% of all DC plan assets were invested in stocks and stock mutual funds. This ratio varied little by age, indicating that many workers nearing retirement were heavily invested in stocks and risked substantial losses in a market downturn like that in 2008. Investment education and target date funds could help workers make better investment decisions.

5. *Fee disclosure.* Retirement plans contract with service providers to provide investment management, record-keeping, and other services. There can be many service providers, each charging a fee that is ultimately paid by participants in 401(k) plans. The arrangements through which service providers are compensated can be very complicated and fees are often not clearly disclosed.

6. *Leakage from retirement savings.* Pre-retirement withdrawals from retirement accounts are sometimes called "leakages." Current law represents a compromise between limiting leakages from retirement accounts and allowing people to have access to their retirement funds in times of great need. In general, borrowing from a 401(k) plan poses less risk to retirement security than a withdrawal. Pre-retirement withdrawals can have adverse long-term effects on retirement income.

7. *Converting retirement savings into income.* Retirees face many financial risks, including living longer than they expected, investment losses, inflation, and possible large expenses for medical care and long-term care. Annuities can protect retirees from some of these risks, but few retirees purchase them. Developing polices that motivate retirees to convert assets into a reliable source of income will be a continuing challenge for Congress and other policymakers.

Chapter 2 - While many factors influence workers' decisions to retire, Social Security, Medicare, and pension laws also play a role, offering incentives to retire earlier and later. Identifying these incentives and how workers respond can help policy makers address the demographic challenges facing the nation.

GAO assessed (1) the incentives federal policies provide about when to retire, (2) recent retirement patterns and whether there is evidence that changes in Social Security requirements have resulted in later retirements, and (3) whether tax-favored private retiree health insurance and pension benefits influence when people retire. GAO analyzed retirement age laws and SSA data and conducted statistical analysis of Health and Retirement Study data. Under the Comptroller General's authority, GAO has prepared this report on its own initiative.

Chapter 3 - The Economic Growth and Tax Relief Reconciliation Act of 2001 (P.L. 107-16) authorized a non-refundable tax credit of up to $1,000 for eligible individuals who contribute to an IRA or an employer-sponsored retirement plan. The credit was first available in 2002, and as enacted in 2001, it would have expired after the 2006 tax year. The Pension Protection Act of 2006 (P.L. 109-280) made the retirement savings tax credit permanent. Beginning in 2007, the eligible income brackets were indexed to inflation. The maximum credit is 50% of retirement contributions up to $2,000. The credit can reduce the amount of taxes owed, but the tax credit itself is non-refundable. The maximum credit is the lesser of $1,000 or the tax that the individual would have owed without the credit. Eligibility is based on the taxpayer's adjusted gross income. Taxpayers under age 18 or who are full-time students are not eligible for the credit.

The Economic Growth and Tax Relief Reconciliation Act of 2001 (P.L. 107-16) authorized a tax credit to encourage low- and moderate-income families and individuals to save for retirement. Eligible taxpayers who contribute to an individual retirement account (IRA) or to an employer-sponsored plan that is qualified under §401, §403 or §457 of the tax code can receive a non-refundable tax credit of up to $1,000. This credit is in addition to the tax deduction for contributing to a traditional IRA or to an employer- sponsored retirement plan. In determining the amount of the credit, neither the amount of any refundable tax credits for which the taxpayer is eligible nor the adoption credit are taken into consideration. The retirement savings credit was first available in 2002, and as enacted in 2001, it would have expired after the 2006 tax year. Section 812 of the Pension Protection Act of 2006 (PPA, P.L. 109-280) made the retirement savings tax credit permanent. Section 833 of the PPA provided that for years after 2006, the eligible income brackets will be indexed to inflation in increments of $500.

Chapter 4 - In December of 2008, Congress unanimously enacted the Worker, Retiree, and Employer Recovery Act of 2008 (WRERA) (P.L. 110-455), which makes several technical corrections to the Pension Protection Act of 2006 (P.L. 109-280) and contains provisions designed to help pension plans and plan participants weather the current economic downturn. This report highlights the provisions of WRERA relating to the economic crisis, such as the temporary waiver of required minimum distributions and provisions that temporarily relax certain pension plan funding requirements. This report also discusses certain technical corrections to the Pension Protection Act made by WRERA, and certain other notable provisions of the Act affecting retirement plans and benefits.

There has been a great deal of concern over the effect of the current economic downturn on retirement plans. One company recently reported that at the end of 2008, the "chaos" in the financial markets led to a $409 billion deficit in defined benefit pension plan funding for the plans of S&P 1500 companies. The report indicated that this deficit will negatively affect corporate earnings in 2009. Due in part to the large investment losses in pension plans and other retirement accounts, in December of 2008, Congress unanimously enacted H.R. 7327, the Worker, Retiree, and Employer Recovery Act of 2008 ("WRERA" or "the Act"). While several provisions of WRERA make technical corrections to the Pension Protection Act of 2006 ("PPA"), the Act also provides some temporary relief from certain requirements that may be difficult for pension plans to meet due to current economic conditions. This report provides an overview of some of the key provisions of WRERA, in particular, the provisions relating to the funding of single and multiemployer plans, the temporary waiver for required minimum distributions, as well as certain technical corrections and other provisions that affect the two primary types of pension plans, defined benefit and defined contribution plans, as well as individual retirement accounts and annuities (IRAs).

Chapter 5 - Longer life spans and other demographic changes are making it increasingly expensive to finance an adequate retirement income. One way to reduce this burden is for older workers to participate longer in the workforce. Policy makers should consider ways to remove barriers to continued work at older ages with the objective of improving the economic security of American workers in their retirement years.

Over the past 50 years, Americans have enjoyed steadily increasing life spans, and they have also been retiring earlier. The combined effect of these two trends is that the average American worker today can now be expected to spend 50 percent more time in retirement than a similar worker 50 years ago. Experts project life spans will continue to increase.

As a result, the amount of income that must be put aside to fund workers' retirement must grow. Funding retirement is becoming more expensive for individual workers and for our public retirement systems, and the expense is growing to the point where it is putting strains on the ability of workers and society to bear it. Under our retirement systems that depend on workers and/or firms putting aside earnings during the working years to fund retirement income, the period of accumulation is getting shorter while the payout period is getting longer. Under our Social Security system, which uses the contributions of today's workers to pay today's retirees, the declining number of workers relative to retirees raises costs directly.

Although the need to set aside income has grown, many workers have not been accumulating enough savings in their personal or retirement accounts. Rapidly rising health care costs also consume a growing share of earnings and retirement incomes. Experts project these costs will continue to rise faster than national income. Social Security benefits, the major source of income in retirement for most workers, are on track to replace a smaller share of pre-retirement income (about 4 percent less) as the normal retirement age rises to 67, owing to reforms enacted in 1983. Most individuals choose to receive the earliest yet smallest Social Security benefit available to them. The long-term financing imbalances in Social Security remain an unresolved issue.

For some share of our population, economic security in retirement is at risk. The problem is greater for widows and single women, who on average live longer than men, and tend to accumulate fewer savings and earn lower Social Security benefits.

In the past, this Advisory Board has recommended that policy makers address the long-term financial health of our Social Security system, and we have drawn attention to the predictable but growing threats to retirement security. In this report, the Board adds its voice to a growing consensus that one effective way to shore up retirement security in the future is to find ways to extend individual working careers when possible.

Continuing to work and/or postponing retirement benefits can significantly increase the resources available to individuals in retirement. Every additional year spent working provides income, reduces the need to draw down one's assets, provides an additional opportunity to save, and allows already accumulated savings to grow. This can be especially important for those approaching retirement with inadequate savings and for those who will experience longer than average lifetimes.

More Americans choose to begin receiving Social Security benefits at the earliest age of eligibility than at any other age. But for each year they delay taking benefits, they can significantly increase their monthly benefit for the rest of their lives. This choice can be critical for economic security at older ages.

At the same time, delaying retirement also has the potential to enhance economic security for those covered by employer-sponsored retirement plans. In most traditional defined benefit plans and in cash balance plans today, benefit accruals continue for many workers at advanced ages. In defined contribution plans, extending work has two beneficial effects: (1) it extends the period over which contributions are made; and (2) it shortens the period where accumulated savings are relied on for retirement income.

Having a greater share of older Americans continuing to work will also provide additional tax revenue to improve the financial condition of the Social Security system as well as state and federal government budgets. Extending individual working lives should ameliorate the projected decline in national labor force growth and add to national income.

We recommend that older workers should be given information about the personal advantages of remaining employed for a longer period of their lifetimes to the extent they are able. We also recommend that individuals be encouraged strongly to consider under what circumstances it would be advantageous for them to delay the age they choose to begin receiving Social Security benefits.

We recommend that the Social Security Administration continue to provide the most accurate and objective information possible to help the public make appropriate choices about when to claim benefits. The agency should review all communication with the public to ensure it is not inadvertently encouraging people to claim at the earliest date possible.

There are already signs that older workers are beginning to reverse a decades-long trend toward earlier retirement, perhaps responding to the pressures described above. In addition, fewer people are applying for Social Security benefits at the earliest possible age. Some recent survey data suggest that those nearing the usual retirement ages desire and intend to work to older ages.

A substantial share of older Americans, however, will not be able to work longer because of ill health, disability, or a lack of employment opportunities. And even for those who wish to work longer, important barriers to remaining employed still exist. Our current patchwork of laws and regulations should be changed to do a better job of helping those who can work a few years longer and secure a better standard of living in retirement.

We believe there are opportunities to reform policies and regulations that affect Social Security, public and private pensions, health care, and tax and labor laws that can assist workers to stay in the workforce longer and reward their efforts adequately.

We recommend that public policy should be geared toward removing barriers and improving incentives to continued employment at older age. A set of coordinated and coherent policies should encourage and support those who want to extend their working lives, while providing adequate support for those who are unable to do so.

We reiterate that our nation's systems of providing economic security to those who cannot work should be maintained and improved. Nothing in this report should be seen to contradict this strong belief.

Raising awareness of the benefits of longer working lives and supporting the choices of those who desire to do so will require more than just a more coherent set of policies:

We encourage employers to evaluate how older workers can continue to contribute in the workplace and, to the extent it is economically feasible, to adopt policies and practices that can accommodate a greater share of those who desire to extend their working lives. Older workers and their advocates, for their part, should consider the requirements they will have to meet so that continued employment benefits employer and employees alike.

In addition, individuals, institutions and public policies should recognize the importance of making lifelong investments that enhance a worker's ability to remain productive at older ages and adapt to the changing needs of the economy. Adequate preparation for retirement is a life-long endeavor.

In: When to Retire: Issues in Working and Saving for a Secure...   ISBN: 978-1-60876-982-7
Editor: Maurice R. Davenworth   © 2010 Nova Science Publishers, Inc.

Chapter 1

401(K) PLANS AND RETIREMENT SAVINGS: ISSUES FOR CONGRESS

Patrick Purcell and John J. Topoleski

SUMMARY

Over the past 25 years, defined contribution (DC) plans—including 401(k) plans—have become the most prevalent form of employer-sponsored retirement plan in the United States. The majority of assets held in these plans are invested in stocks and stock mutual funds, and the decline in the major stock market indices in 2008 greatly reduced the value of many families' retirement savings. The effect of stock market volatility on families' retirement savings is just one issue of concern to Congress with respect to defined contribution retirement plans.

This report describes seven major policy issues with respect to defined contribution plans:

1. *Access to employer-sponsored retirement plans.* In 2007, only 61% of employees in the private sector were offered a retirement plan of any kind at work. Fifty-five percent were offered a DC plan. Only 45% of workers at establishments with fewer than 100 employees were offered a retirement plan of any kind in 2007. Forty-two percent were offered a defined contribution plan.

2. *Participation in employer-sponsored plans.* Between 20% and 25% of workers whose employer offers a DC plan do not participate. Workers under age 35 are less likely than older workers to participate.

3. *Contribution rates.* On average, participants in DC plans contributed 6% of pay to the plan in 2007. The median contribution by household heads who participated in a

DC plan in 2007 was $3,360. This was just 22% of the maximum allowable contribution of $15,500 in that year.

4. *Investment choices.* At year-end 2007, 78% of all DC plan assets were invested in stocks and stock mutual funds. This ratio varied little by age, indicating that many workers nearing retirement were heavily invested in stocks and risked substantial losses in a market downturn like that in 2008. Investment education and target date funds could help workers make better investment decisions.

5. *Fee disclosure.* Retirement plans contract with service providers to provide investment management, record-keeping, and other services. There can be many service providers, each charging a fee that is ultimately paid by participants in 401(k) plans. The arrangements through which service providers are compensated can be very complicated and fees are often not clearly disclosed.

6. *Leakage from retirement savings.* Pre-retirement withdrawals from retirement accounts are sometimes called "leakages." Current law represents a compromise between limiting leakages from retirement accounts and allowing people to have access to their retirement funds in times of great need. In general, borrowing from a 401(k) plan poses less risk to retirement security than a withdrawal. Pre-retirement withdrawals can have adverse long-term effects on retirement income.

7. *Converting retirement savings into income.* Retirees face many financial risks, including living longer than they expected, investment losses, inflation, and possible large expenses for medical care and long-term care. Annuities can protect retirees from some of these risks, but few retirees purchase them. Developing polices that motivate retirees to convert assets into a reliable source of income will be a continuing challenge for Congress and other policymakers.

NEW CHALLENGES TO A SECURE RETIREMENT INCOME

Over the past 25 years, defined contribution (DC) plans have become the most prevalent form of employer-sponsored retirement plan in the United States. According to the Bureau of Labor Statistics (BLS), 51% of workers in the private sector participated in an employer-sponsored retirement plan of some kind in 2007. Only 20% of all private-sector workers were covered by traditional pensions—also called defined benefit or "DB" plans—whereas 43% participated in 40 1(k) plans and other DC plans.[1] Twelve percent of workers participated in both types of plan.[2]

One of the key distinctions between a defined benefit plan and a defined contribution plan is that in a DB plan, it is the employer who bears the investment risk. The employer must ensure that the pension plan has sufficient assets to pay the benefits promised to workers and their surviving dependents. In a DC plan, the worker bears the investment risk. The worker's account balance at retirement will depend on how much has been contributed to the plan over the years and on the performance of the assets in which the plan is invested. In a typical

401(k) plan, a worker must decide whether to participate, how much to contribute, how to invest the contributions, what to do with the account if he or she changes jobs, and how to take money out of the account after retiring.

The majority of assets held in DC plans are invested in stocks and stock mutual funds, and as a result, the decline in the major stock market indices in 2008 greatly reduced the value of many families' retirement savings.[3] According to the Federal Reserve Board, assets held in DC plans fell from $3.73 trillion at year-end 2007 to $2.66 trillion at year-end 2008, a decline of 28.7%.[4] The decline would have been even greater if not for ongoing contributions to the plans by workers and employers.

The effect of stock market volatility on families' retirement savings is just one issue of concern to Congress with respect to DC plans. Other issues that have received attention in hearings and through proposed legislation include increasing access to employer-sponsored plans, raising participation and contribution rates, helping participants make better investment choices, requiring clearer disclosure of fees charged to plan participants, preserving retirement savings when workers face economic hardship or change jobs, and promoting life annuities as a source of retirement income.

This CRS report describes these seven major policy issues with respect to DC plans:

- access to employer-sponsored retirement plans,
- participation in employer-sponsored plans,
- contribution rates,
- investment choices,
- fee disclosure,
- leakage from retirement savings, and
- converting retirement savings into income.

Table 1. Participation in Employer-Sponsored Retirement Plans, 2003 and 2007 Private-Sector Workers; in Percentages

Establishment Size	2003	2007	2003	2007	2003	2007
	Offered any plan		Participated in any plan		Take-up rate	
100 or more workers	75	78	65	66	87	85
Under 100 workers	42	45	35	37	83	82
All Workers	57	61	49	51	86	84
	Offered a DB Plan		Participated in DB plan		Take-up rate	
100 or more workers	34	34	33	32	97	94
Under 100 workers	9	9	8	9	89	100
All Workers	20	21	20	20	100	95
	Offered a DC Plan		Participated in DC plan		Take-up rate	
100 or more workers	65	70	51	53	78	76
Under 100 workers	38	42	31	33	82	79
All Workers	51	55	40	43	78	78

Source: U.S. Department of Labor, Bureau of Labor Statistics, National Compensation Survey.

Notes: Data represent 102 million workers in 2003 and 108 million workers in 2007. The take-up rate is the percentage of workers offered a plan who participated in the plan. In 2007, for example, 55% of workers were offered a DC plan and 43% of workers participated in a DC plan. Therefore, the take-up rate was .43/.55 = .78.

ACCESS TO EMPLOYER-SPONSORED RETIREMENT PLANS

According to the National Compensation Survey (NCS), 61% of private-sector workers were employed at establishments that offered one or more retirement plans in 2007. Twenty-one percent worked for employers that offered a DB plan, 55% worked for employers that offered a DC plan, and 15% worked for employers that offered both types of plan.[5] Thus, almost 4 out of 10 workers in the private sector did not have the opportunity to participate in a retirement plan where they worked. Moreover, there is a substantial disparity in sponsorship of retirement plans between large employers and small employers. Workers at establishments with fewer than 100 employees are much less likely to have access to an employer-sponsored retirement plan than are workers at larger establishments. (See **Table 1**.) Policies that would increase the number of small employers that offer retirement plans could expand access to these plans to include millions more workers.

Plan Sponsorship by Small Employers

Surveys of households and employers illustrate the gap in retirement plan sponsorship between large and small employers. Data collected by the Bureau of the Census indicate that there were 75 million private-sector workers between the ages of 25 and 64 who were employed year-round, full-time in 2007. Thirty million of these workers, or 40%, worked for employers that did not sponsor a retirement plan of any kind. Of these 30 million workers, 19.1 million, or 64%, worked for firms with fewer than 100 employees.[6] Likewise, data from the Department of Labor's 2007 National Compensation Survey show that 78% of workers at establishments with 100 or more employees worked for employers that sponsored retirement plans in 2007, compared with just 45% of workers at establishments with fewer than 100 employees.

Although workers at small establishments are less likely to be offered a retirement plan, when one is offered, they are as likely as employees at larger businesses to participate in the plan. In 2007, for example, 70% of workers at establishments with 100 or more employees were offered a DC plan, and the take-up rate among those offered a DC plan was 76%. At establishments with fewer than 100 employees, 42% of workers were offered a DC plan, and the take-up rate among those offered a DC plan was 79%.[7]

Workers at firms with fewer than 100 employees comprised 44% of all private-sector workers in the United States in 2007. If employees at small firms had been offered DC plans at the same rate as employees of larger firms, an additional 11.4 million workers would have had the opportunity to participate in employer-sponsored retirement plans in 2007. If take-up rates among these employees had been the same as at firms that already offered DC plans, an additional 9.0 million workers would have participated in DC plans in 2007.[8]

Defined Contribution Plans for Small Employers

Qualified retirement plans, including 401(k) plans, must comply with the Employee Retirement Income Security Act (ERISA) and the Internal Revenue Code (IRC). Among the requirements for retirement plans to receive favorable tax treatment is that they are prohibited from discriminating in favor of highly-compensated employees (HCEs) in terms of contributions or benefits.[9] This assures that rank and file employees as well as owners and managers benefit from the tax breaks that Congress has granted to tax-qualified retirement plans. The nondiscrimination tests compare the participation rates and plan contributions for HCEs to those of other employees.[10] In a small firm, relatively modest changes in employee participation or contributions can make the difference between the plan passing or failing the nondiscrimination test. If the plan fails, some of the contributions made by HCEs must be returned to them and included in their taxable income for the year. A plan that fails the nondiscrimination test also can lose its tax-qualified status, but this penalty is applied only in rare circumstances.

To encourage more employers, especially small employers, to sponsor retirement plans, Congress has authorized several kinds of defined contribution plans that are exempt from some administrative requirements that otherwise would apply. In some cases, plans that adopt certain characteristics that favor rank-and-file workers are exempt from nondiscrimination testing.

"Safe-Harbor" 401(k) Plans

In 1996, Congress authorized a "safe-harbor" 401(k) plan that exempts the plan sponsor from the annual nondiscrimination tests in exchange for the employer agreeing to make contributions to the plan. In a safe-harbor 401(k), the employer must either contribute an amount equal to 3% of pay on behalf of each *eligible* employee or match the first 3% of salary deferrals of each *participating* employee on a dollar-for-dollar basis and match the next 2% of employee deferrals at 50 cents per dollar.[11] Any firm with one or more employees can establish a safe-harbor 401(k).

Savings Incentive Match Plans for Employees of Small Employers (SIMPLE)

The Small Business Job Protection Act of 1996 (P.L. 104-188) authorized the Savings Incentive Match Plan for Employees of Small Employers (SIMPLE). In exchange for mandatory employer contributions, the plan is exempt from the nondiscrimination tests. An employer that sponsors a SIMPLE must either contribute an amount equal to 2% of pay on behalf of every *eligible* employee or match 100% of the first 3% of each *participating* employee's contributions to the plan. The maximum allowable employee contribution to a SIMPLE is $11,500 in 2009. Participants aged 50 and older can make additional contributions of up to $2,500 to a SIMPLE plan. SIMPLE plans can be established only by employers with fewer than 100 employees that do not already have retirement plans.

Simplified Employee Pension (SEP)

In the Revenue Act of 1978 (P.L. 95-600), Congress authorized a defined contribution plan called the Simplified Employee Pension (SEP) for firms that do not already sponsor a retirement plan. Only the employer can make contributions to a SEP, and the employer can decide from year to year whether to contribute to the plan. Employer contributions must be made on behalf of all eligible employees, and the contributions must be the same percentage of pay for all eligible employees. Contributions cannot exceed an amount equal to 25% of pay up to a maximum of $49,000 in 2009 (indexed to inflation). Participants are fully and immediately vested in the employer's contributions to the plan. Any firm with one or more employees can establish a SEP.

Plan Sponsorship Remains Low Among Small Employers

Despite the availability of the SEP, SIMPLE, and safe-harbor 401(k), there has been relatively little growth in retirement plan sponsorship among small firms over the past 20 years. According to the Bureau of Labor Statistics, 36% of employees at small private-sector establishments participated in an employer-sponsored retirement plan of some kind in 1990.[12] By 2007, the participation rate in all types of retirement plans among employees at small private-sector establishments had increased by just one percentage point to 37%.[13]

One reason that small firms are less likely than large firms to offer retirement plans is that small employers are much more likely than large employers to go out of business in any given year. For example, over the six years from 2000 through 2005, an average of 10.2% of firms with fewer than 20 employees went out of business each year. Among firms with 20 to 99 employees, an average of 4.6% of firms went out of business annually, whereas among firms with 500 or more employees, an average of 2.3% of firms went out of business each year.[14] Because small firms face relatively greater uncertainty about their survival from year to year, their owners are less likely to offer a retirement plan to their employees.

Policy Issue: Automatic IRAs

Because small employers are less likely to sponsor retirement plans for their employees, policy analysts have continued to search for ways to help employees of these firms save for retirement. One proposal that has received considerable attention is to promote the adoption of payroll deduction IRAs by employers who do not sponsor retirement plans. Some such proposals would require employers above a certain size who do not sponsor a retirement plan to allow employees to contribute to an IRA through payroll deduction.[15]

Payroll deduction IRAs are not subject to the Employee Retirement Income Security Act. Small business owners who are concerned about the administrative burden of complying with ERISA might be willing to set up a payroll deduction IRA for their employees. Although some small business owners who already have retirement plans for their employees might drop these plans in favor of payroll deduction IRAs, many will not because it would reduce their opportunity to save for retirement on a tax-deferred basis. In 2007, the annual contribution limit for an IRA is $5,500 whereas the maximum employee contribution to a 401(k) is $15,500. A small business owner who sponsors and participates in a 401(k) plan can save more for retirement on a tax-deferred basis than he or she could save in an IRA. If IRA contribution limits were the same as 401(k) contribution limits, small business owners would be more likely to drop 401(k) plans for IRAs.

One possible area of concern with respect to payroll deduction IRAs is that because they are not subject to ERISA, workers who save through these plans do not have the same rights and protections as participants in 401(k) plans. The participation and vesting requirements of ERISA are not relevant to payroll deduction IRAs, but ERISA has rigorous fiduciary standards that provide important protections to plan participants. Not all of these protections extend to IRAs.

PARTICIPATION IN EMPLOYER-SPONSORED RETIREMENT PLANS

Even when an employer offers a retirement plan, not all employees choose to participate. In 2007, about 75% of employees whose employer sponsored a 401(k) plan participated in the plan, and about 78% of eligible employees participated in DC plans of all types.[16] Participation in a 401(k) plan usually requires the employee to elect to contribute to the plan. Although some 401(k) plans now automatically enroll eligible employees, almost two-thirds of DC plans continue to require employees to elect to participate.[17]

Sponsorship Rates and Take-up Rates

Participation rates are affected both by access to retirement plans and take-up rates among employees who are offered a plan. The take-up rate is the percentage of employees offered a plan who choose to participate. For example, only 32% of workers under the age of 35 participated in DC plans in 2007.[18] (See Table 2.)

Although this was due in part to the relatively low percentage of these workers whose employers sponsored plans, another important factor was the low take-up rate among younger workers who were offered a plan. Only 70% of workers under age 35 whose employer sponsored a DC plan participated in the plan in 2007. In contrast, the take-up rate among workers aged 35 to 44 was 82%, and the take-up rate among workers aged 45 to 54 was 83%.[19]

In contrast to the lower participation rate of younger workers compared with older workers, participation rates among employees of small firms are lower than those of employees of larger firms mainly because a smaller proportion of workers at small firms are employed by firms that sponsor retirement plans. Among employees who are then offered a retirement plan, take-up the rates are similar for the employees of smaller firms and large firms.

The data presented in Table 2 show that in 2007, only 9% of workers employed at firms with fewer than 20 employees participated in a DC plan, compared with 35% of workers at firms with 20 to 99 employees, 46% of those at firms with 100 to 499 employees, and 57% of those at firms with 500 or more employees. However, only 12% of workers at firms with fewer than 20 employees were *offered* a DC plan, compared with 46% of those at firms with 20 to 99 employees, 59% of those at firms with 100 to 499 employees, and 70% of workers at firms with 500 or more employees. Take-up rates were similar among employees at small firms and large firms. The take-up rate in 2007 among employees at firms with fewer than 20 employees was 77%, whereas the take-up rates among workers at firms with 20 to 99 employees and firms with 100 to 499 employees were 75% and 78%, respectively. The take-up rate at firms with 500 or more employees was slightly higher (81 %).[20]

Table 2. Participation in Defined Contribution Plans: 2004 and 2007
Working Household Heads and Spouses Under Age 65

	Offered a DC Plan		Participated in DC Plan		Take-up Rate	
	2004	2007	2004	2007	2004	2007
Age						
55 to 64	49.9	48.2	43.1	40.2	86.5	83.5
45 to 54	50.1	54.6	40.0	45.3	79.9	83.0
35 to 44	48.4	49.0	38.2	40.2	79.1	82.1
Under 35	42.4	45.6	28.6	31.8	67.5	69.7
Size of Firm						
500+ employees	67.7	70.4	52.8	57.0	78.0	80.9
100-499 employees	56.1	58.7	41.4	45.8	73.7	78.0
20-99 employees	43.6	46.3	34.3	34.9	78.8	75.4
Under 20 employees	14.9	11.9	11.9	9.2	80.1	76.9
Education						
College graduate	58.6	59.5	49.1	50.6	83.8	85.0
Some college	46.3	50.5	35.1	39.3	75.7	77.9
High school less	37.8	39.4	26.5	28.6	70.2	72.7
Household Income						
Top quartile	60.9	61.5	53.0	53.9	87.1	87.5
Second quartile	52.6	54.5	41.4	45.6	78.7	83.8
Third quartile	43.5	46.3	31.1	33.6	71.4	72.5
Bottom quartile	25.8	29.7	13.9	17.0	54.1	57.4
Total	**47.3**	**49.4**	**36.7**	**39.2**	**77.5**	**79.3**

Source: CRS analysis of the Federal Reserve Board's 2004 and 2007 *Survey of Consumer Finances*.
Notes: Data represent 112 million workers in 2004 and 115 million workers in 2007. Education is the
highest level of education completed by the head of household. The take-up rate is the percentage
of workers offered a plan who participated in the plan. In 2007, for example, 49.4% of workers
were offered a DC plan and 39.2% of workers participated in a DC plan. Therefore, the take-up
rate was .392/.494 = .793.

Access to employer-sponsored retirement plans and participation in plans also differ
between better-educated and less-educated workers and between workers in higher-income
and lower- income households. Only 39% of workers in households in which the household
head had a high school education or less worked for an employer that sponsored a DC plan in
2007, compared with 60% of workers in households in which the household head was a
college graduate. The take-up rate among the less-educated group was 73%, compared with
85% for those in the better- educated group. Similarly, only 30% of workers in households in
the bottom quartile of household income worked for an employer that sponsored a DC plan in
2007, compared with 62% of workers in households in the top income quartile. The take-up
rate among workers in the bottom income quartile was just 57%, compared with 88% among
workers in the top income quartile.

These results imply that policies intended to raise participation in retirement plans should
be designed with the situation of the target population in mind. Efforts to increase plan
participation among younger workers should be focused on the low take-up rate among young

employees who are offered a plan, perhaps by encouraging firms to adopt automatic enrollment or to provide more education for workers about the importance of saving for retirement. Policies designed to raise participation among employees of small firms will need to target the low sponsorship rate among small employers, which may require finding new ways to make offering a retirement plan less burdensome and costly to small employers. Less-educated workers may need more guidance, perhaps in the form of investment education and investment advice, than better-educated workers. Workers in lower-income households, who may be hesitant to opt into a 401(k) plan that will reduce take-home pay, may be more receptive to plans that devote a portion of future pay increases to the retirement plan.

Policy Issue: The Retirement Savings Tax Credit

Congress has established tax incentives to encourage employers to sponsor retirement plans and employees to participate in these plans. Employer contributions to qualified plans are a tax- deductible business expense, and neither contributions—whether made by the employer or the employee—nor the investment earnings on those contributions are taxed as income to the employee until they are withdrawn from the plan.[21]

Because higher-earning workers pay higher marginal tax rates than lower-earning workers, the tax deduction for contributing to a retirement plan is worth more to a worker in a higher tax bracket than it is to a worker in a lower tax bracket. For a worker with a marginal income tax rate of 35%, contributing $1 to a 401(k) plan costs just 65 cents after taking the tax deduction into account. For a worker with a marginal income tax rate of 20%, contributing $1 to a 401(k) plan costs 80 cents on an after-tax basis. Moreover, both economic theory and empirical evidence suggest that the propensity to save rises with income. Because higher-earners would save much of their income even without tax incentives to do so, a substantial share of the tax revenue lost through the deduction for contributions to retirement plans does not result in a net increase in national saving. Consequently, some economists have suggested that the tax incentives for retirement saving are "upside down." Most of these tax breaks are enjoyed by higher-wage workers who would be likely to save part of their income even without a tax deduction, rather than by low-wage workers who might respond to an effective tax incentive with new saving.

One strategy for increasing contributions to retirement plans would be to provide tax incentives that are targeted to low- and middle-income workers. To provide an additional incentive for lower-income workers to contribute to retirement savings plans, Congress in 2001 authorized a new retirement savings tax credit, sometimes called the "saver's credit." In 2009, single taxpayers with adjusted gross income (AGI) up to $16,500 are eligible for a credit of 50% on qualified retirement contributions up to $2,000. For single filers with AGI of $16,501 to $18,000, the credit is 20%, and for single filers with AGI of $18,001 to $27,750, the credit is 10%. Married couples filing jointly with AGI up to $33,000 are eligible for a credit of 50% on qualified retirement contributions up to $2,000. For married couples with AGI of $33,001 to $36,000, the credit is 20%, and for married couples with AGI of $36,001 to $55,500, the credit is 10%.

The saver's credit is now claimed on about 5 million tax returns each year.[22] The maximum credit is $1,000. The average credit in 2006 was $172. Although the saver's credit provides an incentive for lower-income workers to save for retirement, its effect has been limited because the credit is non-refundable and phases out steeply over a range of income that is relatively low. A nonrefundable credit reduces taxes owed by the amount of the credit. However, if the individual or family owes no income tax after having taken the exemptions and deductions for which they are eligible, a nonrefundable credit has no value. [23] This is the case for many households with modest earnings who might benefit from the saver's credit if the credit were refundable. [24]

H.R. 1961(Pomeroy) of the 111th Congress would increase the rate of the tax credit for retirement savings contributions, make the credit refundable, and require the credit to be paid into retirement accounts. The income limit for the maximum credit of 50% of contributions would be increased to an adjusted gross income of $32,500 for individuals and $65,000 for couples. The credit would phase out between $32,500 and $42,500 for individuals and between $65,000 and $85,000 for married couples filing jointly. The bill would set the maximum amount of an employee contribution that is eligible for the credit at $500 for an individual and $1,000 for a couple. The contribution limits would increase by $100 and $200, respectively, each year until 2020. After that time, the limits would be indexed to the rate of inflation.

CONTRIBUTIONS TO RETIREMENT SAVINGS PLANS

If an employee elects to participate in a 401(k) plan, the next important decision he or she must make is how much to contribute to the plan. Studies have shown that employees are more likely to contribute to a plan if it provides matching contributions, and the amount that an employee contributes to a plan can be influenced by the formula for the matching contribution. [25] About two- thirds of all 401(k) plans offered an employer matching contribution in 2007. [26] The most common matching formula was 50% of the first 6% of pay contributed by the employee, for a total employer contribution equal to 3% of employee pay.

The maximum permissible annual contribution to a retirement plan is limited by federal law, but very few workers contribute amounts near the annual legal maximum. [27] Many employees contribute only enough to receive the full amount of the employer matching contribution. Those who elect not to contribute to a plan that offers a match, or who contribute less than the amount necessary to receive the full match, are in effect choosing to reduce their own compensation below the maximum available to them. [28]

In defined contribution plans, the benefit available to the worker at retirement is the amount in his or her account. The account balance depends on the amount that the employer and employee have contributed to the plan, the investment gains or losses on those contributions, and the fees charged to participants. Research has shown that, historically, the most important factors affecting workers' retirement account balances at retirement are the number of years over which they have contributed and the amounts that they contributed each year to their retirement plans. [29] Consequently, persuading workers to save more and to begin saving earlier are two of the most effective ways of increasing workers' income in retirement.

Household Contributions to DC Plans in 2007

Table 3 shows households' monthly contributions to DC plans in 2007 both in dollars and as a percentage of household earnings. The top panel of the table shows contributions categorized by the age of the household head, the middle panel shows contributions categorized by household income, and the bottom panel shows contributions by all households that contributed to a DC plan.

In 2007, the median monthly contribution to defined contribution plans by households in which at least one worker aged 25 to 64 participated in a DC plan was $290. This is equivalent to $3,480 on an annual basis.[30] As a percentage of household earnings, the median contribution by households in which one or more workers participated in a DC plan was 5.1% of earnings. Twenty-five percent of households that contributed to a DC plan in 2007 contributed $660 or more per month, and 25% contributed $130 per month or less. As a percentage of earnings, 25% of households participating in DC plans contributed 8.3% of earnings or more to the plan in 2007, and 25% of participating households contributed 2.9% of earnings or less to the plan.

Household Contributions by Age of Household Head

Households headed by persons under age 35 contribute less to DC plans, both in dollars and as a percentage of household earnings, than households headed by individuals aged 35 and older. In 2007, the median monthly contribution to DC plans by households headed by persons under age 35 in which at least one worker participated in a plan was $190. Among households headed by persons aged 35 to 44, the median monthly contribution was $310, and among households headed by persons aged 45 to 44, the median monthly contribution was $368. The median monthly DC plan contribution among households headed by persons aged 55 to 64 was $330 in 2007.

As a percentage of total household earnings, the median monthly contribution to DC plans by households headed by persons under age 35 in which at least one worker participated in a plan was 4.2% of earnings. The median contribution among households headed by persons aged 35 to 44 was 5.2% of earnings. Among both households headed by persons aged 45 to 54 and households headed by persons aged 55 to 64, the median contribution to DC plans in 2007 was 5.7% of household earnings.

Household Contributions by Household Income

As one might expect, household contributions to DC plans vary substantially by household income. This is likely to be the case both because higher-income households have more disposable income to save and also because, as was discussed earlier, the tax deduction for retirement savings is more valuable to higher-income households than to lower-income households. In addition, higher-income households are more likely than lower-income households to have more than one worker contributing to a DC plan.

In 2007, the median monthly contribution to DC plans among households in the top income quartile in which one or more workers participated in a plan was $750. Among households in the bottom income quartile in which one or more workers participated in a DC plan, the median monthly contribution to DC plans was $100. As a percentage of income, the median contribution among households in the top income quartile was 6.6% of household earnings, whereas among households in the bottom income quartile, the median contribution was 4.3% of household earnings.[31]

Policy Issue: Automatic Contribution Escalation

Employer matching contributions have been shown to raise participation rates in 401(k) plans. Many employees, however, contribute just enough to receive the full employer match. Employer matching contributions usually phase out at relatively low employee contribution rates. Matching contributions on employee salary deferrals of more than 6% of pay are relatively uncommon. Consequently, employer matching contributions are not as effective at raising employee contribution rates over time as they are at inducing employees to start contributing to the plan. Just as automatic enrollment has proven to be an effective means of raising participation rates in 401(k) plans, automatic contribution escalation can raise contribution rates.

The Pension Protection Act of 2006 sought to encourage employers to adopt automatic enrollment as a feature of their retirement plans by granting an exemption to certain regulations to plans that include a "qualified automatic contribution arrangement."[32] One of the features that a qualified automatic contribution arrangement must include is automatic escalation of employee contributions. Employee deferrals must be equal to specific percentages of pay unless the employee elects a different percentage. The minimum required deferral amount is 3% of pay in the employee's first year of participation, 4% in the second year, 5% in the third year, and 6% in the fourth and later years. The automatic deferral cannot exceed 10% of pay, but participants can elect a higher deferral rate, provided their total deferrals for the year do not exceed the annual limit under I.R.C. § 402(g). In 2009, this limit is $16,500.

A qualified automatic contribution arrangement also must include employer contributions. The employer contribution can be either a non-elective contribution equal to at least 3% of pay for all employees or a matching contribution equal to 100% of the first 1% of salary deferred and 50% of deferrals from 1% of pay to 6% of pay. Other matching formulas are permitted if they result in matching contributions that are at least equal to the amount provided under the prescribed matching formula, do not increase as the employee's rate of deferral increases, and do not apply to deferrals in excess of 6% of pay.

In 2007, the median employee salary deferral into employer-sponsored defined contribution plans was 6% of pay; however, 25% of workers who contributed to a DC plan deferred 3.9% of pay or less. Qualified automatic contribution arrangements that include automatic contribution escalation could raise employee contribution rates for a substantial percentage of participants. Employees could elect not to participate or to lower their contributions. The experience of most plans with automatic enrollment has been that the majority of participants who are automatically enrolled continue to participate. There is less evidence on the long-term effects of automatic contribution escalation on employee contributions because not as many plans have yet adopted automatic escalation.

Table 3. Monthly Household Contributions to Defined Contribution Plans in 2007

	Monthly Contributions in Dollars	Percentage of Household Earnings
Age of Householder		
55 to 64		
75th percentile of contributions	$790	9.9%
50th percentile of contributions	330	5.7
25th percentile of contributions	133	3.1
45 to 54		
75th percentile of contributions	810	8.5
50th percentile of contributions	368	5.7
25th percentile of contributions	158	3.1
35 to 44		
75th percentile of contributions	750	8.6
50th percentile of contributions	310	5.2
25th percentile of contributions	150	2.9
Under 35		
75th percentile of contributions	360	6.0
50th percentile of contributions	190	4.2
25th percentile of contributions	87	2.5
Household Income		
Top income quartile		
75th percentile of contributions	1,292	10.0
50th percentile of contributions	750	6.6
25th percentile of contributions	380	3.6
Second income quartile		
75th percentile of contributions	500	8.2
50th percentile of contributions	303	5.1
25th percentile of contributions	170	3.0
Third income quartile		
75th percentile of contributions	250	6.1
50th percentile of contributions	160	4.4
25th percentile of contributions	90	2.5
Bottom income quartile		
75th percentile of contributions	160	6.2
50th percentile of contributions	100	4.3
25th percentile of contributions	50	2.5
All Contributing Households		
75th percentile of contributions	660	8.3
50th percentile of contributions	290	5.1
25th percentile of contributions	130	2.9

Source: CRS analysis of the Federal Reserve Board's 2007 Survey of Consumer Finances.

Notes: Households are grouped by total income, including earnings and all other income. Contributions are reported as a percentage of total household earnings. Among households in which there was a worker under age 65 in 2007, those with income of $100,780 or more were in the top income quartile and those with income under $33,940 were in the bottom income quartile. Median income for these households was $59,650.

INVESTMENT CHOICES AND INVESTMENT RISK

A worker who has elected to participate in a 401(k) plan and has decided how much to contribute to the plan usually also must decide how to invest these contributions. More than 90% of 401(k) plans allow employees to direct the investment of their contributions, and three-fourths of plans allow employees to direct the investment of the employer's contributions.[33] In order for a plan sponsor to be relieved of liability for investment losses in a participant-directed retirement plan, participants must be given a choice of at least three investment alternatives, each of which must have different risk and return characteristics.[34] Most plans offer participants more than the minimum number of investment choices required by law. In 2007, the average 401(k) plan offered participants 18 investment options.[35] The investment options most commonly offered were actively managed U.S. stock funds (77% of plans), actively managed international stock funds (73%), indexed U.S. stock funds (70%), and actively managed U.S. bond funds (64%).[36]

Participants in 401(k) plans bear the risk of investment losses. An individual's retirement account might suffer investment losses because the particular stocks, bonds, or other assets in which he or she has chosen to invest decline in value. Diversification can reduce the risk associated with investing in specific assets because declines in the value of some assets may be fully or partially offset by gains in the value of other assets. Stock and bond mutual funds, for example, help protect individuals from investment risk by purchasing securities from many companies in a variety of industries. In a stock mutual fund, investment losses from companies that are performing poorly may be offset by investment gains from companies that are performing well.

A broader form of investment risk is *market risk*, which is the possibility of an overall decline in a broad class of assets, such as stocks. Even a well-diversified portfolio of stocks, for example, will not protect the value of an individual's retirement account from depreciating if stock values fall across the board, as they did in 2008. This is why most investment advisors recommend diversification not only within a class of assets—by buying broadly diversified stock mutual funds instead of individual stocks, for example—but also diversification across asset classes. Bond prices have historically been less volatile than stock prices, and there have been long periods when returns on stocks and bonds have not been closely correlated. Life-cycle funds and target date funds diversify across classes of assets by buying shares in stock mutual funds, bond funds, and sometimes other investments as well.

Although most financial advisors recommend diversifying investments across classes of assets and periodically re-balancing accounts to maintain appropriate diversification, relatively few plan participants put this advice into practice. The assets of DC plans are heavily invested in stocks and stock mutual funds. At year-end 2007, 78% of all DC plan assets were invested in stocks and stock mutual funds. Investment in stocks and stock mutual funds varied little by age, indicating that many workers nearing retirement were heavily invested in stocks, and risked substantial losses in a market downturn like that in 2008. According to the 2007 Survey of Consumer Finances, nearly 30% of DC plan participants between the ages of 35 and 54 had 100% of their account balance invested in stocks in 2007. Twenty-eight percent of participants aged 55 to 64 had their entire account balance invested in stocks and stock mutual funds. (See **Figure 1**.)

Because many plan participants lack basic financial literacy, policy analysts have suggested that plans should take steps to help participants make better investment choices or adopt plans that automatically allocate contributions among various classes of investments. Investment education and target date funds are two approaches to achieving asset diversification in DC plans.

Policy Issue: Investment Education and Investment Advice

To make informed decisions about how much to save for retirement and how to invest these savings, plan participants need to understand certain basic principles of finance. For example, an individual who understands the risk-and-return characteristics of stocks and bonds will be better able to balance the risk of investment losses with the expected rate of return from each kind of investment compared to someone who lacks this understanding. Not everyone understands investment risk, however, and many people make decisions about their investments that are not well-informed. Some 401(k) plan sponsors have attempted to help employees make better investment decisions by providing investment education, offering investment advice, and adding "life-cycle funds" or "target date funds" to their plans.

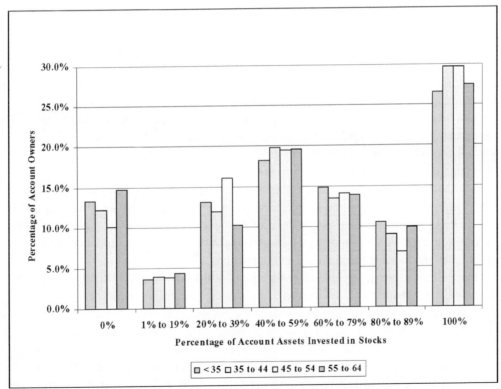

Source: CRS analysis of the Federal Reserve Board's 2007 Survey of Consumer Finances.
Notes: Household heads under age 65 with a defined contribution plan.

Figure 1. Percentage of Defined Contribution Plan Assets Invested in Stocks, 2007
By Age of Account Owner

Investment Education

According to Hewitt Associates, more than 90% of all 401(k) plans offer some form of investment education. Typically, investment education is offered through enrollment kits, seminars and workshops, and internet sites. Investment education helps plan participants understand the importance of saving for retirement. It typically focuses on educating individuals about basic tenets of finance, such as the effects of compound interest and the difference between stocks and bonds. Employees who understand how investment gains compound over time are more likely to start contributing to the plan, to continue to contribute to the plan, and to raise their contributions as their earnings rise over time. Participants who understand that the higher expected rate of return on stocks compared to bonds comes at the cost of greater price volatility will be better able to balance their tolerance for risk with their desire for higher returns when choosing investments. Even with more investment education, some employees will choose not to participate in retirement savings plans because they prefer higher current income to higher income in retirement. For workers who discount future income heavily, changing their default participation status to automatic enrollment may be more effective than investment education.

Investment Advice

Investment education consists mainly of giving plan participants general information about the basic principles of finance that they need to be informed investors. Investment advice, on the other hand, is tailored to the individual and often involves recommending specific investments. Some plan sponsors have been reluctant to offer investment advice both because of the cost of paying professional advisors and concerns about possible legal liability for investment losses incurred by plan participants. Almost half (49%) of all 40 1(k) plans offered investment advice to plan participants in 2007, up from 35% in 2000.[37]

Even if a plan offers a range of low-cost, diversified investment options and offers investment education and investment advice, it is not unusual for some participants to make investment choices that may prove to be unwise in the long run. For example, some participants invest too much of their retirement savings in the stock of their employers. This exposes them to the risk of losing their retirement savings as well as their jobs if the firm goes out of business. Others invest too conservatively while they are young—putting most of their contributions into low-yielding money market funds, for example—even though their longer investment horizon would suggest that they could take on more risk. Sound investment advice can help plan participants avoid these common mistakes.

Under ERISA, providing investment advice is a fiduciary act. A plan sponsor could be held liable for investment losses incurred by a participant who follows investment advice offered by a plan or its agent. The Pension Protection Act of 2006 (PPA) amended ERISA to allow plan sponsors who follow certain procedures to provide investment advice without being held liable for investment losses of participants who act on the advice.[38] In general, to be permissible under the provisions of the PPA, the advice must be provided for a fee rather than a commission, or it must be based on a computer model that meets requirements set forth in statute and regulations. The advisors must disclose their fee arrangements to plan participants and inform them of their affiliations with investments they recommend and with the developer of the computer model. The model on which the advice is based must "operate in a manner that is not biased in favor of investments offered by the fiduciary adviser or a person with a material affiliation or contractual relationship with the fiduciary adviser."[39]

Investment Advice Regulations and Legislation

On January 21, 2009, the Department of Labor published a final regulation on the investment advice provisions of the PPA. On March 19, the department delayed the effective date of the regulation for 60 days, pending further review and receipt of additional public comments. On May, 21, 2009, the department announced that the regulation would not be implemented until November 18, 2009.[40]

The investment advice provisions of the PPA allow investment advice to be provided to plan participants by individuals with a financial interest in the investments that they recommend, provided that they disclose this information to plan participants. On April 23, 2009, Representative Robert Andrews introduced H.R. 1988, the Conflicted Investment Advice Prohibition Act of 2009. This bill would allow investment advice to be provided to plan participants only by independent investment advisers who are registered under the Investment Advisers Act of 1940 and who meet certain other qualifying requirements. The bill would prohibit advisers from managing any investments in which any of the assets of the plan are invested, and it would prohibit plans in which individuals direct the investment of their accounts from contracting with investment advisers who are not independent advisers. Independent advisers would be required to provide participants with documentation of the historic rates of return of investment options available to the plan, and to notify participants that the investment adviser is acting as a fiduciary of the plan.

Policy Issue: Life-cycle Funds and Target Date Funds

Even if a plan participant understands the basic principles of finance, he or she may have neither the time nor the inclination to monitor and manage a retirement account. Because many plan participants lack either the aptitude, interest, or time to manage their retirement accounts, plan sponsors have begun to add "life-cycle funds" or "target date funds" to their 401(k) plans. These plans are designed to allocate the participant's investments between stocks and bonds in a way that takes into account his or her risk tolerance and expected date of retirement. Although these funds have proved popular with participants and have won the approval of many investment professionals, the sharp downturn in stock prices in 2008 showed that they are not without problems. Many target-date funds for people expecting to retire in 2010 or 2011 were heavily invested in stocks and lost 25% to 30% of their value in 2008.

Life-cycle funds and target date funds are similar. Many financial analysts consider target date funds to be a subset of the category of funds called life-cycle funds. A life-cycle fund is a mutual fund in which the allocation of assets among stocks, bonds, and cash-equivalents (money market funds, for example) is automatically adjusted during the course of the participant's working life. As the participant nears retirement age, the investment allocation is shifted away from higher-risk investments, such as stocks, and moves toward lower-risk investments, such as bonds and cash equivalents. A target-date fund is a life-cycle fund designed to achieve a particular (generally conservative) mix of assets at a specific date in the future, which is usually the year when the participant expects to retire.

Although life-cycle funds and target date funds are typically designed with the intent of achieving more rapid growth in the early years of the participant's career and greater stability of asset values in the later years, they can contain any mix of stocks, bonds, and cash. There are no industry standards or federal regulations that specify what allocation of assets is required for a life-cycle fund or a target date fund that is intended for plan participants of a given age or with a particular investment time horizon. Currently, less than 5% of DC plan assets are invested in life-cycle funds. Analysts expect this percentage to rise over the next 10 years because the Pension Protection Act allows companies to use life-cycle funds as the default investment option for employees who are automatically enrolled in a 401(k) plan and who do not select an investment fund for their 401(k) contributions.[41]

Allocation of assets among stocks, bonds, and cash-equivalents varies greatly among target date funds with the same target retirement date. A recent study by Morningstar, Inc. found that among target-date 2010 funds that were at least three years old, stock allocations ranged from 14% of assets to 63% of assets. In December 2008, the average 2010 fund had more than 45% of its assets invested in stocks. Fund performance also varied greatly during the bear market of 2008. The S&P Target Date 2010 Index Fund, a benchmark of fund performance, fell 17% in 2008. The fund holds 60% of its assets in bonds and other fixed-income securities and 40% in equities. In comparison, the Deutsche Bank DWS Target 2010 Fund fell just 4% in 2008, whereas Oppenheimer's Transition 2010 fund fell 41%. In January, 2009, the Thrift Savings Plan's "L2010 Fund" for federal employees who plan to retire in 2010 held 70% of its assets in bonds and 30% in stocks. Shares of the L2010 Fund fell 10.5% in 2008.

In a letter sent to Secretary of Labor Hilda Solis in February 2009, Senator Herb Kohl, chairman of the Senate Special Committee on Aging, urged the Secretary to "immediately commence a review of target date funds and begin work on regulations to protect plan participants."[42] In her reply to Senator Kohl on March 26, Secretary Solis stated that the Department of Labor would, in coordination with the Securities and Exchange Commission, begin a review of target date funds to determine if these funds should be subject to further federal regulation.[43]

FEES AND FEE DISCLOSURE

Another issue that has concerned Congress is the effect of fees on retirement account balances. Retirement plans contract with service providers to provide investment management, record- keeping, and other services. There can be many service providers, each charging a fee that is ultimately paid by plan participants. The arrangements through which service providers are compensated can be very complicated. Because the structure of 401(k) fees is opaque to most plan participants, it is very difficult for them to judge whether they are receiving services at a price they would be willing to pay in a more transparent market transaction.

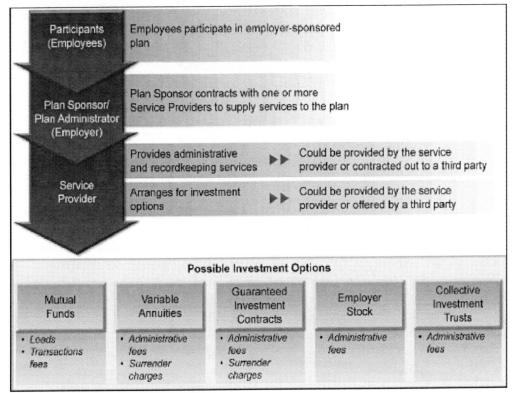

Source: Congressional Research Service.

Figure 2. The Structure of a Typical Defined Contribution Plan

The Administrative Structure of 401(k) plans

Figure 2 illustrates the administrative structure of a typical 401(k) plan. Plan participants have individual accounts to which the employees, the employer, or both contribute. As the plan sponsor, the employer arranges for one or more third parties to provide various services for the plan. Services include recording transactions, arranging for loans, cashing out departing employees' accounts, and contracting with the funds into which participants can direct their contributions. Employers can purchase services separately from several service providers or they might purchase two or more services from a single service provider. Services may be priced individually or purchased in a bundled arrangement. In a bundled arrangement, several services are offered to the plan for a single fee. The service provider sometimes contracts out the provision of these services to one or more third parties.

Fees vary from plan to plan. They are affected by the amounts and kinds of services offered to plan participants and also by the size of the plan. As a percentage of plan assets, fees are negatively correlated with the number of plan participants and the average account balance. In general, the greater the number of plan participants and the larger the average account balance, the lower the fees will be as a percentage of plan assets. A recent survey conducted by Deloitte Consulting for the Investment Company Institute looked at fees in plans ranging in size from those with fewer than 100 participants and less than $1 million in total assets to plans with more than 10,000 participants and assets of more than $500 million.[44] The study looked at fees for administration, recordkeeping, and investment management, which were combined into a single "all-in" fee, expressed as a percentage of plan assets. The median fee for all plans in the survey was 0.72% of plan assets, or approximately $350 for an account with the median balance of plans in the survey, which was $48,500. The study found that 10% of plans had total fees of 0.35% of assets or less and that 10% of plans had total fees of 1.72% of assets or more.

Policy Issue: Requiring Clearer Disclosure of Fees

The firms that provide record-keeping, investment management, and other services to 401(k) plans charge fees for these services, and many of these fees are passed on to plan participants. Fees for some services are charged for each transaction, while others are charged as a flat fee per account per year, and still others—such as investment management—are typically charged as a percentage of total plan assets. Small differences in fees can yield large differences in account balances at retirement, especially in the case of yearly or recurring fees.[45] For example, after 20 years, an initial $20,000 account balance earning 7% yearly would be worth about $70,000 if fees were equal to 0.5% of plan assets each year. The account would have a balance of about $58,000, or 17% less, if fees amounted to 1.5% per year. Over the course of 30 years, a participant in a plan charging fees equal to 1.5% of assets would pay almost $33,000 more in fees than he or she would have paid if the annual fees were 0.5% of assets.[46]

Section 404(a) of ERISA states that plan sponsors are responsible for "defraying reasonable expenses of administering the plan." This has been interpreted by the Department of Labor as imposing a duty on plan sponsors to assure that expenses—including fees—are reasonable. Plan sponsors are not required to minimize fees, but they are required to make sure that plan fees are "reasonable." This standard allows for wide variation in fees across plans. Although sponsors of DC plans are required by law to assure that fees are reasonable, they do not have the same financial incentive to keep fees low as do the sponsors of DB plans. In a DC plan, many fees are passed through to the plan participants, while in a DB plan most fees are paid by the plan sponsor.[47] If plan participants were better-informed about the fees that they pay and the services they receive in return for those fees, they could question plan sponsors about fees that they believe to be unreasonable. Therefore, policies that increase the transparency of fee arrangements could result in participants paying lower fees.

Plans are required by law to disclose some of the fees that plan participants pay. However, the information is not always easily accessible or easily understood by the average participant. The Department of Labor is developing regulations to improve the disclosure of fees to participants in 401(k) plans. On November 16, 2007, the department issued regulations that require plan administrators to disclose the compensation received by service providers. On July 23, 2008, the department issued proposed regulations that would require plan fiduciaries to disclose to participants the dollar amount charged to each participant's account during the preceding quarter for individual services, such as fees for processing plan loans. These regulations were not final as of June 30, 2009.[48]

Members of Congress have been developing legislation that would require greater disclosure of fees to participants. On February 10, 2009, Senator Tom Harkin introduced S. 401, the Defined Contribution Fee Disclosure Act. On April 21, 2009, Representative George Miller introduced H.R. 1984, the 401(k) Fair Disclosure for Retirement Security Act. On June 24, the House Education and Labor Committee ordered the 401(k) Fair Disclosure and Pension Security Act reported to the House. The bill reported by the committee was numbered H.R. 2989. This bill combined H.R. 1984 with H.R. 1988, the Conflicted Investment Advice Prohibition Act, which was introduced by Representative Robert Andrews. On June 9, 2009, Representative Richard Neal introduced H.R. 2779, the Defined Contribution Plan Fee Transparency Act, which was referred to the Committee on Ways and Means.

LEAKAGE FROM RETIREMENT SAVINGS PLANS

The tax incentives that Congress has authorized for retirement savings accounts are designed to assure that the money workers have set aside for retirement remains in the account until they are near retirement age. In recognition of needs that may arise over the course of an individual's life, Congress has allowed certain exceptions to the general restriction on access to these accounts before retirement. Each exception, however justifiable on its own merits, increases the danger that workers will reduce their retirement savings before they have reached retirement.

Pre-retirement withdrawals from retirement accounts are sometimes described as "leakages" from the pool of retirement savings. Congress has used a combination of regulation and taxation to limit and discourage pre-retirement access to money in retirement accounts, but it has not completely prohibited pre-retirement access to these accounts because this access is important to many plan participants. Research has shown that workers are less likely to put money into a retirement account if they believe that the money will be inaccessible in the event of emergency. Consequently, current law represents a compromise between limiting leakages from retirement accounts and allowing people to have access to their retirement funds in times of great need.

Leakages from retirement plans can take a variety of forms, including "hardship" withdrawals from the plan prior to retirement, borrowing against plan assets, and cashing out plan assets upon separation from employment.

Hardship Distributions

The tax code permits 401(k) plans to make distributions available "upon hardship of the employee."[49] Although the Internal Revenue Code (IRC) allows plans to make these distributions available, it does not require them to do so. Federal regulations specify that a hardship distribution can be made only on account of "an immediate and heavy financial need of the employee" and cannot exceed the amount of the employee's previous elective contributions.[50] Qualifying expenses include medical care for the participant or family members, the purchase of a principal residence, college tuition and education expenses, expenses to prevent eviction or foreclosure on a principal residence, and funeral expenses.

A hardship distribution must be limited to the amount needed to meet the employee's immediate financial need plus any taxes that will result from the distribution. Plan participants are prohibited from making contributions to a plan for a period of six months after a hardship distribution, and consequently they forego any employer match on contributions during that time. Hardship distributions are always subject to ordinary income taxes, and unless the distribution is used for a purpose specifically designated in law, the distribution will be subject to a 10% early withdrawal tax penalty unless the plan participant is over age 59½.[51]

Borrowing from Retirement Plans

The IRC allows participants in employer-sponsored retirement plans to borrow from their accounts, but plans are not required to allow such loans. A loan cannot exceed the greater of $10,000 or 50% of the participant's vested benefit in the plan, up to a maximum of $50,000. Most loans from retirements plans must be paid back within five years, although loans used to purchase a home can be repaid over 15 years. If repayment ceases, the IRS will treat the full amount of the loan as a distribution from the plan, and it will be subject to income tax and possibly to an early distribution penalty. Most plans require employees who separate from the employer before the loan is repaid to repay the balance immediately or the loan will be treated as a taxable distribution from the plan. [52]

For the plan participant, borrowing from a 401(k) plan is usually preferable to taking a hardship withdrawal. With a loan, the account balance is not permanently reduced because the loan will be repaid into the account, generally within five years. Unlike a hardship distribution, after which employee contributions must be suspended for six months, the participant can continue to contribute to the plan while the loan is outstanding. Also unlike hardship distributions, loans are not subject to income taxes or the early withdrawal penalty if repayments continue on schedule.

According to the Federal Reserve Board's Survey of Consumer Finances, 9.5% of households in which the householder or spouse participated in a DC plan had one or more plan loans outstanding in 2007. The mean balance of all loans from DC plans was $6,683 and the median loan balance was $5,000. Ten percent of households with loans from DC plans had outstanding loan balances of $15,000 or more and 10% of households had loan balances of $1,000 or less.

Leakages When Switching Jobs

Leakages from retirement savings can occur when workers change jobs.[53] A participants in retirement plans usually has several options from which to choose from when leaving a job. He or she can:

- keep the account in the former employer's plan;
- roll over the account into the new employer's retirement plan;
- roll over the account into an Individual Retirement Account (IRA); or
- receive the account balance directly as a distribution from the plan.[54]

Policy Issue: Preserving Retirement Savings

Congress has amended the IRC several times to encourage workers who change jobs to leave their accrued retirement benefit in the former employer's plan or to roll over the account into an IRA or another qualified retirement plan. For example:

- Section 72(t) of the IRC imposes a 10% tax in addition to ordinary income taxes on distributions from retirement plans received before age 59½ that are not rolled over into an IRA or another tax-qualified plan within 60 days.[55]
- The Unemployment Compensation Amendments of 1992 (P.L. 102-318) require employers to give departing employees the option to transfer a distribution directly to an IRA or to another employer's plan. If the participant instead chooses to receive the distribution, the employer is required to withhold 20%, which is applied to any taxes due on the distribution.[56]
- IRC §411(a)(11) allows a plan sponsor to distribute to a departing employee his or her accrued benefit under a retirement plan without the participant's consent only if the present value of the benefit is less than $5,000.[57] The Economic Growth and Tax Relief Reconciliation Act of 2001 (P.L. 107-16) requires that if the present value of the distribution is at least $1,000, the plan sponsor must deposit the distribution into an IRA unless otherwise instructed by the participant.

In developing policies to prevent leakages from retirement savings, Congress has attempted to promote the preservation of savings until workers retire while recognizing that they may have to take money from their accounts in times of financial hardship. An example of how these goals have been balanced is the treatment of distributions when a worker leaves a job in which he or she participated in a retirement plan. In this situation, Congress has sought to *encourage* recipients to roll over pre-retirement distributions from retirement plans, but it has not *required* such distributions to be rolled over into an IRA or another retirement plan. Current law allows accrued benefits worth less than $5,000 to be cashed out automatically, but it requires the plan participant to agree in writing to a distribution of more than $5,000. The law allows workers to take cash distributions from plans when they leave a job, but it requires 20% to be withheld against taxes owed, and it places an additional 10% tax on amounts that are not rolled over into another retirement account within 60 days of the distribution.

Current law on pre-retirement distributions represents a compromise between competing goals. Stricter limits on access to retirement savings prior to retirement could lower participation or contributions. Research has shown that participation in plans that do not permit plan loans or hardship distributions is lower than in plans that allow these kinds of access to funds held by the plan. Allowing easier pre-retirement access to retirement accounts could lead to more leakages from the plans, depleted account balances, and poorer retirements for many. Moreover, to the extent that retirement accounts could be freely tapped before retirement, they would not be retirement accounts at all, but merely tax-deferred general-purpose savings accounts.

In summary, the laws that Congress has passed with respect to taxation of early distributions from retirement plans represent a compromise among several competing objectives, including

- encouraging employees to participate in retirement plans;
- promoting the preservation of retirement assets;
- allowing participants to have access to their retirement savings when they would otherwise face substantial economic hardship; and
- assuring that the tax preferences granted to retirement savings plans are not used for purposes other than to fund workers' financial security during retirement.

CONVERTING RETIREMENT SAVINGS INTO INCOME

A retiree who is deciding how to convert retirement savings into income will have to take into account many risks. Increases in average life expectancy mean that many retirees will have to ensure that their savings will last through a retirement that could span 30 or 40 years. Volatility in equity markets, the effects of inflation on purchasing power, and the possibility of substantial expenses for medical treatment and long-term care will further complicate this decision. Many retirees may find it more challenging to manage their financial assets in retirement than it was during their working years.[58]

There are a number of ways to convert retirement savings into income. One option is to purchase an annuity. A life annuity—also called an immediate annuity—is an insurance contract that provides regular income payments for life in return for an initial lump-sum premium. Life annuities can help protect retirees against some of the financial risks of retirement, especially longevity risk and investment risk. A life annuity pays income to the purchaser for as long as he or she lives, and in the case of a joint-and survivor annuity, for as long as the surviving spouse lives. Some annuities offer limited protection against inflation through annual increases in income; however, the annual increases must be paid for by accepting a lower initial monthly annuity income. Other annuities allow the purchaser to share in investment gains from growth in equity markets as a way to offset the effects of inflation. These annuities also require the purchaser to share in the investment losses if markets fall.

Relatively few 401(k) plans provide the opportunity for retiring workers to convert all or part of their 401(k) accounts into life annuities at retirement. Only 21% of plans offered an annuity option in 2007, down from 26% in 2000.[59] One reason few plans offer annuities is that they have proven to be unpopular in plans that offer them. Fewer than 10% of participants in plans that offer an annuity choose this option.[60] At retirement, most DC plan participants either take periodic withdrawals or roll the account balance into an IRA from which they take withdrawals.

Few people purchase life annuities for a number of reasons. Social Security provides benefits in the form of an inflation-adjusted annuity, and some retirees may consider this to be sufficient protection against the risk of spending all of their retirement assets before they die. In addition, about one-third of retirees receive income from defined benefit pensions, and they therefore have less need to purchase an annuity with their retirement savings. Some potential purchasers of annuities are concerned that the fees charged by insurers are too high and that the insurance companies do a poor job of explaining the fees that they charge. Others are concerned that purchasing an annuity will reduce the financial assets that they have available to meet unexpected expenses. Finally, some older persons prefer not to purchase an annuity in the hope that they will be able to leave their assets as an inheritance for their children. For these and other reasons, the number of retirees who purchase income annuities has remained relatively low compared with the number who elect to take periodic withdrawals from their retirement accounts.

Policy Issue: The Role of Income Annuities in Retirement

Defined benefit pension plans are required by law to offer participants a joint and survivor annuity as the default form of benefit.[61] No such requirement applies to defined contribution plans. Congress could require DC plan sponsors to contract with insurance companies to offer participants the option of taking their retirement benefits in the form of an annuity, but most policy proposals have focused on making annuities a more appealing option rather than a mandatory form of benefit. For example, H.R. 2748of the 111th Congress (Pomeroy) would amend the Internal Revenue Code to exclude from gross income up to 50% of annuity income up to an annual maximum of $5,000 for single tax filers and $10,000 for couples filing jointly.

Because most 401(k) plans do not offer an annuity option, retirees who wish to purchase annuities have to withdraw money from their accounts and buy annuities in the individual market. Individual annuities are more expensive than group annuities, and they place the responsibility for finding the best deal from a financially sound insurer on individuals who usually have had little or no experience shopping for annuities. Many consumers may not feel competent to do this on their own. They may be more comfortable taking periodic withdrawals from their accounts. Some retirees are reluctant to purchase a life annuity because canceling the annuity contract can be costly. The charge for canceling an annuity—the "surrender charge"—can account for more than 10% of the principal in the first year of the contract.[62]

Many economists have found the low demand for life annuities to be puzzling in light of the protection they provide against longevity risk. Recent research has found that the appeal of annuities to potential purchasers depends greatly on whether prospective buyers understand and appreciate the value of the income security that annuities provide. Researchers have found that when annuities are portrayed—or "framed"—as investment vehicles, the lower rates of return on life annuities (which are backed mainly by bonds) can put them at a competitive disadvantage with respect to stocks and stock mutual funds.

However, when the insurance aspects of annuities are emphasized—in particular, the insurance against outliving one's assets—potential buyers have been found to be more receptive to the idea of buying a life annuity.[63]

Automatic Trial Income

As a way to familiarize people with annuities, researchers at the Retirement Security Project have suggested a strategy they call "automatic trial income." This would allow retirees to "test drive" an annuity for 24 months.[64] They suggest that if the default form of benefit from a 401(k) plan were a monthly check, even for only a 24-month period with the option to take the remainder as a lump-sum at the end of two years – it would help change the public's perception of retirement accounts by framing them as an income stream rather than as a lump sum.

Under automatic trial income, at least part of the assets in a worker's 401(k) account would be automatically paid out as income at retirement unless the individual chooses another option. Retirees would receive monthly payments from the automatic trial income plan for 24 months, at the end of which they could choose to take the remainder as a lump sum or have it converted to an annuity. To assure that only people who are near retirement have their accounts distributed as income when they leave an employer, automatic trial income could apply only to those who are 55 or older when they leave a job. To prevent small account balances from being converted to annuities, the policy could apply only to accounts above a minimum value of perhaps $50,000.

Advanced Life Deferred Annuity

Another annuity product, the Advanced Life Deferred Annuity (ALDA) is purchased at retirement but does not begin paying income until the purchaser reaches an advanced age, such as 80 or 85. If the purchaser dies before the age at which income payments are scheduled to begin, he or she forfeits the premium. On the other hand, because income payments are deferred until an advanced age, premiums would be relatively low compared to immediate income annuities. A recent analysis concluded that "this product would provide a substantial proportion of the longevity insurance provided by an immediate annuity, at a small fraction of the cost," and that "few households would suffer significant losses were it used as a 40 1(k) plan default."[65] Although the ALDA could provide substantial insurance against living into very old age for a comparatively low premium, "it remains to be seen whether such a product would overcome annuity aversion."[66]

One way to help participants in 401(k) plans to begin thinking of their accounts as a source of retirement income rather than as a savings account would be to report the value of the participant's accrued benefits as a stream of monthly income beginning at age 65 in addition to reporting the account balance. To make these presentations comparable across plans, it might be necessary for the federal government to set standards on the appropriate interest rates and mortality tables for plans to use in restating account balances as streams of future income.

Some financial firms are designing managed withdrawal programs as alternatives to annuities. These are typically investment accounts with periodic distributions that are designed to assure that the account balance will not be exhausted before a specified number of years have passed. Unlike annuities, however, these accounts do not provide longevity insurance. The account owner bears the risk that investment losses or living longer than he or she anticipated will result in the account being exhausted during his or her lifetime.

CONCLUSION

About half of all workers in the United States participate in employer-sponsored retirement plans, a proportion that has remained essentially unchanged since the early 1970s. Since the 1980s, the proportion of workers in defined benefit pension plans has fallen while the proportion in defined contribution plans has risen. Sponsorship of retirement plans is substantially lower among small employers than among large employers. Efforts to increase retirement plan sponsorship among small employers have had only limited success. Some policy analysts have suggested that expanding access to payroll deduction IRAs could greatly increase the number of employees at small firms who have a retirement savings account.

Even among employers who offer a retirement plan, not all workers participate. Roughly 20% to 25% of workers employed at firms that sponsor a defined contribution plan do not participate in the plan. Participation rates may rise if more firms adopt automatic enrollment, but currently, almost two-thirds of DC plans continue to require employees to elect to participate in the plan.

On average, individual workers who participate in DC plans contribute about 6% of their pay to the plan, and households with one or more participants contribute about 5% of total household earnings. One way to boost employee savings rates would be for employers to adopt automatic escalation of contributions. Employee contributions can be increased slightly each year until reaching a target contribution rate, such as 10% of pay. As with automatic enrollment, employees must be permitted to opt out of the increase or to choose another contribution rate.

In most DC plans, workers must decide not only whether to participate in the plan and how much to contribute, but also how to invest the contributions. As employers have become more aware of how daunting these choices can be for their employees, some have begun to add life-cycle funds that automatically adjust the allocation of contributions between stocks, bonds, and other investments based on the employee's expected date of retirement. The majority of plan sponsors also offer investment education for participants. Some employers arrange for financial planners or other professionals to offer investment advice to their employees.

Excessive fees can substantially reduce retirement account balances, but plan participants often are unable to discern from their account statements how much they are paying in fees and what services they are receiving in exchange for the fees charged to their accounts. Improving the disclosure of fees charged to participants in 401(k) plans could help to drive down fees because participants and plan sponsors would be better able to compare fees across plans and to evaluate the services provided relative to the fees charged for those services.

Although pre-retirement access to money held in 401(k) plans is limited by law, money sometimes "leaks" from workers' accounts before they retire. This happens when a worker withdraws funds from a 40 1(k) plan when changing jobs, or through a hardship distribution from the plan. Current law imposes a 10% tax penalty on most withdrawals from 401(k) plans before age 591/2. The tax penalty creates a disincentive for withdrawing money from the account before retirement and also helps assure that 401(k) accounts remain dedicated to preparing for retirement rather than functioning as tax-deferred general-purpose savings accounts.

Workers who are approaching retirement today are less likely than those who retired 20 or more years ago to have a defined benefit pension. Those who have retirement savings in a 401(k) plan or an IRA will have to decide how to convert their retirement savings into retirement income. One of the risks that they will face is the possibility that if they withdraw money too quickly, they might exhaust their savings while they still have many years to live. Income annuities insure retirees against the possibility of outliving their retirement savings, but for a variety of reasons income annuities have not yet proved to be a popular option for providing retirement income. One of the most important public policy challenges of the next several years will be to develop strategies that will help retirees manage their retirement savings wisely so that they can remain financially independent throughout retirement.

End Notes

[1] Not all DC plans are 401(k) plans, but 401(k) plans hold about 67% of DC plan assets. Other DC plans include 403(b) plans for non-profit employers, 457 plans for state and local governments, and miscellaneous other DC plans. Increasingly, 403(b) plans and 457 plans operate similarly to 40 1(k) plans. In this report the terms "40 1(k)" plan and "defined contribution" plan are used interchangeably unless a distinction is noted in the text.

[2] U.S. Department of Labor, Bureau of Labor Statistics, *National Compensation Survey: Employee Benefits in Private Industry in the United States, March 2007*, Summary 07-05, August 2007. The sample represented 108 million workers.

[3] On October 11, 2007, the Standard & Poor's 500 Index of common stocks reached an intra-day high of 1,576, an all-time record for the index. On March 6, 2009, the S&P 500 fell to an intra-day low of 667, a decline of 57.7% from its all-time high. Over the next three months, stock prices climbed 41%. The S&P 500 closed at a value of 943 on June 1, 2009. This was 40% lower than the index's highest level in October 2007. By July 7, the S&P 500 had fallen to 881.

[4] Board of Governors of the Federal Reserve System, *Flow of Funds Accounts of the United States: Flows and Outstandings*, Fourth Quarter 2008, March 12, 2009, p. 113.

[5] U.S. Department of Labor, Bureau of Labor Statistics, *National Compensation Survey, March 2007*, Summary 07-05, August 2007. In contrast, the BLS data indicate that 89% of workers in state and local governments were offered a retirement plan of some kind. Eighty-three percent of state and local workers were offered a DB plan, 29% were offered a DC plan, and 23% were offered both types of plan. See *National Compensation Survey: Employee Benefits in State and Local Governments in the United States, September 2007*, Summary 08-01, March 2008.

[6] The Census Bureau data are from a CRS analysis of the March 2008 Current Population Survey (CPS). The National Compensation Survey is a survey of business establishments. The CPS is a survey of households. The CPS asks households about the number of workers employed by the firm where the respondent is employed. A firm may consist of more than one establishment. Some small establishments are operating units of larger firms.

[7] Bureau of Labor Statistics, National Compensation Survey, March 2007.

[8] CRS calculations based on analysis of the Census Bureau's March 2008 Current Population Survey.

[9] Under I.R.C. §414(q), for 2009 a highly compensated employee is anyone who owned 5% or more of the firm at any time during 2008 or 2009 or anyone whose compensation in 2009 exceeds $110,000. The employer can elect to count only workers in the top 20% of employee compensation as an HCE, but must count all 5% owners.

[10] A plan must satisfy one of two tests: either the proportion of non-highly compensated employees (NHCEs) covered by the plan must be at least 70% of the proportion of highly compensated employees (HCEs) covered by the plan, or the average contribution percentage for NHCEs must be at least 70% of the average contribution percentage for HCEs. Plans that have employer matching contributions are subject to the "actual contribution percentage" (ACP) test, which measures the contribution rate to HCEs' accounts relative to the contribution rate to NHCEs' accounts.

[11] The maximum annual employee salary deferral into a 401(k) plan is $16,500 in 2009 (I.R.C. §402(g)). Employees aged 50 and older can contribute an additional $5,500. The total annual addition to a 40 1(k) plan—comprising the sum of employer and employee contributions—is limited to $49,000 in 2009 (I.R.C. §415(c)).

[12] U.S. Department of Labor, Bureau of Labor Statistics, *Employee Benefits in Small Private Establishments, 1990,* Bulletin 2388, September 1991.

[13] U.S. Department of Labor, Bureau of Labor Statistics, *National Compensation Survey, March 2007*, Summary 07-05, August 2007.

[14] U.S. Small Business Administration, Office of Advocacy.

[15] See, for example, H.R. 2167and S. 1 141of the 110th Congress.

[16] U.S. Department of Labor, Bureau of Labor Statistics, *National Compensation Survey, March 2007*, Summary 07-05, August 2007.

[17] The participation rate in 401(k) plans is from the Profit Sharing/401(k) Council of America's 51st Annual Survey of Profit Sharing and 401(k) Plans. The participation rate in DC plans of all types is from the Department of Labor's National Compensation Survey.

[18] This participation rate is based on a CRS analysis of the Federal Reserve Board's 2007 Survey of Consumer Finances. Similarly, a CRS analysis of the Census Bureau's Survey of Income and Program Participation (SIPP) showed that only 30% of workers under age 35 participated in a defined contribution plan in 2006.

[19] The take-up rate is calculated as the percentage of workers who participated divided by the percentage offered a plan. For workers under age 35, the take-up rate in 2007 was .318/.456 = .697.

[20] All figures cited in this paragraph are from the Federal Reserve Board's 2007 Survey of Consumer Finances.

[21] A notable exception to this rule is the Roth 401(k). In a Roth 401(k), the employee's salary deferrals into the plan are made with after-tax income. In retirement, the part of the withdrawals attributable to the employee's contributions and investment earnings on those contributions is tax free.

[22] For more information, see CRS Report RS2 1795, *The Retirement Savings Tax Credit: A Fact Sheet*, by Patrick Purcell.

[23] Some tax credits – such as the earned income tax credit (EITC) for low-income families – are refundable.

[24] Consider, for example, a young married couple with one child, for whom the husband is the sole breadwinner. In 2007, 25% of all workers aged 18 to 34 who worked year-round, full-time had earnings of $21,000 or less. Taking into account the standard deduction in effect for 2007 ($10,700) and three personal exemptions ($3,400 X 3 = $10,200), a couple with gross income of $21,000 would have had taxable income of $100. The child tax credit of $1,000 would reduce their tax liability to zero. For this couple, the saver's credit would have no value because it is not refundable.

[25] See, for example, CRS Report RL33116, *Retirement Plan Participation and Contributions: Trends from 1998 to 2006*, by Patrick Purcell, and CRS Report RL30922, *Retirement Savings and Household Wealth in 2007*, by Patrick Purcell.

[26] Employers often suspend the match during difficult times. According to the Pension Rights Center, between June 2008 and June 2009, nearly 300 medium and large employers had announced plans to suspend, reduce, or delay their 401(k) matching contributions.[26] See http://www.pensionrights.org/pubs/facts/401(k)-match.html#.

[27] The limit in 2009 is $16,500 (I.R.C. §415(c)).

[28] With respect to after-tax income, even non-participants in plans that do not offer a matching contribution are reducing their total income by not contributing. Nevertheless, because contributions to a 401(k) plan reduce a worker's take-home pay, some workers are willing to give up higher future retirement income for higher current income.

[29] For more information, see CRS Report RL33845, *Retirement Savings: How Much Will Workers Have When They Retire?*, by Patrick Purcell and Debra B. Whitman.

[30] This takes into account contributions by both the household head and his or her spouse. Among household heads who contributed, the median monthly contribution was $280, or $3,360 on an annual basis. This was just 22% of the maximum permissible employee salary deferral under I.R.C. §402(g) in 2007, which was $15,000.

[31] In **Table 3**, households are grouped by income quartile. Income includes earnings and unearned income, such as interest, dividends, rent, and transfer payments. Contributions are reported as a percentage of total household earnings.

[32] Section 902 of P.L. 109-280exempts plans with a qualified automatic contribution arrangement from the nondiscrimination tests.

[33] U.S. Department of Labor, Bureau of Labor Statistics, National Compensation Survey.

[34] ERISA §404(c). Employer stock cannot be one of the three core investment choices.

[35] Profit Sharing/401(k) Council of America, 51st Annual Survey.

[36] Profit Sharing/401(k) Council of America, 51st Annual Survey.

[37] Profit Sharing/401(k) Council of America, 44th Annual Survey and 51st Annual Survey.

[38] Section 406(a)(1)(C) of ERISA prohibits a fiduciary from engaging in a transaction when he knows or should know that such transaction constitutes a direct or indirect furnishing of goods, services, or facilities between the plan and a party in interest. Section 601 of the PPA amended §408(b) of ERISA to add an exception to the transactions prohibited by ERISA for an "eligible investment advice arrangement." For more information, see CRS Report RS22514, *Investment Advice and the Pension Protection Act of 2006*, by Jon O. Shimabukuro.

[39] 29 U.S.C. § 1 108(g)(3)(B)(i)-(v).

[40] *Federal Register*, Vol. 74, No. 98, Friday, May 22, 2009, p. 23951.

[41] Under the PPA, a target date fund is a "qualified default investment alternative" (QDIA).

[42] See http://aging.senate.gov/record.cfm?id=308665.

[43] *Investment News*, "Labor Department, SEC to probe target date funds," April 3, 2009.

[44] Defined Contribution/401(k) Fee Study, Deloitte Consulting LLP, Spring 2009. The report is available on the ICI website at http://www.idc.org/pdf/rpt_09_dc_401k_fee_study.pdf.

[45] See CRS Report RL34678, *Fee Disclosure in Defined Contribution Retirement Plans: Background and Legislation*, by John J. Topoleski.

[46] The examples are based on an account with an initial balance of $20,000 growing at an average annual rate of 7.0%.

[47] Even if fees charged to a DB plan are paid for from plan assets, this increases the sponsor's funding obligation.

[48] *Federal Register*, Vol. 73, No. 142, Wednesday, July 23, 2008, p. 43014.

[49] 26 U.S.C. §401(k)(2)(B)(i)(IV). All distributions are taxable, except any portion that is attributable to after-tax contributions. I.R.C. §72(t) lists limited cases in which distributions made before age 591/2 are not subject to the 10% additional tax on early distributions.

[50] 26 C.F.R. § 1.40 1(k)-1(d). Regular matching contributions and discretionary profit-sharing contributions may also be distributed on account of hardship if the plan so provides. See 26 C.F.R. §1.401(k)-1(d)(3)(ii).

[51] The exceptions to the 10% additional tax are listed at 26 USC, §72(t).

[52] Loans are not permitted from IRAs, but money in an IRA can, in effect, be "borrowed" for 60 days because the law states that any distribution from an IRA that is not deposited in the same or another IRA within 60 days is a taxable distribution. (26 U.S.C. § 408(d)).

[53] More information is available in CRS Report RL30496, *Pension Issues: Lump-Sum Distributions and Retirement Income Security*, by Patrick Purcell, *Pension Issues: Lump-Sum Distributions and Retirement Income Security*, by Patrick Purcell.

[54] If the individual chooses this option, federal law requires 20% of the account balance to be withheld and forwarded to the IRS toward any income tax and tax penalties owed.

[55] Under IRC §72(t), the 10% penalty is waived if the distribution is made in a series of "substantially equal periodic payments" based on the recipient's life expectancy or if the recipient has retired from the plan sponsor at age 55 or older. Other exceptions to the 10% additional tax apply under special circumstances. See CRS Report RL3 1770, *Individual Retirement Accounts and 401(k) Plans: Early Withdrawals and Required Distributions*, by Patrick Purcell.

[56] If the distribution is not rolled over within 60 days, the 20% withheld is applied to the taxes owed on the distribution. If the distribution is rolled over within 60 days, the 20% withheld is credited toward the income tax that the individual owes for the year. If the participant has received the distribution in cash, then to roll over the full amount of the distribution, the recipient must have access to other funds that are at least equal to 20% withheld by the employer.

[57] Distributions of $5,000 or more require the participant's written consent. The $5,000 limit was established by the Taxpayer Relief Act of 1997 (P.L. 105-34). The amount had been set at $3,500 by Retirement Equity Act of 1984. It was originally established at $1,750 by ERISA in 1974.

[58] For more information, see CRS Report R40008, *Converting Retirement Savings into Income: Annuities and Periodic Withdrawals*, by Janemarie Mulvey and Patrick Purcell.

[59] Profit Sharing/401(k) Council of America, 51st Annual Survey.

[60] Hewitt Associates, survey of 401(k) plans, various years.

[61] ERISA § 205; 29 USC § 1055.

[62] Typically, surrender charges drop by about one percentage point per year, eventually allowing penalty-free withdrawals from the annuity.

[63] See "Why Don't People Insure Late Life Consumption? A Framing Explanation of the Under-Annuitization Puzzle," by J. R. Brown, J. R. Kling, S. Mullainathan, and M. V. Wrobel, TIAA-CREF Institute, April 2008.

[64] See *Increasing Annuitization in 401(k) Plans with Automatic Trial Income* by William Gale, J. Mark Iwry, David C. John, and Lina Walker at http://www.retirementsecurityproject.org/pubs/File/RSP_TrialIncomev4(2).pdf.

[65] Guan Gong and Anthony Webb, *Evaluating the Advanced Life Deferred Annuity*, Boston College Center for Retirement Research, Working Paper no. 2007-15, September 2007.

[66] Ibid.

In: When to Retire: Issues in Working and Saving for a Secure…   ISBN: 978-1-60876-982-7
Editor: Maurice R. Davenworth   © 2010 Nova Science Publishers, Inc.

Chapter 2

RETIREMENT DECISIONS: FEDERAL POLICIES OFFER MIXED SIGNALS ABOUT WHEN TO RETIRE

United States Government Accountability Office

WHY GAO DID THIS STUDY

While many factors influence workers' decisions to retire, Social Security, Medicare, and pension laws also play a role, offering incentives to retire earlier and later. Identifying these incentives and how workers respond can help policy makers address the demographic challenges facing the nation.

GAO assessed (1) the incentives federal policies provide about when to retire, (2) recent retirement patterns and whether there is evidence that changes in Social Security requirements have resulted in later retirements, and (3) whether tax-favored private retiree health insurance and pension benefits influence when people retire. GAO analyzed retirement age laws and SSA data and conducted statistical analysis of Health and Retirement Study data. Under the Comptroller General's authority, GAO has prepared this report on its own initiative.

WHAT GAO RECOMMENDS

Congress may wish to consider changes to law, programs, and policies that support retirement security, including retirement ages, in order to provide a set of signals that work in tandem to encourage work at older ages.

GAO received comments from HHS, and technical comments from SSA and the departments of Labor and the Treasury, which were incorporated where appropriate.

WHAT GAO FOUND

Federal policies offer incentives to retire both earlier and later than Social Security's full retirement age depending on a worker's circumstances. The availability of reduced Social Security benefits at age 62 provides an incentive to retire well before the program's age requirement for full retirement benefits; however, the gradual increase in this age from 65 to 67 provides an incentive to wait in order to secure full benefits. The elimination of the Social Security earnings test in 2000 for those at or above their full retirement age also provides an incentive to work. Medicare's eligibility age of 65 continues to provide a strong incentive for those without retiree health insurance to wait until then to retire, but it can also be an incentive to retire before the full retirement age. Meanwhile, federal tax policy creates incentives to retire earlier, albeit indirectly, by setting broad parameters for the ages at which retirement funds can be withdrawn from pensions without tax penalties.

Nearly half of workers report being fully retired before turning age 63 and start drawing Social Security benefits at the earliest opportunity—age 62. Early evidence, however, suggests small changes in this pattern. Traditionally, some workers started benefits when they reached age 65. Recently, workers with full retirement ages after they turned 65 waited until those ages to start benefits. Also, following the elimination of the earnings test, some indications are emerging of increased workforce participation among people at or above full retirement age.

GAO's analysis indicates that retiree health insurance and pension plans are strongly associated with when workers retire. After controlling for other influences such as income, GAO found that those with retiree health insurance were substantially more likely to retire before the Medicare eligibility age of 65 than those without. GAO also found that men with defined benefit plans were more likely to retire early (before age 62) than those without, and men and women with defined contribution plans were less likely to do so.

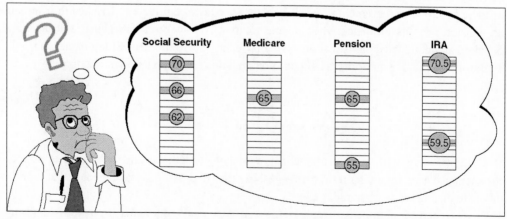

Sources: GAO (analysis); Art Explosion (images).

Federal Retirement Age-Related Rules

ABBREVIATIONS

BEPUF	Benefit and Earning Public Use File
CPS	Current Population Survey
DB	defined benefit
DC	defined contribution
EBRI	Employee Benefit Research Institute
ERISA	Employee Retirement Income Security Act
HRS	Health and Retirement Study
IRA	individual retirement account
NBDS	New Beneficiary Data System
PBGC	Pension Benefit Guarantee Corporation
SSA	Social Security Administration

July 11, 2007

Congressional Committees

The first wave of the 78 million member baby boom generation is now reaching retirement age. The number of people age 62, the earliest age of eligibility for Social Security retired worker benefits, is expected to be 21 percent higher in 2009 than in 2008. In addition, by 2030, the number of workers supporting each retiree is projected to be 2.2, down from 3.3 in 2006. This demographic shift poses challenges to the economy, federal tax revenues, the nation's old-age programs, and individuals' financial security in retirement. For those who are able to work longer, later retirement can strengthen the economy and also retiree incomes by postponing the time at which people will start drawing retirement benefits rather than working. A wide range of factors including the features of employers' benefit plans, personal finances, social norms, health, and individual attitudes influence workers' decisions about when to retire. Federal policies may also play a role: these include Social Security, Medicare, and tax policies related to certain private retiree health and defined benefit (DB) and defined contribution (DC) pension plans.[1] Identifying both the incentives posed by these policies and the extent to which workers respond to them can help to inform policy makers as they consider ways to address the demographic challenges facing the nation.

To determine the extent to which federal policies—directly and indirectly —pose incentives and are influencing individuals' decisions about the age at which they retire, we have pursued the following questions: (1) What incentives do federal policies provide about when to retire? (2) What are the recent retirement patterns, and is there evidence that recent changes in Social Security requirements have resulted in later retirements? (3) Is there evidence that tax-favored private retiree health insurance and pension benefits have influenced when people retire?

We have prepared this report under the Comptroller General's authority to conduct evaluations on his own initiative as part of a continued effort to provide Congress with relevant information on the aging of the American workforce.

To identify which federal policies may influence the age at which workers retire, we reviewed the relevant literature and interviewed agency experts. To answer our second and third objectives, we used two main data sources: (1) Social Security Administration (SSA) data and (2) longitudinal data from the Health and Retirement Study (HRS) conducted by the University of Michigan, which looks at the circumstances under which recent retirees or people who are approaching retirement are making their decisions to retire. We used the SSA data to determine when workers who reached ages 66 through 71 in 2006 started drawing Social Security retired worker benefits. We conducted various statistical analyses of the HRS survey data to determine which factors were associated with decisions to retire at early ages (before age 62) and decisions to retire at later ages (at or after age 65). We focused on workers who were born from 1931 to 1941 (reaching age 62 at some point between 1993 and 2003) and who were in the labor force when the HRS survey began in 1992. To select appropriate variables to consider in our analyses, we reviewed relevant literature and interviewed experts in the field. We conducted reliability assessments of these data and found them to be sufficiently reliable for our study. As is the case with most statistical analyses, our work is limited by factors such as the unavailability of information and the inability to account for influences that cannot be quantified or observed. In addition, our analysis of the HRS survey, which includes only one cohort of workers, may not apply to older or younger groups of workers. In different parts of our analysis we considered workers to be retired based on four different definitions:

- *Reported retirement:* Workers who described themselves as completely retired in response to HRS interviews.

- *Full retirement:* Workers who described themselves as fully retired in response to HRS interviews and who were no longer working for pay.

- *Partial retirement:* Workers who described themselves as retired in response to HRS interviews who were working part-time or for a portion of the year.

- *Social Security retirement:* Workers who received Social Security retired worker benefits as indicated in Social Security administrative data.

These definitions can be used to examine different aspects of retirement whether it be the decision to leave the workforce or the decision to start drawing Social Security benefits. These definitions are not mutually exclusive. For further discussion of these definitions of retirement and details concerning our scope and methodology, see appendix I. We conducted our work between July 2006 and June 2007 in accordance with generally accepted government auditing standards.

RESULTS IN BRIEF

Federal policies offer incentives to retire at different ages depending on a worker's circumstances. The availability of reduced Social Security benefits at age 62 provides an incentive to retire well before the full retirement age, particularly for those in poor health or with short life expectancies. However, the incremental rise in the Social Security full retirement age from 65 to 67 makes it more costly for future cohorts to draw benefits early because of the progressively higher reductions in benefits. This increase in full retirement age gives workers born after 1937 a greater incentive to remain in the workforce longer in order to secure full benefits. The elimination in 2000 of the Social Security earnings test for those at or above full retirement age also provides an incentive (or removes a disincentive) to continue working. With regard to Medicare, the age 65 eligibility requirement for nearly all workers is a strong incentive for those without retiree health insurance to wait until then to retire, since most have only expensive alternatives in the form of extended employer coverage or individual policies. On the other hand, Medicare's availability at 65 can be an incentive to retire before the rising full retirement age. Meanwhile, federal tax policy creates incentives to retire earlier, albeit indirectly, by setting broad parameters for the ages at which retirement funds can be withdrawn without penalty from employer-sponsored pension plans. For example tax laws generally allow workers to begin withdrawing funds from individual retirement accounts (IRAs) and pension plans starting at age 59½ without penalty or earlier under certain circumstances. Withdrawals must generally begin by about age 70½. Additionally, the Employee Retirement Income Security Act (ERISA) allows employer-sponsored, DB pension plans to set earlier eligibility ages without tax penalties. Many of these plans allow workers to retire with reduced benefits at age 55.

Considering how these incentives affect retirement behavior, we found that nearly half of all workers fully retire by the time they reach age 63, but early evidence suggests that alterations in Social Security policy may be fostering some later retirements. Despite Social Security's full retirement age of 65 and above, 46 percent of the workers we studied in the HRS reported having completely retired before their 63rd birthday. In addition, Social Security administrative data shows that 62 remains the median age for starting to draw Social Security benefits—meaning that half of recipients born in the years 1935 through 1940 began drawing benefits before they reached age 62½. There is, nevertheless, evidence that some workers have started drawing benefits later than workers born in earlier years—changes that coincide with changes in Social Security policy. First, there is a slightly smaller proportion of people subject to the higher full retirement age who are drawing Social Security benefits at age 62. Second, although in years past many workers started Social Security benefits when they reached age 65, more recently workers have had full retirement ages some months after they turned 65 and often waited until those ages to start benefits. Third, there are indications that a somewhat higher proportion of people are working in their late 60s following the elimination of the Social Security earnings test for people at or above full retirement age.

Our analysis indicates that employer-provided retiree health insurance and pension plans are strongly associated with when workers retire. After controlling for other factors, we found that those with retiree health insurance in our HRS study group were substantially more likely to retire before the Medicare eligibility age of 65 than those who lacked such coverage. This may reflect the scarcity of affordable options workers have for obtaining health insurance on their own. With regard to our analysis of current employer-sponsored pension plans, we found that men with DB plans were about 28 percent more likely to retire before age 62 than those without these pensions. We found no statistically significant relationship between DB pensions and the age at which women retired. On the other hand, we found that men and women with DC plans were less likely to retire before age 62 than those without DC pensions.

The results of any given policy change continue to be difficult to project given the many countervailing forces at work and workers' sometimes limited understanding of the incentives they face. Nonetheless, as policy makers consider reforms to the Social Security and Medicare programs, it will be important to consider the consolidated impact of the incentives that such reforms might create and act to send signals that consistently encourage those able to continue working to do so. In light of the range of challenges facing the country in the 21st century, Congress may wish to consider changes to laws, programs and policies that support retirement security, including retirement ages, in order to provide a set of signals that work in tandem to encourage work at older ages.

We provided a draft of this report to the Social Security Administration, the departments of Labor, Health and Human Services, and Treasury. The Department of Health and Human Services commented on the report, generally agreeing with our findings on the incentives posed by Medicare and retiree health insurance. (See appen. V.) In addition, SSA and the departments of Labor and the Treasury provided technical comments, which we have incorporated as appropriate.

BACKGROUND

Demographic Changes

In the 21st century, older Americans are expected to make up a larger share of the U.S. population, live longer, and spend more years in retirement than previous generations. The share of the U.S. population age 65 and older is projected to increase from 12.4 percent in 2000 to 19.6 percent in 2030 and continue to grow through 2050. In part, this is due to increases in life expectancy. The average number of years that men who reach age 65 are expected to live is projected to increase from just over 13 in 1970 to 17 by 2020. Women have experienced a similar rise—from 17 years in 1970 to a projected 20 years by 2020. These increases in life expectancy have not, however, resulted in an increase in the average number of years people spend in the workforce. While life expectancy has increased, labor force participation rates of older Americans only began to increase in recent years.[2] As a result, individuals are generally spending more years in retirement. In addition to these factors, fertility rates at about the replacement level are contributing to the elderly population's increasing share in the total population and a slowing in the growth of the labor force. Also contributing to the slowing in the growth of the labor force is the leveling off of women's labor force participation rate. While women's share of the labor force increased dramatically between 1950 and 2000—from 30 percent to 47 percent—their share of the labor force is projected to remain at around 48 percent over the next 50 years. While hard to predict, the level of net immigration can also affect growth in the labor supply.[3] Taking each of these factors into account Social Security's trustees project that the annual growth rate in the labor force, about 1.2 percent in recent years, will fall to 0.3 percent by 2022.

The aging of the baby boom generation, increased life expectancy, and fertility rates at about the replacement level are expected to significantly increase the elderly dependency ratio—the estimated number of people aged 65 and over in relation to the number of people aged 15 to 64 (fig. 1). In 1950, the ratio was 12.5 percent. It increased to 20 percent in 2000 and is projected to further increase to 33 percent by 2050. As a result, there will be relatively fewer younger workers to support a growing number of Social Security and Medicare beneficiaries. The age at which workers choose to retire has implications for these trends. If workers delay retirement, the ratio of workers to the elderly will decrease more slowly.[4]

The aging of the population also has potential implications for the nation's economy. As labor force growth continues to slow as projected, there will be relatively fewer workers available to produce goods and services. In addition, the impending retirement of the baby boom generation may cause the net loss of many experienced workers and possibly create skill gaps in certain occupations. Without a major increase in productivity or higher than projected immigration, low labor force growth will lead to slower growth in the economy compared with growth over the last several decades and potentially slower growth of federal revenues. Social Security's trustees project that real (inflation-adjusted) GDP growth will subside from 2.6 percent in 2007 to 2.0 percent in 2040, in part due to slower growth in the labor force. The prospect of slower economic growth is likely to accentuate the pressures on the federal budget from growing benefit claims and the shrinking proportion of workers to beneficiaries. Later retirement and increases in labor force participation by older workers could help diminish those pressures.

Retirement Dynamics

Retirement has traditionally been thought of as a complete one-time withdrawal from the labor force. However, such transitions are no longer as common. A recent study found that only half of first-time retirees fully retired from the workforce and remained fully retired after 3 to 5 years.[5] The other half chose to partially retire by reducing their work hours or taking bridge jobs—transitional jobs between career work and complete retirement—or they re-entered the labor force after initially retiring.[6] According to our analysis of the HRS, about one in five workers who fully retire later re-enter the workforce on at least a part-time basis sometime over the next 10 years. There are various reasons behind these trends. In some cases, older workers need the income or benefits a job provides; in other cases, they wish to start a new career in a different field. With no universal definition of retirement, researchers use different definitions depending on their purpose. Since our focus is on labor force participation, we are using definitions of retirement that combine whether or not people say they are retired with measures of their labor force participation.[7]

Workers have generally been retiring at younger ages over the last several decades, but over more recent periods, retirement ages appear to have stabilized. This finding holds for a variety of definitions of retirement. Census Bureau data indicate that the average age at which workers left the labor force dropped from about 71 and 70 years for men and women respectively in 1960, to about age 65 for both men and women in 1990 (figure 2).[8] Since that time, retirement trends appear to have stabilized for men, with their retirement occurring on average between 64 and 65. The retirement age for women continued to decline. Similar trends appear in the age at which workers start drawing Social Security benefits. From 1960 to 1990, the average age of workers starting to draw Social Security benefits declined 3 years for men (from 66.8 to 63.7) and about 2 years for women (from 65.2 to 63.5).[9] Since 1990, these averages have changed little. The averages were 63.7 years for men and 63.8 for women in 2005. In addition, in the 2007 Retirement Confidence Survey, workers responded on average that they planned to retire at age 65, up from age 62 in 1996.[10] We, along with others, have suggested that increasing labor force participation for older workers could lessen problems for the economy and the Social Security and Medicare trust funds, and boost income security for retirees as well.[11]

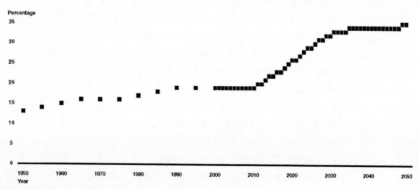

Source: GAO analysis of Census Bureau estimates and projections.
Note: Population age 65 and older as a percent of population age 15 to 64. Data for 2006 through 2050 are projected. The elderly dependency ratio equals the number of people age 65 and older divided by the number between age 15 and 64, expressed as a percentage.

Figure 1. U.S. Elderly Population is Rising Compared to the Working-Age Population

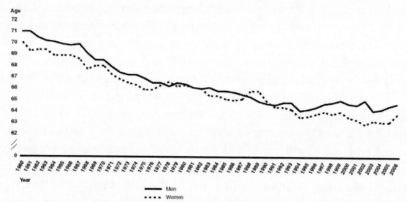

Source: OECD analysis of Census Bureau data.
Note: This is a 5-year moving average based on labor force participation data in the Current Population Survey. For each 5-year period ending in the year shown in the figure, the effective age of retirement corresponds to the average age of exit for all labor force participants initially aged 40 and over who were no longer in the labor force 5 years later.

Figure 2. Average Effective Retirement Ages, 1960 to 2006

Workers retire for a variety of reasons, some of which are under their control while others are not. Some personal reasons for retiring include workers' job situation, their financial situation, and social norms regarding retirement. In addition, there are often factors outside of a person's control that may lead to retirement. According to focus groups that we conducted in 2005 with workers and retirees, we found that health problems and layoffs were common reasons to retire and that few focus group members saw opportunities to gradually or partially retire. Workers also cited what they perceived as their own limited skills and employers' age discrimination as barriers to continued employment.[12] Similarly to our focus group results, the Employee Benefit Research Institute (EBRI) found that an estimated 37 percent of workers retire sooner than they had expected.[13] Of those, the most often cited reasons were health problems or disability, changes at their company, such as downsizing or closure, or having to care for a spouse or another family member. The role federal policies play in influencing retirement behavior needs to be considered as well. Depending on workers' circumstances, these policies can provide incentives to retire at certain ages, and send signals or set norms about when it is appropriate to retire. In addition, many employers have structured their own retirement benefits, such as pension eligibility ages, based on federal policies.

FEDERAL POLICIES PROVIDE INCENTIVES FOR BOTH EARLY AND LATE RETIREMENT

Federal policies present a mix of retirement incentives, some of which encourage individuals to retire well before their Social Security full retirement age and others that promote staying in the workforce. (See figure 3 below.) The effect of these incentives also varies substantially with personal circumstances. In general, the availability of Social Security benefits at age 62 offers an incentive to retire before full retirement age, though changes in program rules are progressively weakening that incentive. The recent elimination of the Social Security earnings test for those at full retirement age and beyond, which had formerly reduced benefits for those beneficiaries who had earnings above a certain threshold, also may discourage drawing benefits early. The fact that most individuals are eligible for Medicare at age 65 generally deters them from leaving the labor force before then, especially if they are not covered by retiree health insurance.[14] Federal pension tax policies give employers discretion to set pension plan rules that provide incentives for many workers to retire somewhat earlier than the norms established by Social Security, often age 55, or in some cases earlier. However, these incentives to retire early apply to fewer workers, due to the diminished prevalence of DB plans.

Social Security Policies Provide Mixed Incentives, While Recent Program Changes Reward Later Retirement

Several characteristics of the Social Security program—including eligibility ages and the earnings test—provide incentives to retire at different ages. The Social Security full retirement age, which has traditionally been age 65, is gradually rising to 67. However, workers can begin receiving reduced benefits at 62; benefits are progressively larger for each month workers postpone drawing them, up to age 70.[15] In general, benefits are "actuarially neutral" to the Social Security program; that is, the reduction for starting benefits before full retirement age and the credit for starting after full retirement age are such that the total value of benefits received over one's lifetime is approximately equivalent for the average individual.[16] However, Social Security creates an incentive to start drawing early retirement benefits for those who are in poor health or otherwise expect to have a less than average lifespan.[17] If a worker lives long enough—past a "break-even" age—he or she will receive more in lifelong retired worker benefits by starting benefits at a later, rather than an earlier date. (See figure 4 below for examples of the kinds of considerations workers face in making a decision about when to begin drawing Social Security benefits.)

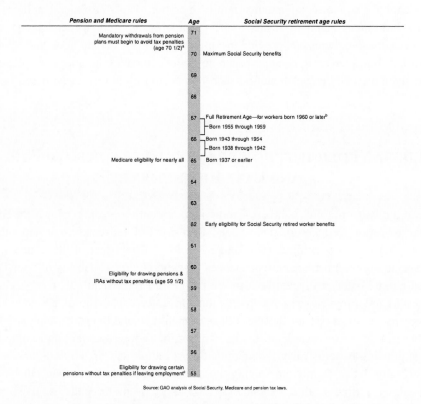

Source: GAO analysis of Social Security, Medicare and pension tax laws.

^aᵃ The age 70½ rule applies by April 1 of the year following the year in which the participant turns 70½. Some exceptions apply, but not for IRAs.

ᵇ For workers born in 1937 or earlier the Social Security full retirement age is 65 and 0 months. For those born in later years it is as follows: 1938 – 65 years and 2 months; 1939 – 65 years and 4 months; 1940 – 65 years and 6 months; 1941 – 65 years and 8 months; 1942 – 65 years and 10 months; 1943 through 1954 – 66 years and 0 months; 1955 – 66 years and 2 months; 1956 – 66 years and 4 months; 1957 – 66 years and 6 months; 1958 – 66 years and 8 months; 1959 – 66 years and 10 months; 1960 and later – 67 years and 0 months.

ᶜ Distributions without tax penalty are allowed at any age in cases where distributions are a series of substantially equal periodic payments for the beneficiary's life or life expectancy, or in other cases including rollover distributions, total and permanent disability, and death.

Figure 3. Federal Retirement Age-Related Rules

The increase in full retirement age and the larger penalty for early retirement reduce the incentive to start drawing Social Security benefits and retiring early.[18] Because the early retirement age has remained fixed at 62 while full retirement age is gradually rising to 67, workers taking early retirement benefits are progressively incurring bigger reductions. For example, workers who reached 62 in 1999 and started drawing benefits that year faced a reduction of 20 percent because their full retirement age was 65. In contrast, workers drawing benefits when they turn 62 in 2022, when their full retirement age will be 67, will face a 30 percent reduction. On the other hand, workers with health problems may now have a greater incentive to apply for Social Security Disability Insurance as these benefits are not based on age.[19]

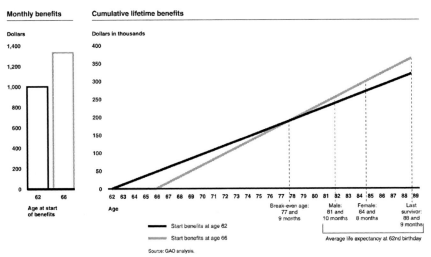

Source: GAO analysis.

Notes: This figure illustrates the case of a worker born in 1950 (with a full retirement age of 66) who would be entitled to a monthly retired worker benefit of $1,000 beginning at age 62 or a monthly benefit of $1,333 beginning at age 66—a 33 percent increase. This assumes no increase in adjusted indexed monthly earnings. If earnings during additional years of work from age 62 through age 65 are high enough to increase the workers' adjusted average earnings over the best 35-years of credited work, the break-even age would be lower. The break-even age varies depending on the ages at which the worker is considering starting benefits and the amounts of benefits available at each age.

As Social Security benefits are adjusted annually for changes in the CPI for wage earners, dollar amounts are shown in constant (inflation-adjusted) terms as of the worker's 62nd birthday. These calculations do not reflect discounting or adjustments for interest rates that may increase the break-even age if, for example, a worker would increase debt or decrease savings as a result of delaying the start of retired-worker benefits. The average last survivor life expectancy is the average life expectancy as of the 62nd birthday for the longest-lived spouse if a man and a woman are born on the same day in 1950.

Figure 4. Lifetime Social Security Retired Worker Benefits are Higher if a Worker Starts Benefits Later and Lives Past His or Her Break-Even Age, Analysis of a Hypothetical Case

Social Security rules can pose different incentives for married workers because their decision about when to start drawing benefits has important implications for the surviving spouse. For example, if a retired worker who is entitled to a larger benefit than his spouse starts drawing early benefits and dies shortly thereafter, his widow may be left for many years with a relatively small survivor benefit since her payment would be limited to what he was receiving.[20] This risk affects female survivors in particular. Widow beneficiaries are one of the largest and most vulnerable groups with a relatively high incidence of poverty.[21]

The Social Security earnings test gives some workers a disincentive to earn more than a specified amount. Because of the earnings test, people collecting Social Security benefits before their full retirement age who continue to work are subject to further reduction or withholding in their benefits if they earn above a threshold. For example, in 2007, $1 of benefits is withheld for every $2 of earnings over $12,960.[22] Although early beneficiaries generally recoup the amounts withheld because of the earnings test in the form of higher recalculated benefits after they reach full retirement age, workers typically view the earnings test as a tax on work.[23] As such, it provides an incentive to reduce the number of hours worked or stop working altogether.[24] Since 2000, beneficiaries who reach their full retirement age are exempt from the earnings test. The elimination of the test for these individuals is an incentive to start benefits at full retirement age and continue working.[25]

Medicare's Age Requirement Generally Provides an Incentive Not to Retire before 65

Because Medicare provides health insurance coverage for virtually all individuals 65 and older, it has important implications for the decision about when to retire.[26] The Medicare eligibility age, fixed at 65 since the program's inception, is a strong incentive not to retire before that age, particularly for people who do not have employer-sponsored health benefits as retired workers. These individuals would either have to purchase expensive private coverage if they retired before 65, or remain uninsured until they qualify for Medicare because private health insurance may be difficult to obtain at older ages, especially for those with preexisting medical conditions.[27] Given the steep rise in health care costs and the high health risks older people face, Medicare's eligibility age encourages them to delay retirement until age 65.[28] Workers with no employer-based health insurance during their working years are arguably less affected by Medicare eligibility rules because their decision to retire does not affect their health coverage. However, to the extent that they are exposed to the same potentially expensive health problems as they get older, Medicare does provide an incentive to postpone retirement until age 65 because retirement often involves a significant drop in income.

The incentive posed by Medicare may become more important if the proportion of workers with no retiree health insurance continues to increase. The share of large private employers offering retiree health insurance declined from an estimated 66 percent in 1988 to 35 percent in 2006.[29] Similarly, a 2003 study found that only about one-quarter of private sector employees worked for companies that offered retiree health insurance.[30] Further, the value of the coverage for retirees is eroding because of higher costs, eligibility restrictions, and other benefit changes. A recent study estimated that the percentage of after-tax income spent on health care by the typical older married couple will almost double from 16 percent in 2000 to 35 percent in 2030.[31]

On the other hand, Medicare's availability at 65 can be an incentive to retire before Social Security's rising full retirement age. Eligibility for Medicare upon reaching age 65 encourages workers to retire then, rather than wait to collect somewhat higher Social Security benefits when they reach their later full retirement age.[32]

Certain Tax Laws for Pension Plans Enable Employers to Create Incentives for Retirement before Age 62

Federal tax and pension laws, including the Employee Retirement Income Security Act (ERISA), give employers some discretion to set retirement ages and other terms and conditions that support earlier retirement for workers who have employer-sponsored pension plans. For example, IRS rules on tax-qualified pensions put an upper limit on what may be treated as a "normal retirement age" (NRA).[33] For a DB plan, this can be no greater than age 65.[34] In practice, some employers have set their NRA lower.[35]

According to the Department of Labor's 2003 National Compensation Survey, 17 percent of private workers with DB plans had an NRA less than 65 and 6 percent had no age requirement. Many workers with DB plans could retire with reduced benefits at age 55.[36] IRS rules also state that payouts with specified minimum amounts must generally begin by about age 70½.[37] Additionally, tax rules generally permit withdrawals without penalty from both DB and DC plans (including IRAs) as early as age 59½. Exceptions to this rule allow for even earlier withdrawals. For example, participants can access their funds without penalty beginning at age 55 if they leave their current employer.[38] Workers taking distributions prior to age 59½ may do so without the tax penalty if they receive the distribution in the form of a fixed annuity.[39] For those who are no longer working for the plan's sponsor, tax law generally requires at a minimum that such a series of payments begin at about age 70½ at the latest or that they receive a lump sum payment of the entire amount. If a plan participant is working for the plan sponsor at age 70½ the required distributions must generally begin in the calendar year in which he or she stops working for the employer maintaining the plan.[40]

Workers who have employer-sponsored pension plans from their current employer constitute only about half of full-time private sector workers. Employers have increasingly shifted from traditional DB to DC pension plans.[41] Specifically, in 1992, about 29 percent of heads of household had a DB plan; by 2004, the figure had dropped to 20 percent. Over this same period, the proportion of household heads with DC plans increased from about 28 percent to 34 percent.

As the prevalence of DC plans has increased relative to DB plans, workers face a different set of incentives.[42] The benefits of a worker covered by a DB plan often reach their high value when the worker attains a specific age, and as a result, may offer little incentive to work past that age.[43] The predetermined retirement benefit generally depends on years of service and wages or salaries, and changes little after its peak value, especially if subsequent salary increases are not substantial.[44] Additional years of work after the NRA, often age 65 for private sector workers in 2003, do not necessarily change lifetime retirement benefits because of the shortened retirement period.[45] (See table 1 for an example showing the effect of another year of work with a hypothetical DB pension.)

With DC plans, benefit levels depend on total employer and employee contributions and investment earnings; as such, DC plans do not offer the same age-related retirement incentive as DB plans. Individuals typically allocate the balance of their DC accounts among bonds, stocks, and money market funds, bearing all of the investment risks. In addition, since at retirement most DC plans allow people to receive the accumulated value of the funds in their account as a lump sum, individuals also bear the risk of outliving their resources. The fact that different people will make different contribution and investment decisions is likely to lead to a greater variability in retirement ages. (See table 2 below for an example showing the effect of another year of work on lifetime benefits with a DC pension.)

While a DB pension plan generally does not encourage continued work after a certain age, recent changes in DB pension provisions have created an incentive to remain in the workforce somewhat longer. First, recent IRS regulations permit workers to receive money from their DB plans while still working after they have reached the plan's NRA.[46] These regulations also include rules restricting a plan's NRA. Those reaching a plan's NRA or age 62 who want to reduce the number of hours they work for a particular employer may be able to do so and at the same time receive prorated pension benefits. As a result, these workers are able to ease out of their jobs while maintaining their previous level of income by combining paycheck and pension.[47] The new provisions are likely to encourage longer careers by formally allowing more flexible work arrangements and the opportunity to gradually transition into retirement rather than make a sudden shift. By comparison, participants in DC plans can often begin receiving their pension at age 59½ while continuing to work (if allowed by their plan administrator), so they often face fewer limitations to phased retirement.[48]

Table 1. A Delay in Retirement Can Result in Lower Lifetime Benefits from a DB Pension, Analysis of a Hypothetical Case

	Retire at 62	Retire at 63	Difference
Annual pension beginning age 62 1.5% x $31,177 x 35 years of service	$16,368		
Annual pension beginning age 63 1.5% x $ $32,112 x 36 years of service (adjusted for inflation at 3 percent)		$16,836	
Increase in annual pension as a result of the 36th year of work			$468
Total pension expected over a retirement based on remaining life expectancy at 62nd birthday (average for men and women) $16,368 x 21.2 years adjusted for inflation	248,965		
Total pension expected over a retirement beginning on 63rd birthday based on remaining life expectancy at 62nd birthday $16,836 x 20.2 years adjusted for inflation		246,694	
Increase (decrease) in lifetime benefit for retirement at age 63 compared with retirement at age 62			(2,270)

Source: GAO analysis.

Table 2. A Delay in Retirement Can Result in Higher Lifetime Benefits from a DC Pension, Analysis of a Hypothetical Case

	Retire at age 62	Retire at age 63	Difference
401(k) balance on 62nd birthday	$200,000	$200,000	
Expected interest on the balance (at 5.125 percent) during an additional year of work		10,250	
Worker's contribution during additional year of work		3,000	
Employer's matching contribution during additional year of work		1,500	
Expected earnings during the year on additional contributions		115	
Total expected balance on 63rd birthday		214,865	
Total expected balance on 63rd birthday adjusted for inflation at 3%		208,607	
Annuity beginning age 62 based on balance of $200,000 (annual amount)	16,368		
Annuity beginning age 63 based on a balance of $214,865 adjusted for inflation (annual amount)		17,417	
Increase in annual pension as a result of the 36th year of work			$1,049
Total pension expected over the period of retirement (lifetime benefit) based on life expectancy at 62nd birthday $16,368 x 21.2 years (adjusted for inflation at 3 percent)	248,965		
Total pension expected over the period of retirement beginning on 63rd birthday (lifetime benefit) based on life expectancy at 62nd birthday $16,917 x 20.2 years (adjusted for inflation at 3 percent)		255,220	
Increase (decrease) in lifetime benefit for retirement at age 63 compared with retirement at age 62			6,255

Source: GAO analysis.

Note: Both pension holders in tables 1 and 2 would receive the same annual pension if they retire on their 62nd birthdays. Both would realize an increase in their annual pension income if they worked another year and retired on their 63rd birthday, but the amount of the DC annual pension would increase more. The worker with a DB pension wouldn't receive enough of an increase to compensate for the shorter expected period of retirement.

HALF OF WORKERS RETIRE WELL BEFORE THEIR FULL RETIREMENT AGE, ALTHOUGH EARLY EVIDENCE POINTS TO SOME CHANGES FOLLOWING RECENT IMPLEMENTATION OF SOCIAL SECURITY POLICIES

About half of those in the HRS study group reported being fully retired by the time they reached age 63, and over the last several years SSA data indicate that nearly half started drawing benefits at age 62 and 1 month, their earliest opportunity to do so.[49] However, there is some evidence that this behavior is starting to change to a limited extent. With the graduated rise in full retirement ages for persons born after 1937, a somewhat smaller proportion of these workers are starting to draw benefits at 62. Others are waiting to draw benefits until the higher full retirement ages that apply to them. Also, since the January 2000 elimination of the earnings test for workers at full retirement age and beyond, labor force participation among such older workers has increased.

Nearly Half of Workers Fully Retire before Reaching Age 63

Despite Social Security's full retirement age of 65 and later, we found that about half of the workers in the HRS study group reported that they fully retired by age 63. Specifically, an estimated 46 percent of workers born in 1931 through 1941 reported fully retiring before their 63rd birthday, based on our analysis of workers interviewed in the HRS sample.[50] As shown in figure 5 below, we found a pattern of retirement marked by a steady increase in retirements among people in their late 50s until ages 62 and 65, when the numbers increase sharply. For workers in the study group the estimated probability of fully retiring prior to age 60 was 28 percent, and the estimated probability prior to age 65 was 60 percent.

Social Security Administration data provide similar indications of early retirement patterns. Many workers begin drawing Social Security benefits at age 62. Half the workers born 1935 through 1940 started to draw Social Security benefits before they reached age 62½. The most common age was 62 and 1 month—the earliest age at which most workers are eligible. Only about 13 to 17 percent of workers born in these years started to draw benefits at their full retirement age.

In a 2005 study, researchers analyzing the characteristics of workers who began drawing Social Security benefits at age 62 found that many had no earnings or comparatively low earnings in the years before they reached age 62.[51] Among workers in this study born in 1937 (who reached 62 in 1999), for example, 20 percent had no earnings at age 55, and this figure rose to 32 percent at age 61 for men who started drawing Social Security benefits at age 62.[52] The comparable figures for those who started drawing benefits between age 63 and 65 ranged from 11 to 12 percent. It is not clear to what extent these low earners or non-earners had chosen to retire before reaching age 62 or whether they were in the labor force, but not able to find work before reaching age 62. As discussed above, EBRI found that an estimated 37 percent of workers retire sooner than they had expected to. The most often cited reasons were health problems or disability, changes at their company, such as downsizing or closure, or having to care for a spouse or another family member.

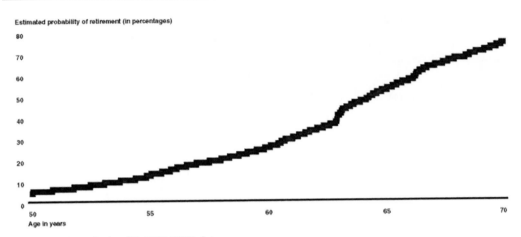

Source: GAO analysis of RAND HRS data.

Note: This analysis is for workers born 1931 through 1941. It excludes outliers among workers born in 1937, 1938, and 1939. Workers born in 1940 or 1941 had not reached age 65 by the end of the study period, so the probabilities at later ages are not shown. Those who reached 65 during the study period were classified as having the following labor force status at that age: 56 percent were fully retired; 15 percent were partially retired; 19 percent were working full time; 5 percent were working part time; 4 percent were not in the labor force; 2 percent were disabled; and 0.4 percent were unemployed.

Figure 5. Retirement Pattern among Workers Born from 1931 to 1941

Early Evidence Points to Small Changes in the Ages at Which Workers Start Drawing Social Security Benefits

Social Security administrative data for those born between 1935 and 1940 provide evidence of some modest changes in retirement behavior among the first group of workers subject to the increases in the Social Security full retirement age. First, a declining proportion of workers are starting to draw benefits as soon as they are eligible. Whereas 46 or 47 percent of those with a full retirement age of 65 and 0 months (born in 1935 through 1937) started benefits at the earliest opportunity, 45 to 42 percent of those who were subject to an increased full retirement age did so, as shown in table 3 below.[53] That many workers continue to start drawing benefits at the earliest opportunity may, in part, reflect workers' lack of knowledge about their full retirement age. A 2007 survey indicated that an estimated 56 percent of workers aged 55 and over incorrectly identified or did not know the age at which they can receive unreduced Social Security benefits.[54]

Second, along with changes in the proportion of workers drawing Social Security retired worker benefits at the earliest opportunity, we see early indications of changes at workers' full retirement ages. The traditional rise in the proportion of workers beginning to draw benefits at their 65th birthday has largely shifted in concert with the gradual rise in the age required by Social Security for full retired worker benefits.[55] As shown in figure 6 below, some of the workers in successive cohorts who were born after 1937 have waited additional months to start drawing benefits—that is, until their higher full retirement ages.[56]

Table 3. Early Evidence That Some Workers Are Delaying the Start of Social Security Retired Worker Benefits

Birth year	Full Retirement Age	Percent of workers starting to draw benefits			
		At the earliest opportunity[a]	At full retirement age[b]	By month before 65th Birthday[c]	By month before 66th Birthday[d]
1935	65 and 0 months	47	17	78	97
1936	65 and 0 months	47	16	79	97
1937	65 and 0 months	46	15	80	96
1938	65 and 2 months	45	13	77	96
1939	65 and 4 months	43	13	73	95
1940	65 and 6 months	42	13	71	95

Source: GAO analysis of SSA data.

Note: Rows for birth years 1938, 1939, and 1940 identify workers subject to a full retirement age after their 65th birthday. The estimated percentage of workers born in 1936 through 1940 who are expected to draw benefits, but had not done so by the end of 2006 was 0, 1, 2, 3, and 5 percent, respectively.

[a] Cumulative percent from 62 and 0 months through 62 and 1 month.

[b] Percent of workers at 65 and 0 months for workers born 1935 through 1937, at 65 and 2 months for those born in 1938; 65 and 4 months for those born in 1939; and 65 and 6 months for those born in 1940.

[c] Cumulative percent from 62 and 0 months through 64 and 11 months.

[d] Cumulative percent from 62 and 0 months through 65 and 11 months.

Following Elimination of the Earnings Test, More Workers Are Remaining in the Labor Force beyond Full Retirement Age

Along with these modest delays in claiming Social Security benefits that are associated with the rising full retirement age, we found that some increases in labor force participation coincided with the elimination of the earnings test in January 2000. Our analysis of all workers in the HRS sample found that the proportion of 66 and 67 year olds who were employed (full-time, part-time, or partially retired) increased between 2000 and 2004 by 4 percentage points.[57] Another researcher's analysis of BLS data found that between 1994 and 2005, the proportion of 65 to 69 year olds in the labor force increased by about 7 percentage points for men and by about 6 percentage points for women. While there may be a variety of reasons for this upward trend, some researchers attribute it to the elimination of the Social Security earnings test. After controlling for other factors associated with retirement, one study concluded that the labor force participation rate among those 65 to 69 increased by 0.8 to 2 percentage points and that earnings for this group increased.[58] The authors hypothesized that this increase resulted from the retention of older workers who were still in the workforce instead of attracting retirees to return to work. This study also found that applications for Social Security benefits among individuals at ages 65 or above increased and that earnings for this group increased as well. A second study also concluded that the elimination of the earnings test had increased labor force participation among older workers, and that there was some indication that participation rates among younger workers increased in anticipation of this policy change.[59] A third study found that men aged 66 to 69 had an increase in annual earnings of $1,326 following the earnings test elimination.[60] This study did not find that labor force participation increased overall, but rather that the hours per week worked by men increased. A final study found the effect of the elimination of the earnings test has not only been confined to those above full retirement age. Rather, this change has resulted in men with earnings above the earnings test threshold reporting an increased probability that they will work after full retirement age.[61]

These studies also indicate that relatively more workers in the upper- middle income range have responded to the elimination of the earnings test by continuing to work. Specifically, two studies found that earnings increased for those in the higher income percentiles, but not for those in lower income groups.[62] See appendix III for more information on these studies.

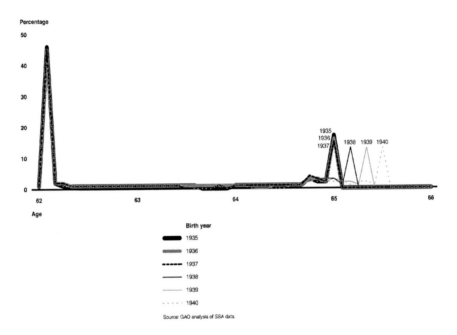

Source: GAO analysis of SSA data.

Note 1. This graph shows estimates for ages 62 and 0 months through 66 and 0 months. The maximum proportion for ages 66 and 1 month through 70 and over was 1 percent. Although the proportion of workers starting benefits each month after age 62 and 1 month and before age 65 is relatively low, the cumulative percent of workers starting benefits during this period was substantial —ranging from 29 percent for those born in 1940 to 33 percent for those born in 1936 and 1937.

Note 2. These percentages are calculated as the number of workers starting to draw benefits at each age in months divided by the total number of workers born in the same year who have or are expected to eventually draw benefits. These figures for benefits awarded in 1997 through 2006 exclude workers who had previously drawn disability benefits and subsequently begun drawing retired worker benefits. The workers born in 1940 reached age 66 in 2006 and those born in 1935 reached age 71 in 2006.

Figure 6. People Typically Begin Drawing Retired Worker Social Security Benefits at Age 62 or at Full Retirement Age

TAX-FAVORED PRIVATE RETIREE HEALTH INSURANCE AND PENSION PLANS MAY INFLUENCE RETIREMENT PATTERNS

We found employer-provided retiree health insurance and pension plans are strongly associated with when workers retire based on our analysis of retirement behavior using the HRS.[63] We found that workers with access to retiree health insurance were more likely to retire before age 65 than those without it.[64] However, other factors, such as poor health, could become an overriding factor for some of these workers, in terms of their retirement decisions. At the beginning of the study period (1992), those workers who lacked retiree health insurance tended to be those with lower incomes and levels of education.[65] Pension plans also influenced the timing of workers' retirements, though this varied by type of pension plan. Men with DB plans were more likely to retire earlier, whereas both men and women with DC plans tended to retire later compared to those who did not have these plans.[66]

Workers with Employer- Provided Retiree Health Benefits Have Been More Likely to Retire before 65

Our analysis of retirement behavior suggests that workers who have access to health insurance in retirement are substantially more likely to retire before becoming eligible for Medicare at age 65 than those without such access.[67] Men with retiree health insurance either through their own or their spouse's current or former employer were an estimated 86 percent more likely to retire before they turned 65 than those who were not eligible for benefits in retirement. Women with retiree health insurance were more than twice as likely (139 percent more likely) to retire by this same age. We also found that workers with retiree health insurance were more likely to retire before they became eligible for early Social Security benefits at the age of 62 (109 percent and 76 percent more likely, respectively for men and women). For a complete discussion of our model results, please see appendix II. The population without access to retiree health insurance tended to be those with lower incomes and less education. See Appendix IV for information on the demographic characteristics of people with access to retiree health insurance at the beginning of the study period.

These findings are consistent with a larger body of research indicating a strong link between health insurance availability and retirement decisions. For example, a 2002 study found that having retiree health insurance available increased the likelihood of workers retiring before age 65 by an estimated 15 to 35 percent.[68] According to the 2003 Health Confidence Survey, almost 80 percent of current workers over age 40 consider their access to health insurance in planning the age at which they expect to retire.[69] That people without access to retiree health insurance are more likely to wait until they are eligible for Medicare to retire may reflect the scarcity of options for affordable health insurance outside of employer-based plans. Particularly for those in poor health, market-based health insurance coverage may be prohibitively costly.

Health problems that limit work lead to earlier retirement for many workers regardless of the availability of retiree health benefits. After controlling for other factors, including whether one had access to retiree health insurance, we found that men who said that their health limited their work were over two times more likely to retire by age 62 and that women were

96 percent more likely to do so. Similarly, men and women reporting these limitations were more likely to retire by age 65 (71 percent and 72 percent, respectively).[70]

Pension Plans May Influence Retirement Timing, but This Effect Differs by Pension Type

We found that men with DB plans generally retired earlier than those without, while both men and women with DC plans generally retired later, based on our analysis of the HRS data.[71] After controlling for other factors, men with DB plans through either their employer or their spouse's employer were 28 percent more likely to retire before age 62.[72] Results for women were not statistically significant. On the other hand, we found that men with DC plans were 47 percent less likely to retire by 62 than those without DC plans.[73] We found a similar effect for women as well; those with DC plans were 37 percent less likely to retire before 62 than those without DC plans. Looking at retirements before or after age 65, we did not find a significant effect of having a DB pension plan. However, we continued to find a diminished likelihood of retiring before age 65 among those with DC plans, with men 35 percent less likely to retire by age 65 and women 45 percent less likely to retire than those without DC plans.

Our finding that men with DB pensions were more likely to retire before age 62 is consistent with a larger body of research that finds that the structure of DB plans can lead to earlier retirements. One study found that the differences in retirement patterns for those with DB or DC pensions were related to the ability of DB plans to subsidize retirements at ages as early as age 55. Some of these pensions allow long-tenured individuals to collect early benefits that are high enough to provide an incentive to retire early.[74] DC plans, on the other hand, are generally neutral with regard to retirement age since DC account balances depend on contributions made by both employers and employees instead of years of service. Another study found that retirement patterns for those with DB plans and those with DC plans began to differ at around age 55. Differences increased at around age 60, when the value of lifetime benefit began decreasing for most workers with DB plans.[75] This same study found that the absence of retirement incentives tied to age in DC plans led people with those plans to retire on average almost two years later than those with DB plans.

CONCLUSIONS

The age at which workers retire is important for the sake of their retirement income security, the cost of federal programs for the elderly, federal tax revenue, and the strength of the U.S. economy. In deciding when to retire, workers weigh their personal circumstances, the features of employers' benefit plans as well as the mix of incentives and disincentives posed by federal policies. Some of these policies encourage earlier retirement; others encourage later retirement; and different groups of workers face differing incentives. While preliminary evidence indicates that some workers subject to full retirement ages after their 65th birthday are drawing Social Security benefits a little later and working more after age 65 than their predecessors, more time is needed to determine whether these changes foretell any substantial shifts. With so many factors influencing workers' decisions about when to retire, changes may be gradual and limited. Moreover, changes made to one program have the potential to create an inconsistent set of incentives. For example, as Social Security's full retirement age rises to age 67, Medicare's eligibility age remains at 65. Medicare's eligibility age may become increasingly important in workers' decisions about when to retire as the availability of employer-sponsored retiree health insurance declines.

In recent years, federal policy makers have considered various options to modify policies in hopes of promoting later retirements and continued work in later years. However, the results of any given policy change continue to be difficult to project given the many countervailing forces at work and workers' sometimes limited understanding of the incentives they face. To date, we see indications of some changes in retirement behavior, but do not yet see large changes. At the same time, trends in employer- provided retirement benefits have clear implications for workers' retirement decisions. Our results suggest that with declining access to retiree health insurance and DB pension plans, those individuals who can, may indeed choose to work longer. This trend suggests the need for federal initiatives to help support workers who make that choice. These may include policies that encourage employers to hire or retain older workers and provide them with flexible options for continued work. In addition, there will be a continued need for federal policies to ensure that workers are informed about the advantages of continued work, as well as to protect and support those who, due to poor health or disability, are unable to work at older ages.

Given the increased pressures that demographic shifts will place on entitlement programs, the mix of incentives offered by programs such as Social Security and Medicare, as well as pension law, becomes more questionable. Ultimately, it will be important for policy makers to understand the incentive structures that their policies create, and to coordinate their decisions to allow for individual flexibility, but send signals that consistently encourage those who are able to continue working to do so.

MATTER FOR CONGRESSIONAL CONSIDERATION

Accordingly, in light of the range of challenges facing the country in the 21st century, Congress may wish to consider changes to laws, programs, and policies that support retirement security, including retirement ages, in order to provide a set of signals that work in tandem to encourage work at older ages.

AGENCY COMMENTS

We provided a draft of this report to the Social Security Administration and the departments of Labor, Health and Human Services, and the Treasury. The Department of Health and Human Services commented on the report, generally agreeing with our findings on the incentives posed by Medicare and retiree health insurance. (See appen. V.) In addition, SSA, and the departments of Labor and the Treasury provided technical comments, which we incorporated where appropriate.

Barbara D. Bovbjerg, Director
Education, Workforce, and Income Security Issues

List of Congressional Committees

The Honorable Max Baucus
Chairman
The Honorable Charles E. Grassley
Ranking Member
Committee on Finance
United States Senate

The Honorable Edward M. Kennedy
Chairman
The Honorable Michael B. Enzi
Ranking Member
Committee on Health, Education, Labor, and Pensions
United States Senate

The Honorable Herb Kohl
Chairman
The Honorable Gordon H. Smith
Ranking Member, Special Committee on Aging
United States Senate

The Honorable Tom Davis
Ranking Member
Committee on Oversight and Government Reform
House of Representatives

The Honorable Charles B. Rangel
Chairman
The Honorable Jim McCrery, Ranking Member
Committee on Ways and Means
House of Representatives

The Honorable Michael R. McNulty
Chairman
The Honorable Sam Johnson
Ranking Member
Subcommittee on Social Security
Committee on Ways and Means
House of Representatives

APPENDIX I. OBJECTIVES, SCOPE, AND METHODOLOGY

Our objectives were to 1) identify incentives federal policies provide about when to retire; (2) determine recent retirement patterns and whether there is evidence that recent changes in Social Security requirements have resulted in later retirements; and 3) determine if there is evidence that tax-favored private retiree health insurance and pension benefits influence when people retire.

To answer our first objective, we reviewed the relevant literature and interviewed agency officials to identify which federal policies may influence the age at which workers retire.

To answer our second objective, we analyzed data from the Social Security administration and reviewed studies of the effects of changes in SSA rules. We used the SSA data to look at when workers, who were between the ages of 66 to 71 in 2006, chose to start Social Security retired worker benefits. While these data allowed us to examine patterns in men's and women's claiming of Social Security benefits, they did not contain any other personal information that would allow us to control for differences between workers. Therefore, we were able to use these data for descriptive purposes only. We analyzed these data and found them to be reliable for our purposes.

To answer the third objective, we first analyzed data from the Health and Retirement Study (HRS), a national, longitudinal survey of older Americans produced by the University of Michigan.[76] In particular, we used a data set that the RAND Corporation compiled on the HRS, which is a more user-friendly subset of the HRS. This rich data set contains information on retirement timing and a wide variety of associated factors, such as demographic characteristics, income, assets, health, health care insurance, workforce status, pensions, and retirement expectations. In addition, it tracks respondents over time, allowing us to look at the initial HRS cohort (those born from 1931 to 1941) over a 12 year period from 1992 to 2004.[77] We conducted both bivariate and multivariate analyses to determine what factors were associated with workers' decisions about when to retire, with special attention to Social Security, health care, and pension availability. See appendix II for a full description of these analyses. We analyzed this dataset and found it to be reliable for our purposes.

We conducted our work between July 2006 and June 2007 in accordance with generally accepted government auditing standards.

This appendix is organized into three sections to more fully describe the methods we used to analyze our data, with particular focus on our analysis of the RAND HRS data: Section 1 describes the definitions of retirement used in this analysis. Section 2 describes how we selected our different samples for analysis. Section 3 describes limitations to our analysis.

Retirement Definitions

As other researchers have done, we used different definitions for retirement in different parts of our analysis. In particular, we considered workers to be retired based on one of four different definitions, which are explained in table 4 below:

Table 4. Definitions of Retirement

	Source of data	Definition
Reported retirement	HRS	The respondent reports being either completely or partly retired to the question "At this time do you consider yourself completely retired, partly retired, or not retired at all."
Full retirement[a]	HRS	To be considered fully retired, a respondent must report not working for pay at all, and report being retired in response to the question above or another question concerning retirement and employment status.
Partial retirement[a]	HRS	The respondent reports working between 1 and 35 hours per week or less than 36 weeks per year, and reports being retired in response to either of the questions referred to above.
Social Security retirement	SSA administrative data	The worker has started drawing Social Security retired worker benefits, excluding people who earlier drew disabled worker benefits and automatically converted to retired worker benefits.

Source: HRS and SSA.

[a] A respondent is considered fully or partially retired based on a labor force status variable that the RAND Corporation constructs using several questions in the HRS. If a respondent reports working full-time he or she is classified as working full-time rather than retired, whether or not he or she also reports being retired.

We conducted our multivariate analysis based on two of these retirement definitions. Since our focus in this study is on when people decided to fully withdrawal from the labor force, our primary analysis was of those who had fully retired. We also ran an analysis on those who had fully or partially retired and received similar results. For our analysis of the claiming of Social Security benefits, we used the definition of Social Security retirement. Finally, for some of our descriptive results of those who said they retired prior to the beginning of the HRS, we used our definition of reported retirement.

Sample Selection

Just as we used different definitions of retirement, we also chose different samples of workers. Since our goal in analyzing the HRS data was to model retirement behavior, we sought to look at individuals who had a chance to retire; in other words, they had reached traditional ages of retirement. Therefore, we focused our analysis on those in the HRS cohort who were born between 1931 and 1941. These individuals were between the ages of 63 and 73 in 2004, when the most recent data for the HRS were collected. Second, we chose individuals who had been in the labor force for at least 10 years so that they could qualify for Social Security retired worker benefits based on their own work history. To calculate certain descriptive statistics, we just applied the above two criteria to create a worker sample. For our regression analyses, we added the stipulation that a respondent was in the workforce in 1992 when the HRS began.[78] Applying these criteria excludes respondents who had retired, were out of the labor force (such as homemakers), or those who were not working due to disability in 1992.[79] This allowed us to model the act of retiring from the labor force. In addition, we were not able to observe the behavior of those who retired outside of the 1992 to 2004 study period. See table 5 below for the criteria we used to construct these samples.

Although the HRS cohort is a nationally representative sample of those born from 1931 to 1941, the samples that we constructed may not be.[80] In comparing some of the descriptive statistics of our samples with those from the larger HRS sample, there are differences, as shown in table 6 below. In particular, the sample used to analyze full retirement decisions had a greater proportion of those in better health, those with access to retiree health insurance, and higher income than either the HRS cohort or the worker sample.

Table 5. Selection of Samples for Analysis of Health and Retirement Study Respondents

Sample	Criteria applied	Respondents dropped	Unweighted number of respondents remaining
RAND HRS Sample[a]			12,652
Health and Retirement Study Worker Sample	Respondents born 1931 through 1941	2,903	9,749
	Had 10 years of work experience prior to age 62[b]	1,133	8,616
Sample for Logistic Regression Analysis of Full Retirement	Respondents born 1931 through 1941		9,749
	Had ten years of work experience by age 62[b]	1,133	8,616
	In labor force in 1992 (working full time, working part time, unemployed, or partially retired in wave 1)[c]	1,834	6,782[d]

Source: GAO Analysis of RAND HRS data.

Note: This table includes only respondents with a positive respondent statistical weight. The respondent level weight is non-zero for living noninstitutionalized respondents born in the appropriate years. It is zero for nonrespondents, deceased respondents and respondents residing in nursing homes. It is scaled so as to yield weight sums which correspond to the number of individuals in the U.S. population as measured by the March Current Population Survey (CPS) for the year of data collection.

[a] RAND HRS file release F, October 2006. See Patricia St. Clair et al., RAND HRS Data Documentation, Version F (Santa Monica, Calif.: May 2006).

[b] Based on responses to question concerning work history and job tenure in any HRS study wave 1992 through 2004.

[c] Based on RAND's construction of a labor force status variable, RxLBRF. RAND assigned respondents to these categories: works full-time, works part-time, unemployed, partly retired, retired, disabled, or not in the labor force.

[d] The number of respondents studied who fully retired is greater than the number who partially or fully retired, because 313 respondents who were partially retired in wave one were excluded from our analysis of full or partial retirement but included in our analysis of full retirement.

Table 6. Descriptive Statistics for Our Different Samples

Weighted Demographics as of wave 1 (1992)	HRS cohort individuals born 1931 – 1941	Worker sample	Full retirement sample
Percent male	48%	52%	55%
Percent married	74%	75%	75%
Percent white non-Hispanic	81%	82%	83%
Percent with high school education or more	77%	80%	82%
Percent who have access to retiree health insurance through respondent's or spouse's current employer	52%	54%	55%
Percent who have DB plan from respondent's or spouse's current employer[a]	45%	47%	53%
Percent who have good, very good, or excellent health	80%	82%	88%
Annual earned income in 2003 dollars[b]			
Percent less than $10,000	38%	31%	18%
Percent $10,000 or more, but less than $25,000	18%	20%	23%
Percent $25,000 or more, but less than $50,000	25%	28%	33%
Percent $50,000 or more	19%	21%	26%

Source: GAO analysis of RAND HRS data.

[a] Those with a DB plan may have also had a DC plan. Those without a DB plan may have had a DC plan or no pension plan. Similarly, in our analysis of DC plans, we grouped respondents with both DB and DC plans along with those reported having only a DC plan.

[b] This includes the respondent's earnings (including wages, salary, and bonuses from employment or self-employment), but not their spouse's income. It excludes other types of income, such as interest, dividends, and rent.

Limitations

We identified factors associated with the decision about when to retire rather than the causes of that decision. Our analysis of the factors associated with retirement timing is limited to the definition of retirement that we used; others may have different definitions of retirement. Some people working part-time consider themselves retired; others do not. In addition, we cannot generalize our findings beyond the group of workers included in our sample. Our findings do not necessarily apply to younger groups of workers, who may not behave in the same way or face the same constraints. As mentioned earlier, our sub-sample of workers from the larger HRS sample cohort is not entirely representative of the larger US population. In addition, we were unable to observe the retirement behavior of those who retired before and after the study period. Finally, due to limitations in the data and the methods that we used, we did not include in our analysis some variables identified during our research that could potentially affect workers' retirement timing. For example, the RAND

HRS includes information on a respondent's pension from a current job, but not prior jobs. Our analysis did not include measures of wealth or income other than earnings. Also, we did not analyze lump sum payments from pensions, which could influence retirement decisions. In addition, the RAND HRS data rely heavily on people's knowledge of their finances, work history, pension options, et cetera. Studies show that workers are sometimes misinformed about the details of their pension benefits or the age at which they are eligible for full Social Security benefits.[81]

APPENDIX II. LOGISTIC REGRESSION ANALYSIS OF FACTORS ASSOCIATED WITH WORKERS' RETIREMENT TIMING

This appendix describes the results of two separate analyses we did to determine what factors were associated with whether or not men and women retired 1) before or after age 62, and 2) before or after age 65. We conducted both of these analyses separately for men and women due to sizable gender differences in labor force participation and because data published by the census suggested that the factors that affected retirement decisions may be different for the two groups.[82] The data we used in our analyses were from the HRS cohort of men and women who were born from 1931 to 1941 and thus were between the ages of 63 to 73 in 2004, which was the last year for which we had data. We restricted our attention to workers who had been in the labor force for at least 10 years prior to age 62. In our analysis of whether workers retired before age 62, we limited the analysis to those who had reached age 62 at some point in the study period. Similarly, in our analysis of whether workers retired before age 65, we limited the analysis to those who had reached age 65 at some point in the study period, and we eliminated workers who, based on their birth year, could not reach age 65 by 2004. In addition, we excluded those individuals who were not part of the labor force in the first wave of data collection (1992); see comparison of samples in appendix I.

The HRS dataset is a longitudinal dataset, meaning there are multiple observations per respondent. Respondents were interviewed every 2 years. Each observation is called a wave. In our data set there were seven waves of data (1992 to 2004). For our analysis we limited the data set to one observation per respondent. We selected the observation by taking the first wave the respondent was noted as retiring in the age specific analysis (62 and 65). If the respondent did not retire in that time frame, we selected the wave closest to when the participant was age 62 or 65. For each observation we calculated an age of retirement if the respondent noted that he or she retired. For example, if the respondent noted retiring in wave five and reported a retirement date that fell between waves four and five, we used the reported retirement date as the age of retirement and used wave 4 responses in our analysis. However, if the respondent did not report a retirement date or if the retirement date did not fall between two previous waves of data collection and the current wave, then we imputed the retirement date using the midpoint between the waves. For example, if a respondent noted retiring in wave six but did not report a retirement date and had data for wave five we imputed their age of retirement as the midpoint between wave five and six. For those respondents who did not retire by the specified age used in our analyses (by age 62 or by age 65), we used their age at the end of the interview to select the observation closest to that specified age.

These restrictions meant we had samples of 2,840 men and 2,519 women in our analyses of whether retirement occurred by age 62, and 1,978 men and 1,779 women in our analyses of whether retirement occurred by 65. It should be noted that the sample sizes represent unweighted samples. Our samples differed slightly from the overall HRS sample (see appendix 1 for comparison). The data are from a complex sample, and all analyses were performed using statistical weights and adjusting the standard errors for the sample design. Only respondents with statistical weights greater than zero were included in the analyses (based on HRS documentation for statistical weights). The (weighted) percentages reported in some of the tables of this appendix do not exactly match what would be derived from the (unweighted) numbers reported.

The factors or independent variables we considered in the two sets of analyses are shown in table 7, along with the unweighted numbers and weighted percentages of men and women in each category of those factors. These factors included selected demographic characteristics, including occupation, race/ethnicity, education, marital status, age difference with spouse, income (specifically earnings), work tenure, and birth year. Occupation was divided into three categories: white collar, services, and blue collar. White collar included managerial, professional, sales, clerical, and administrative support occupations. Services included cleaning business services, protection, food preparation, health services, and personal services. Blue collar included farming, forestry, fishing, mechanics and repair, construction and extraction, precision production, operators, and members of the armed forces. We based these categories on a previous GAO report that utilized the HRS data.[83] The income variable—the respondent's earned income—was adjusted for inflation using CPI values to make all dollars comparable to 2003 dollars.[84] The factors also included a general measure of health status, an indicator of whether health limited the ability to work, and measures indicating whether the workers in our sample had any health insurance. In addition, we considered whether the spouse or respondent had retiree health insurance, a DB plan, and a DC plan. For many of our variables, we lagged them to the prior wave to capture workers' preretirement characteristics. For example, if the respondent is noted as retiring in wave 4, the income variable from wave 3 was used in the regression. If the prior wave was missing, that respondent was not included in the analysis. For all of the lagged variables the data collected from 2 years prior was used in the analysis (the HRS respondents were interviewed every two years). Table 7 also shows the numbers and percentages of men and women who had and had not retired by ages 62 and 65. An estimated 25 percent of the men and 28 percent of the women in our sample had retired by age 62, and of those who had reached age 65 by 2004, an estimated 48 percent of the men and 53 percent of the women had retired. The following results are based on our full retirement definition (see appendix I for definition of full retirement).

We used bivariate (one variable) and multivariate (multiple variables) logistic regression models to estimate the likelihood of men and women being retired, first at age 62 and then at age 65. Logistic regression is a widely accepted method of analyzing dichotomous outcomes—variables with two values such as retired or not—when the interest is in determining the effects of multiple factors that may be related to one another. While it is somewhat more common to consider how different categories of workers differ in their likelihoods of being retired by calculating and comparing differences in the percentages of retired and non-retired workers across categories, the use of these models in our analysis requires us to express differences in the likelihoods of being retired using odds ratios.

Table 7. Numbers and Percentages of Men and Women in Different Categories of the Variables Used in Analyses of Full Retirement Timing

	N (and weighted percentage)			
	For full retirement before age 62		For full retirement before age 65	
	Male (N=2840)	Female (N=2519)	Male (N=1978)	Female (N=1779)
Retirement decision				
Retired	700 (24.6)	726 (28.1)	990 (48.3)	967 (52.7)
Not retired	2140 (75.4)	1793 (72.0)	988 (51.7)	812 (47.3)
Demographic characteristics				
Previous wave occupation				
White collar	1283 (50.2)	1630 (70.3)	918 (51.5)	1129 (69.2)
Services	171 (5.8)	500 (17.6)	109 (5.1)	361 (18.0)
Blue collar	1277 (44.1)	334 (12.1)	882 (43.4)	250 (12.8)
Race/ethnicity				
White/ non-Hispanic	2213 (84.5)	1844 (82.2)	1559 (85.3)	1321 (83.2)
Black/ non- Hispanic	349 (7.7)	466 (10.6)	241 (7.6)	316 (10.2)
Hispanic/ other	278 (7.8)	209 (7.2)	178 (7.1)	142 (6.6)
Education				
<HS	629 (19.4)	482 (16.5)	446 (19.4)	361 (17.0)
HS/GED	966 (33.5)	1034 (41.4)	680 (34.1)	739 (42.2)
Some college	573 (21.3)	554 (22.6)	373 (20.0)	372 (21.8)
College+	672 (25.9)	449 (19.5)	479 (26.6)	307 (19.0)
Previous wave marital status				
Married	2367 (82.0)	1542 (62.7)	1653 (82.6)	1085 (62.3)
Not married	472 (18.0)	975 (37.3)	321 (17.4)	691 (37.7)
Previous wave spousal age difference				
No spouse/ no diff up to 5 yr	2099 (72.7)	2137 (83.3)	1451 (72.2)	1506 (83.8)
Spouse <5 yr Resp	685 (24.8)	72 (3.3)	491 (25.3)	49 (3.1)
Spouse >5yr Resp	56 (2.5)	310 (13.4)	36 (2.5)	224 (13.1)
Previous wave income categories[a]				
0-<1 0,000	666 (23.3)	753 (29.5)	594 (30.0)	622 (34.3)
10,000-<25,000	418 (13.6)	752 (29.4)	301 (13.7)	511 (28.1)
25,000-<50,000	871 (29.4)	734 (29.0)	535 (26.4)	476 (27.0)
>=50,000	885 (33.7)	280 (12.1)	548 (30.0)	170 (10.6)
Tenure at current job in previous wave-categories				
0-<5	670 (25.7)	557 (25.7)	465 (26.0)	377 (24.4)
5-<15	690 (26.2)	761 (34.8)	463 (25.3)	530 (34.8)
15-<25	467 (16.9)	547 (24.0)	315 (17.0)	400 (24.3)
>=25	808 (31.2)	385 (15.5)	576 (31.8)	286 (16.5)
Birth year categories				
1931, 1932	481 (16.6)	395 (15.5)	443 (21.9)	363 (20.7)

Table 7. (Continued)

	N (and weighted percentage)			
	For full retirement before age 62		For full retirement before age 65	
	Male (N=2840)	Female (N=251 9)	Male (N=1 978)	Female (N=1779)
1933, 1934	487 (16.1)	436 (16.8)	434 (21.0)	415 (22.8)
1935, 1936	524 (17.8)	446 (17.2)	474 (24.1)	411 (22.8)
1937	255 (9.2)	243 (9.8)	241 (12.7)	233 (13.6)
1938, 1939	549 (20.0)	481 (19.0)	386 (20.4)	357 (20.1)
1940, 1941	544 (20.3)	518 (21.8)	n/a	n/a
Health related				
Health status previous wave				
Excellent/ very good/ good	2343 (84.0)	2100 (85.3)	1634 (84.2)	1474 (84.6)
Fair/ poor	496 (16.0)	419 (14.7)	344 (15.8)	305 (15.4)
Previous wave: health limits work				
No	2437 (86.2)	2134 (85.7)	1697 (86.3)	1501 (85.2)
Yes	396 (13.8)	371 (14.3)	273 (13.7)	267 (14.8)
Previous wave: health insurance				
No	643 (21.7)	620 (23.1)	496 (23.8)	501 (26.5)
Yes	2197 (78.4)	1899 (76.9)	1482 (76.2)	1278 (73.5)
Previous wave: retiree health insurance R or S[b]				
No	1405 (49.6)	1343 (53.0)	964 (48.2)	993 (55.3)
Yes	1435 (50.5)	1176 (47.0)	1014 (51.8)	786 (44.7)
Pension related				
Prior wave DB pension type of R or S[b]				
No DB	960 (36.0)	771 (35.4)	657 (35.5)	554 (36.3)
DB pension	1646 (64.0)	1393 (64.6)	1174 (64.6)	967 (63.7)
Prior wave DC pension type of R or S[b]				
No DC	1012 (36.6)	837 (37.3)	700 (36.0)	587 (36.9)
DC pension	1624 (63.4)	1327 (62.7)	1131 (64.0)	934 (63.1)

Source: GAO analysis of RAND HRS data.

[a] Respondent's earned income adjusted for inflation

[b] R= respondent; S= Spouse. The RAND HRS data provided information about DC and DB pensions from current employment during the 1992 through 2004 study period. It did not provide data concerning any pensions from respondents' or spouses' previous employers.

An "odds ratio" is generally defined as the ratio of the odds of an event occurring in one group compared to the odds of it occurring in another group—the reference group. While odds and odds ratios are somewhat less familiar than percentages and percentage differences, they have certain advantages, and can be readily derived from the underlying percentages or from the numbers from which those percentages were calculated. Moreover, odds ratios are amenable to a reasonably simple interpretation, as we show in Table 8. In addition, unadjusted and adjusted odds ratios are the parameters that underlie our logistic regression models.

Table 8 shows the numbers and percentages of men who were retired by age 62, first across marital status categories, and then across categories defined by race/ethnicity. Typically we would compare groups by contrasting the percentages of retired or not retired individuals in each group and noting, in this case for example, that the percentage of individuals retired by age 62 is greater among unmarried men (30.1 percent) than married men (23.3 percent), and lower for Hispanic men (17.4 percent) than for Black men (25.4 percent) and white men (25.1 percent). Alternatively, we can calculate the odds on retiring for each group by simply taking the percentage who retired in each group and dividing it by the percentage who had not retired. The odds on retiring were 30.1/69.9 = 0.43 for unmarried men, and 23.3/76.7 = 0.30 for married men. Making similar calculations, the odds were virtually identical for white men and Black men (0.34, apart from rounding) but lower for Hispanic men (0.21). We can compare groups directly by taking the ratios of these odds, given in the "Odds Ratios" column in table 8. As can be seen, the odds on retiring were higher for unmarried men than for married men, by a factor of 0.431/0.304 = 1.42. To compare race/ethnicity categories, we choose (arbitrarily) one group (white men in this case) as the reference category, make similar calculation by taking the ratios of the odds for the other two groups to the odds for white men, and find that Black men have odds on retiring that are only slightly different than white men (higher by a factor of 1.02), while Hispanic men are less likely than white men to retire, by a factor of 0.63.

Table 8. Full Retirement Status at Age 62, by Marital Status and Race/Ethnicity, among Men

		Full retirement status at age 62		Odds on retired	Odds ratios
		Fully retired	Not fully retired		
Married	N	561	1806		
	%	23.3	76.7	0.30	reference
Unmarried	N	138	334		
	%	30.1	69.9	0.43	1.42
Total	N	**699**	**2140**		
	%	**24.6**	**75.5**		
White	N	557	1656		
	%	25.1	74.9	0.34	reference
Black	N	95	254		
	%	25.4	74.6	0.34	1.02
Hispanic	N	48	230		
	%	17.4	82.6	0.21	0.63
Total	N	**700**	**2140**		
	%	**24.6**	**75.4**		

Source: GAO analysis of RAND HRS data.

Table 9. Odds Ratios and 95 Percent Confidence Intervals Indicating the Gross (Bivariate) Associations between Various Factors and Full Retirement before Age 62 and Age 65, for Men and Women

	Odds ratios (and 95 percent confidence intervals)			
	For full retirement before age 62		For full retirement before age 65	
	Male (N=2840)	Female (N=2519)	Male (N=1978)	Female (N=1779)
Demographic characteristics				
Previous wave occupation			*	
White collar	1(1-1)	1(1-1)	1(1-1)	1(1-1)
Services	1.47(0.98-2.21)	0.87(0.67-1.13)	1.27(0.81-1.99)	0.92(0.73-1.16)
Blue collar	1.11(0.92-1.33)	1.15(0.94-1.39)	1.76(1.43-2.16)	1.37(0.98-1.9)
Race/ ethnicity		*	*	
White/ non-Hispanic	1(1-1)	1(1-1)	1(1-1)	1(1-1)
Black/ non- Hispanic	1.02(0.75-1.39)	0.95(0.74-1.23)	1.22(0.87-1.71)	1.09(0.82-1.43)
Hispanic/ other	0.63(0.4-0.97)	0.58(0.4-0.85)	1.02(0.77-1.35)	0.95(0.68-1.34)
Education	*		*	
<HS	1(1-1)	1(1-1)	1(1-1)	1(1-1)
HS/GED	1.23(0.95-1.6)	0.93(0.7-1.24)	0.93(0.7-1.24)	0.86(0.67-1.09)
Some college	0.91(0.66-1.25)	0.82(0.63-1.07)	0.71(0.53-0.95)	0.72(0.51-1.02)
College+	0.98(0.73-1.32)	0.88(0.61-1.28)	0.48(0.35-0.64)	0.77(0.54-1 .1)
Previous wave marital status	*	*	*	*
Married	1(1-1)	1(1-1)	1(1-1)	1(1-1)
Not married	1.42(1.14-1.76)	0.63(0.5-0.79)	1.36(1.08-1.72)	0.6(0.47-0.76)
Previous wave spousal age difference				*
No spouse/ no diff up to 5 yr	1(1-1)	1(1-1)	1(1-1)	1(1-1)
Spouse <5 yr Resp	0.89(0.71-1.12)	0.96(0.54-1.74)	0.82(0.67-1)	0.79(0.44-1.45)
Spouse >5yr Resp	0.5(0.22-1.14)	1.26(0.93-1.71)	1(0.37-2.72)	1.62(1.2-2.18)
Previous wave Income categories[b]	**	*	*	**
0-<10,000	1(1-1)	1(1-1)	1(1-1)	1(1-1)
10,000-<25,000	0.94(0.69-1.28)	0.65(0.48-0.87)	1.57(1.16-2.13)	1.05(0.83-1.32)
25,000-<50,000	0.88(0.69-1.12)	0.73(0.57-0.95)	1.96(1.57-2.46)	1.47(1.1-1.97)
>=50,000	1.2(0.92-1.58)	0.81(0.6-1.09)	2.08(1.68-2.57)	1.23(0.91-1.66)
Tenure at current job in previous wave-categories	*	*	*	**
0-<5	1(1-1)	1(1-1)	1(1-1)	1(1-1)
5-<15	0.63(0.46-0.86)	0.9(0.7-1.15)	0.98(0.76-1.28)	0.94(0.68-1.31)
15-<25	1.26(0.93-1.7)	1.2(0.9-1.61)	1.39(0.97-1.98)	1.36(1-1.86)
>=25	1.63(1.25-2.13)	1.51(1.11-2.06)	1.81(1.37-2.39)	1.35(0.96-1.89)
Birth year categories	*	*		
1931, 1932	1(1-1)	1(1-1)	1(1-1)	1(1-1)
1933, 1934	2.16(1.5-3.1)	2.05(1.31-3.21)	1.2(0.84-1.71)	1.18(0.84-1.67)
1935, 1936	2.88(1.91-4.34)	2.13(1.41-3.22)	0.99(0.68-1.45)	1.06(0.75-1.49)
1937	2.48(1.48-4.16)	2.75(1.53-4.94)	0.9(0.6-1.37)	1.18(0.73-1.91)

Table 9. (Continued)

	Odds ratios (and 95 percent confidence intervals)			
	For full retirement before age 62		For full retirement before age 65	
	Male (N=2840)	Female (N=2519)	Male (N=1978)	Female (N=1779)
1938, 1939	4.47(3.15-6.35)	2.83(1.75-4.58)	1.39(0.99-1.94)	1.16(0.77-1.76)
1940, 1941	4.2(2.91-6.06)	3.19(2.1-4.85)	n/aa	n/a
Health related				
Health status previous wave	*	*	*	*
excellent/ very good/ good	1(1-1)	1(1-1)	1(1-1)	1(1-1)
fair/ poor	1.67(1.33-2.11)	1.76(1.44-2.15)	1.67(1.27-2.21)	1.65(1.27-2.13)
Previous wave: health limits work	*	*	*	*
no	1(1-1)	1(1-1)	1(1-1)	1(1-1)
yes	2.36(1.8-3.1)	2.13(1.67-2.72)	1.81(1.28-2.55)	1.68(1.3-2.18)
Previous wave: health insurance		*	*	
No	1(1-1)	1(1-1)	1(1-1)	1(1-1)
Yes	1.14(0.86-1.5)	1.08(0.91-1.3)	1.36(1.05-1.75)	1.23(0.99-1.53)
Previous wave: retiree health insurance R or S[c]	*	*	*	*
No	1(1-1)	1(1-1)	1(1-1)	1(1-1)
Yes	1.8(1.49-2.18)	1.56(1.3-1.88)	1.77(1.47-2.14)	2.2(1.76-2.76)
Pension related				
Prior wave DB pension type of R or S[c]	*	*	*	*
No DB	1(1-1)	1(1-1)	1(1-1)	1(1-1)
DB pension	1.66(1.34-2.06)	1.24(1.04-1.49)	1.39(1.14-1.71)	1.19(0.97-1.47)
Prior wave DC pension type of R or Sc			*	*
No DC	1(1-1)	1(1-1)	1(1-1)	1(1-1)
DC pension	0.87(0.72-1.05)	0.82(0.64-1.07)	0.8(0.65-0.99)	0.66(0.53-0.82)

* indicates an overall Satterthwaite adjusted p-value <0.05

** indicates an overall Satterthwaite adjusted p-value <0.10

Source: GAO analysis of RAND HRS data.

Note: The RAND HRS data provided information about DC and DB pensions from current employment during the 1992 through 2004 study period. It did not provide data concerning any pensions from respondents' or spouses' previous employers.

[a] Respondents born in 1940 and 1941 were excluded from the age 65 analysis because they would not have been 65 by the last wave of data collection in 2004.

[b] Respondent's earned income adjusted for inflation

[c] R= respondent; S= Spouse

Table 9 shows the gross effects of each of the factors we considered on the odds on men and women retiring before age 62 (in the first two columns) and before age 65 (in the last two columns). By gross effects, we mean the effects of each factor estimated from bivariate regressions, or regressions that ignore or fail to take account of the effects of other factors which may be related to retirement. Table 10, by contrast, shows the adjusted effects of the factors that we found to be significantly related to retiring at age 62 or age 65 after adjusting for other factors.

In developing our multivariate models, we controlled for income in the previous wave, birth year categories, DB, and DC pension plans in the previous wave, and retiree health insurance in the previous wave even if the overall p-value for these variables is not statistically significant. We adjusted for income in the previous wave because it is a very strong demographic characteristic, and we adjusted for birth year to account for any possible cohort effect in the HRS data. Similarly, we adjusted for pension type (both DB and DC) and retiree health insurance because we are interested in assessing the impact of these policy variables on a respondent's decision to retire.

In order to assess factors associated with the retirement decisions at specific ages in a multivariate setting, we wanted the most parsimonious model without adding additional noise by factors that were not statistically significant. To do this we iteratively fit a model by first adjusting for all of the variables of interest (see Table 9). After keeping in the five variables mentioned above (income, birth year, and DB and DC pension, and retiree health insurance) we then selected the variables that were statistically significant (p-value <0.05) one at a time. Then after the reduced model was fit we re-entered the variables that we excluded to see if any became statistically significant in the presence of the variables from the reduced model. The results from the multivariate models retain the statistically significant associations (p-value <0.05) and exclude those that reflected insignificant effects, or difference in the sample that could reasonably be assumed to be due to chance or random fluctuations. Some factors that were correlated with other variables and were statistically significant in the bivariate analysis were not statistically significant in the final multivariate model when we adjusted for these other factors. We assessed our final model for goodness of fit using the Hosmer Lemeshow goodness of fit statistic, which tests the hypothesis that the data fit the specified model. All our multivariate models fit the data appropriately (p- values for model fit >0.05). We provide the gross or unadjusted effects in table 9 in order to show what effect each factor has when other factors with which they are associated are ignored, or left uncontrolled. By gross effects, we mean the effects of each factor estimated from bivariate regressions, or regressions which ignore or fail to take account of the effects of other factors which may be related to retirement. We focus our discussion here however, as well as in the body of the report, on the adjusted odds ratios from the multivariate models, shown in table 10. The results in the table 10 only reflect the statistically significant adjusted odds ratios. However, all models include income, birth year, retiree health insurance, and DB and DC pension plans. In addition, some of the factors in the multivariate models have missing data; therefore, the overall sample size from the multivariate models differs from the sample size noted in table 9. We have assumed that the missing values are missing at random.

The HRS is based on a probability sample and therefore the estimates are subject to sampling error. The HRS sample is only one of a large number of samples that could have been drawn of this population. Since each sample could have provided different estimates, we express our confidence in the precision of the analysis results as 95 percent confidence intervals. These are intervals that would contain the actual population values for 95 percent of the samples that could have been drawn. As a result, we are 95 percent confident that each of the confidence intervals in this report will include the true values in the study populations.

All multivariate models were run using an alternative definition that included partial and full retirement (see appendix I for definitions). Results from these multivariate models were similar to the results presented here. (Data not shown.)

Table 10 shows that the odds on men retiring before age 62 were affected by income, job tenure, birth year, health limitations, retiree health insurance, and having DB and DC plans. All of the results can be interpreted as adjusted odds ratios and the net effects of those factors on early retirement for men can be described as follows, after adjusting for the other factors:

- Men in the highest income category (who made greater than or equal to $50,000 in the previous wave) were 1.76 times more likely than men making less than $10,000 to retire by age 62. Men earning between $10,000 and $25,000 and men earning between $25,000 and $50,000 were not significantly different from men earning less than $10,000 in their decisions to retire before 62.

- Men who had been working for 15 to less than 25 years were not significantly different from men working less than 5 years at their primary occupation (in the previous wave), but men who had worked 5 to less than 15 years were less likely to retire by age 62 by a factor of 0.61 than men working less than 5 years. However, men working 25 years or more were more likely than men working less than 5 years to be retired by age 62, by a factor of 1.6.

- Men born after 1933 were more likely than those born 1931 to 1932 to be retired by age 62, by factors ranging (fairly linearly) from 2.2 (for those born 1933 to 1934) to 5.7 (for those born 1940 to 1941).

- The odds on retiring before age 62 were more than twice as high for men who reported health limitations as for men without such limitations, and were twice as high for men with retiree health insurance as for those without retiree health insurance.

- The odds on retiring before age 62 were higher for men with a DB plan than for those without, by a factor of 1.3, and lower for men with DC plans than for those without, by a factor of 0.5.

The odds on women retiring before age 62 were affected by marital status, job tenure, birth year, health status, health limitations, retiree health insurance, and having a DC plan. Although not statistically significant the final model also adjusted for income, an important demographic characteristic, and DB plan, to account for policy related variables. The net effects of those factors on early retirement for women can be described as follows, after adjusting for other factors:

- Unmarried women were only roughly half as likely as married women to retire before age 62; that is, the odds on retiring before that age were lower for unmarried women than for married women, by a factor of 0.57.

- Women who had been working for 5 to less than 15 years and 15 to less than 25 years were not significantly different from women working less than 5 years at their primary occupation (in the previous wave). However, women working 25 years or more were more likely than women working less than 5 years to be retired by age 62, by a factor of 1.7.

- As was the case with men, women born after 1933 were more likely than those born 1931 to 1932 to be retired by age 62, by factors ranging (again fairly linearly) from 2.9 (for women born 1933 to 1934) to 4.3 (for women born 1940 to 1941).
- The odds on retiring before age 62 were 1.5 times greater for women who said they were in fair or poor health as for women in good or excellent health, 2.0 times greater for women with health limitations than for women without, and nearly twice as high for women with retiree health insurance as for those without retiree health insurance.
- The odds on retiring before age 62 were lower for women with DC plans than for those without, by a factor of 0.6.

The odds on men retiring before age 65 were affected by categories of occupation, education, marital status, income, job tenure, health limitations, retiree health insurance, and having a DC plan. Although not statistically significant, we adjusted for birth year to control for any possible cohort effects and DB plan to account for policy related variables. The net effects of those factors on late retirement for men can be described as follows, after adjusting for other factors:

- Men in the blue collar occupation category were 1.5 times more likely to retire before age 65 than men in the white collar category. Men in the services category were not significantly different from men in white collar professions in their decision to retire prior to 65.
- Men with college or more education were 0.51 times less likely to retire before age 65 compared to men with less than a high school education. There were no statistically significant differences between men with high school/ GED education and men with some college compared to men with less than a high school education in their decision to retire before age 65.
- The odds that unmarried men would retire before age 65 were 1.5 times those of married men.
- Men with income greater than or equal to $10,000 were more likely to retire prior to age 65 than men earning less than $10,000, by factors ranging (fairly linearly) from 2.0 (for those earning between $25,000 to $50,000) to 3.1 (for those earning greater than or equal to $50,000).
- Men who had been working for 5 to 15 years and those who had been working 15 to 25 years were not significantly different from men working less than 5 years at their primary occupation. But men who had worked greater than or equal to 25 years were more likely than men working less than 5 years to be retired by age 65, by a factor of 1.4.
- The odds on retiring before age 65 were almost twice as high (1.7) for men who reported health limitations as for men without such limitations and were almost twice as high for men with retiree health insurance as for those without retiree health insurance.
- The odds on retiring before age 65 were lower for men with DC plans than for those without, by a factor of 0.7.

Table 10. Adjusted Odds Ratios and 95 Percent Confidence Intervals Indicating the Net (Multivariate) Associations between Various Factors and Full Retirement before Age 62 and Age 65, for Men and Women

	Adjusted odds ratios (and 95 percent confidence intervals)			
	For full retirement before age 62		For full retirement before age 65	
	Male (N=2462)	Female (N=1954)	Male (N=1 640)	Female (N=1 511)
Demographic characteristics				
Occupation in previous wave				
White collar			1(1-1)	
Services			1.18(0.66-2.09)	
Blue collar			1.45(1.13-1.85)	
Education				
<HS			1(1-1)	
HS/GED			1.01(0.71-1.44)	
Some college			0.76(0.51-1.14)	
College+			0.51(0.34-0.78)	
Marital status in previous wave				
Married		1(1-1)	1(1-1)	1(1-1)
Not married		0.57(0.43-0.74)	1.52(1.02-2.25)	0.60(0.46-0.77)
Spousal age difference in previous wave				
No spouse/ no diff up to 5 yr				1(1-1)
spouse <5 yr Resp				0.61(0.31-1.17)
spouse >5yr resp				1.46(1.1-1.94)
Previous wave Income categories[a]				
0-<10,000	1(1-1)		1(1-1)	1(1-1)
1 0,000-<25,000	1.27(0.83-1.95)		1.97(1.28-3.04)	1.23(0.91-1.64)
25,000-<50,000	1.17(0.83-1.64)		2.14(1.59-2.89)	1.62(1.17-2.24)
>=50,000	1.76(1.23-2.5)		3.07(2.13-4.43)	1.27(0.86-1.87)
Tenure at current job in previous wave categories				
0-<5	1(1-1)	1(1-1)	1(1-1)	
5-<1 5	0.61(0.43-0.87)	1.06(0.8-1.39)	0.84(0.6-1.17)	
1 5-<25	1.18(0.86-1.63)	1.23(0.92-1.66)	1.07(0.75-1.52)	
>=25	1.56(1.16-2.09)	1.68(1.21-2.34)	1.44(1.01-2.06)	
Birth year categories				
1931, 1932	1(1-1)	1(1-1)		
1933, 1934	2.19(1.42-3.38)	2.85(1.65-4.91)		
1935, 1936	3.52(2.15-5.77)	2.9(1.76-4.78)		
1937	3.56(2.03-6.25)	3.64(1.78-7.45)		
1938, 1939	6.4(4.05-10.09)	3.73(2.17-6.41)		
1940, 1941	5.72(3.53-9.27)	4.3(2.67-6.94)		
Health related				
Health status previous wave				
Excellent/ very good/ good		1(1-1)		1(1-1)
Fair/ poor		1.45(1.04-2.03)		1.49(1.07-2.07)
Previous wave: health limits work				

Demographic characteristics				
No	1(1-1)	1(1-1)	1(1-1)	1(1-1)
Yes	2.25(1.58-3.21)	1.96(1.43-2.67)	1.71(1.18-2.48)	1.72(1.2-2.45)
Previous wave: retiree health insurance[b]				
No	1(1-1)	1(1-1)	1(1-1)	1(1-1)
Yes	2.09(1.66-2.64)	1.76(1.43-2.17)	1.86(1.49-2.34)	2.39(1.82-3.14)
Pension related				
Prior wave DB pension type of R or S[b]				
No DB	1(1-1)			
DB pension	1.28(1.02-1.61)			
Prior wave DC pension type of R or S[b]				
No DC	1(1-1)	1(1-1)	1(1-1)	1(1-1)
DC pension	0.53(0.43-0.67)	0.63(0.45-0.87)	0.65(0.52-0.81)	0.55(0.45-0.66)

Source: GAO analysis of RAND HRS data.

[a] Respondent's earned income adjusted for inflation

[b] R= respondent; S= Spouse

Notes: The model for male retirement before age 65 includes both education and income. We recognize that education and income have the potential for being highly correlated. However, that does not appear to be the case for this age group and the decision to retire before age 65. We compared the odds ratios in Table 9 to those in the adjusted model in Table 10 and noted that they are quite stable. In addition, both education and income are statistically significant in the multivariate model (p-values <0.01). Therefore, we decided to keep both education and income in the final model.

The RAND HRS data provided information about DC and DB pensions from current employment during the 1992 through 2004 study period. It did not provide data concerning any pensions from respondents' or spouses' previous employers.

All models were run adjusting for income in the previous wave, birth year, DB plan and DC plan. Only statistically significant results (overall p-value<0.05) are presented in the table above.

The odds on women retiring before age 65 were affected by marital status, spousal age difference, income, health status, health limitations, retiree health insurance, and having DC plans. Although not statistically significant, we adjusted for birth year to control for a possible cohort effect and DB plan to account for policy-related variables. The net effects of those factors on late retirement for women can be described as follows, after adjusting for other factors:

- Unmarried women were roughly half as likely as married women to retire before age 65; that is, the odds on retiring before that age were lower for unmarried women than for married women, by a factor of 0.6.

- Women who were at least 5 years younger than their spouse were more likely to retire before age 65 compared to women with no spouse or women who were within 5 years of their spouses' age, by a factor of 1.5. There were no statistically significant differences on the odds of retiring before age 65 for women who were more than 5 years older than their spouse compared to women with no spouse or women who were within 5 years.

- The odds on retiring before age 65 were higher for women earning $25,000 to $50,000 than for those earning less than $10,000, by a factor of 1.6. Women earning between $10,000 to $25,000 and more than $50,000 were not significantly different than the lowest earning women in terms of their odds on retiring before age 65.

- The odds on retiring before age 65 were 1.5 times greater for women who said they were in fair or poor health compared to women in good or excellent health, 1.7 times greater for women with health limitations than for women without, and nearly twice as high (2.4) for women with retiree health insurance as for those without retiree health insurance.
- The odds on retiring before age 65 were lower for women with DC plans than for those without, by a factor of 0.6.

APPENDIX III. PRIOR STUDIES ON THE SOCIAL SECURITY EARNINGS TEST

This appendix summarizes the findings in selected studies concerning changes in labor force participation among older workers following the elimination of the Social Security earnings test for beneficiaries at or above their full retirement age, effective January 1, 2000.

Jae G. Song and Joyce Manchester, "New Evidence on Earnings and Benefit Claims Following Changes in the Retirement Earnings Test in 2000," *Journal of Public Economics*, vol. 91, nos. 3-4 (April 2007).

To examine the effect of the removal of the Social Security earnings test, the authors used SSA administrative data known as the Continuous Work History Sample.[85] The authors examined these data for the years 1996 to 2003 and restricted their sample to those who are fully insured under Social Security. One of the limitations of these data is that they lack information on wages, hours worked, health status, education, and family characteristics for workers. The authors ran two sets of regression models on the following dependent variables: claiming Social Security benefits, work participation, and earnings. They used a "difference in difference" approach for which they compared treatment groups who were affected by this policy change (those turning 65 and those aged 65 to 69) with control groups that were not affected (those aged 62 to 64 and 70 to 72). One of the key assumptions the authors make in running these models is that there was no shock other than the earnings test removal in 2000 that affected treatment groups relative to the control groups. After running these models, the authors concluded that: 1) earnings increased among higher income workers; 2) workforce participation increased among those aged 65 to 69; 3) applications for Social Security benefits among those aged 65 to 69 increased following the test's removal.

Leora Friedberg and Anthony Webb, "Persistence in Labor Supply and the Response to the Social Security Earnings Test," *Working Paper 2006-27* (Boston, Mass.: Center for Retirement Research at Boston College, December 2006).

The authors used data from the HRS and Current Population Survey (CPS) to examine the impact on labor supply of changes made to the earnings test in 1996 and 2000.[86] They examine everyone in the CPS aged 55 to 74 between the years 1992 and 2005, and they use several different birth cohorts from the HRS in their analysis. The authors ran regressions on several dependent variables—employment, full-time employment, and earnings. In their regression analysis, the authors focus on those aged 62 to 74 to capture any effect that the earnings test might have on younger workers. Two key assumptions the authors make are that people view the earnings test as a tax instead of a deferral of benefits and that people can choose the number of hours they work. The authors conclude that the earnings test changes in both 1996 and 2000 increased labor force participation for those both aged 65 to 69 along with younger workers who are anticipating its removal. They also found that earnings increased, particularly for higher-income workers, following the 2000 change.

Steven J. Haider and David S. Loughran, "The Effect of the Social Security Earnings Test on Male Labor Supply: New Evidence from Survey and Administrative Data" (Forthcoming, Journal of Human Resources: 2007).

The authors use data from the CPS, New Beneficiary Data System (NBDS), and the Social Security Benefit and Earnings Public Use File (BEPUF).[87] The authors restrict their analyses to men. Using all three data sources, they conducted a "bunching analysis" to determine the extent to which workers adjust their earnings so that they remain just under the earnings test threshold. They found that the age at which workers adjust their earnings has risen as the earnings test threshold has risen. In addition, they found that the extent of bunching is higher with the administrative data from NBDS and BEPUF. Turning next to labor force responses from the elimination of the earnings test, the authors use CPS and BEPUF data to run a "difference in differences" model. They found that earnings increased among 66 to 69 year-olds along with hours worked per week.

APPENDIX IV. DEMOGRAPHIC CHARACTERISTICS OF WORKERS WITH ACCESS TO RETIREE HEALTH INSURANCE AND DB AND DC PENSIONS

This appendix provides supplementary descriptive statistics concerning the prevalence of retiree health insurance, DB, and DC pensions by demographic group among HRS respondents or their spouses included in our full retirement analysis sample. These respondents were born between 1931 and 1941, had 10 years of work experience by the time they reached age 62 and were in the labor force (working part-time or full-time, unemployed, or partially retired) in 1992—the beginning of the study period.

Of those in our sample with less than $10,000 in household earnings at the beginning of the study, about 40 percent had employer-based retiree health insurance from either their employer or their spouse's employer. By contrast, two thirds of people in our sample whose households earned $50,000 or more per year had access to employer-based retiree health insurance. Similarly, we found that a greater proportion of those with higher levels of education were eligible for employer-based retiree health benefits. (See figure 7.) Others have found similar relationships, with a 2005 study finding declines in the availability of retiree health insurance affecting those with lower levels of education, relative to those with higher levels.[88] Specifically, the authors found that retirees without a college degree have experienced a 34 percent decline between 1997 and 2002 in the likelihood of having retiree health benefits, while those with a college degree experienced a 28 percent decline. On the other hand, those with a post-college degree did not experience any decline in coverage. Finally, we also found that as of the beginning of the study period a lower proportion of Hispanics had retiree health insurance when compared to their White or African-American counterparts.

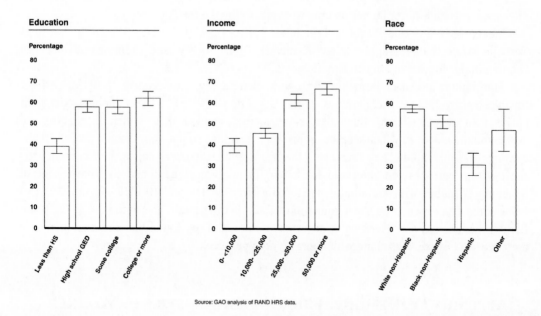

Source: GAO analysis of RAND HRS data.

Source: GAO analysis of RAND HRS data.

Notes: The 95 percent confidence intervals for these estimates are shown with "I" symbols at the top of each bar.

Overall, an estimated 55 percent of workers in our regression study group had access to retiree health insurance in 1992 either through their current or former employer or their spouse's current or former employer. As we mentioned earlier, a 2006 study found that only about one-quarter of private sector employees worked for companies that offered retiree health insurance.

Figure 7. Estimated Percent of Respondents with Retiree Health Insurance by Education, Income Groups, and Race/Ethnicity

As with our analysis of retiree health insurance, we found that as of the beginning of the study period, access to particular types of pensions varied by respondents' income and education level.[89] (See figure 8 and figure 9.) We found that at the beginning of the study period 28 percent of those making less than $10,000 had a DB plan while 65 percent of those making $50,000 or more had them.

We also found that 40 percent of those with less than a high school degree had a DB pension while 62 percent of those with a college degree or more advanced degree had a DB pension. We found similar results for DC plans with a larger proportion of those with higher income and more education having a DC plan compared to those who did not.

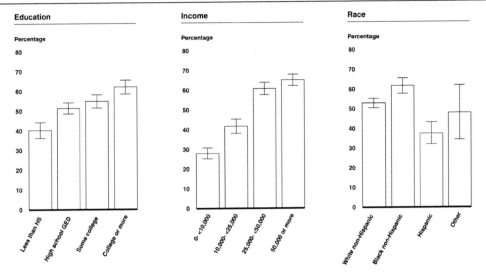

Source: GAO analysis of RAND HRS data.

Notes: The 95 percent confidence intervals for these estimates are with "I" symbols at the top of each bar.

Overall, an estimated 53 percent of respondents or their spouses had a DB plan from an employer during the study period. As we noted earlier, from 1992 to 2004, the proportion of household heads with a DB plan decreased from about 29 percent to 20 percent, respectively.

Figure 8. Estimated Percent of Respondents with DB Pensions by Education Level, Income Groups, and Race/Ethnicity

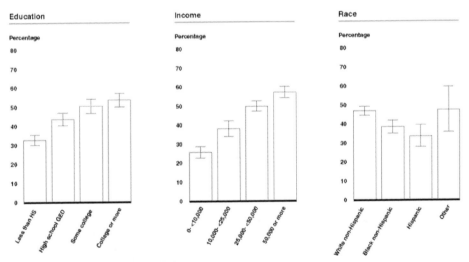

Source: GAO analysis of RAND HRS data.

Notes: The 95 percent confidence intervals for these estimates are shown as "I" lines at the top of each bar.

Overall, an estimated 46 percent of respondents or their spouses had a DC plan from current employment as of 1992. As noted earlier, from 1992 to 2004, the proportion of household heads with a DC plan increased from about 28 percent to 34 percent, respectively.

Figure 9. Estimated Percent of Respondents with DC Pensions by Education Level, Income Groups, and Race/Ethnicity

APPENDIX V. COMMENTS FROM DEPARTMENT OF HEALTH AND HUMAN SERVICES

DEPARTMENT OF HEALTH & HUMAN SERVICES
                      Office of the Assistant Secretary
                      for Legislation

                      Washington, D.C. 20201

JUN 2 0 2007

Barbara D. Bovbjerg, Director
Education, Workforce, and
  Income Security Issues
U.S. Government Accountability Office
Washington, D.C. 20548

Dear Ms. Bovjerg:

Enclosed are the Department's comments on the U.S. Government Accountability Office's
(GAO) draft report entitled, "Retirement Decisions: Federal Policies Offer Mixed Signals
About When to Retire" (GAO 07-753).

The department appreciates the opportunity to comment on this draft before its
publication.

                      Sincerely,

                      Rebecca Hernard

                      for   Vincent J. Ventimiglia
                      Assistant Secretary for Legislation

GENERAL COMMENT ON THE U.S. GOVERNMENT ACCOUNTABILITY OFFICE DRAFT REPORT ENTITLED: RETIREMENT DECISIONS: FEDERAL POLICIES OFFER MIXED SIGNALS ABOUT WHEN TO RETIRE (GAO-07-753).

HHS Comment:

In this draft report, the GAO assessed (1) the incentives federal policies provide about
when to retire, (2) recent retirement patterns and whether there is evidence that changes
in Social Security requirements have resulted in later retirements, and (3) whether tax-
favored private retiree health insurance and pension benefits influence when people
retire.

HHS agrees with the study finding the Medicare eligibility age provides a strong
incentive for those without health insurance to remain in the labor force until they
become eligible for Medicare, as well as the finding that the availability of employment-
based retiree health coverage strongly influences when people retire. We note that as a
Improvement, and Modernization Act of 2003 (MMA), with its incentives for employer
and union plan sponsors to continue offering retiree drug and health coverage,
employment-based retiree health coverage is likely to continue exerting a strong
influence on retirement decisions for the foreseeable future.

End Notes

[1] Types of pension plans include (1) DB plans, which provide a guaranteed benefit generally expressed as a monthly benefit based on a formula that generally combines salary and years of service, and (2) DC plans, which establish individual accounts for employees to which the employer, participants, or both make periodic contributions. DC plan benefits are based on employer and participant contributions to and investment returns (gains and losses) on the individual accounts.

[2] Between 2000 and 2005, for example, the labor force participation rate for those aged 65 to 69 increased from 24.5 to 28.3 percent according to the Bureau of Labor Statistics. See Mitra Toosi, "A New Look at Long-Term Labor Force Projections to 2050" *Monthly Labor Review*, vol. 129, no. 11 (November 2006) 27.

[3] According to SSA's trustees, a substantial increase in net immigration would delay the exhaustion of the Social Security trust fund by 2 years. This projection assumes, for example, that net immigration in each year 2008 through 2016 will be 1.4 million, compared to the estimated 2007 level of 1.075 million, including legal and undocumented immigrants.

[4] Demographers and policy makers pay close attention to the elderly dependency ratio as well as the total dependency ratio (including both the elderly and children as dependents) as these can be important factors influencing trends in the quality of life. For example, the numbers of workers and retirees have implications for the financing of social insurance programs. In 2006 current workers' and their employers' contributions represented 113 percent of Social Security expenditures. The principal sources of Medicare funding are current workers' and their employers' contributions (44 percent of Medicare expenditures in 2006), premiums (12 percent), and general revenue (42 percent).

[5] Nicole Maestas, "Back to Work: Expectations and Realizations of Work After Retirement," *Working Paper WR-196-1* (RAND Corporation, August 2005).

[6] While partial retirement can refer to workers who have reduced hours or changed jobs, phased retirement refers specifically to workers who reduce their hours at their existing (previous full-time) job.

[7] We use definitions of full and partial retirement developed by RAND's HRS researchers. If a respondent identifies himself or herself as retired and works for pay less than 35 hours per week or less than 36 weeks per year, they are classified as partially retired. For details, see appendix I.

[8] This decline reflects, in part, the adoption of age 62 as Social Security's early eligibility age in 1956 for women and 1961 for men and increases in the level of benefits during this period.

[9] These data are from Social Security's *Annual Statistical Supplement* for 2006. Data from 1997-2005 include conversions from nondisabled widow(er)'s benefits to higher retired- worker benefits.

[10] Ruth Helman, Jack VanDerhei, and Craig Copeland, "The Retirement System in Transition: The 2007 Retirement Confidence Survey," *Issue Brief No. 304* (Washington, D.C.: Employee Benefit Research Institute, April 2007) 12.

[11] According to the Social Security and Medicare trustees, the annual cost of Social Security benefits represented 4.2 percent of GDP in 2006 and is projected to be 6.3 percent of GDP in 2081. Meanwhile, Medicare's annual costs were 3.1 percent of GDP in 2006; they are projected to exceed 11 percent of GDP in 2081.

[12] GAO, *Older Workers: Labor Can Help Employers and Employees Plan Better for the Future*, GAO-06-80 (Washington, D.C.: Dec. 5, 2006) 20-22.

[13] Helman, VanDerhei, and Copeland, "The 2007 Retirement Confidence Survey."

[14] Medicare is available at earlier ages for disability insured workers who have end stage renal disease, and Social Security or Railroad Retirement disability beneficiaries after a 2- year waiting period.

[15] SSA reduces retired-worker benefits by 5/9 of 1 percent per month for the first 36 months and 5/12 of 1 percent for each additional month that a worker elects to start benefits in advance of full retirement age. Conversely, delayed retirement credits increase benefits for each month a worker delays the start of benefits after full retirement age until they reach age 70. The factor used to calculate these credits varies by birth year. For workers born 1943 or later the increase is 2/3 of 1 percent each month (8 percent per year).

[16] This is the case if lifetime benefits are calculated on a present value basis with a discount rate equal to the expected return for the Social Security trust fund—a projected 2.9 percent above inflation after 2015, according to the intermediate assumptions in the trustees' 2007 report-- The Board of Trustees, Federal Old-Age and Survivors Insurance and Federal Disability Insurance Trust Funds, *The 2007 Annual Report of the Board of Trustees of the Federal Old-Age and Survivors Insurance and Disability Insurance Trust Funds* (Washington, D.C.:, Apr. 23, 2007) 94.

[17] In addition, people who have cut back on work or otherwise need to supplement their income may also be better off receiving reduced benefits at 62 if they have retirement savings on which they expect a relatively high rate of return. The return on one's savings must exceed the increase in benefits one would receive for waiting to start drawing benefits later.

[18] As noted earlier, in the context of the Social Security program a retired person refers to someone who has started drawing retired worker benefits.

[19] A worker eligible for both retired worker benefits and disability benefits would typically receive a higher benefit as a disabled beneficiary than as a retired worker beneficiary drawing benefits reduced for early retirement. Low-income people with low net worth may also seek Supplemental Security Income. The Congressional Budget Office projects that an increase in the SSA's early eligibility retirement age from age 62 to age 65 phased in over the 2023 to 2040 period would result in an increase in the 75-year present value deficit equal to 0.06 percent of taxable payroll. Increasing the early eligibility age can result in increases in the number of disability beneficiaries.

[20] The amount of survivor benefit ranges from 50 to 67 percent of the combined benefits received by the couple. The closer their earnings, the larger the drop will be at widowhood. Widow or widower's benefits also depend on the age at which he or she starts drawing survivor benefits. Divorced spouses, children, and dependent parents may also be entitled to the same survivor benefits.

[21] Data from SSA show in 2004 about 4 percent of married women 65 and older lived below the poverty line. But among widowed women in that age group, the poverty rate was approximately 15 percent. Poverty rates for elderly women who were divorcees or never married were 21 percent.

[22] The annual exempt amount is pegged to increases in the average wage. When beneficiaries reach the calendar year, but not the month, of their full retirement age, the reduction is $1 for every $3 above $34,440 in 2007.

[23] Recomputed benefits at full retirement age may be even higher if the earnings between 62 and the full retirement age are high enough to increase the "highest 35 years" used in calculating a worker's benefit amount. For a discussion of perceptions that the earnings test is a tax on work, see for example, Jonathan Gruber and Peter Orszag, "What to do about the Social Security Earnings Test?" An Issue in Brief July 1999, no. 1 (Boston, Mass.: Center for Retirement Research at Boston College, July 1999) and Liqun Liu and Andrew J. Rettenmaier, "Work and Retirement," *Policy Backgrounder* no. 162 (Dallas, Tex.: National Center for Policy Analysis, November 2006) 4.

[24] This is especially true for people whose mortality risk is higher than average or people who are risk-averse, i.e. value the certainty of a dollar today more than the promise of a larger amount in the future.

[25] On the other hand, delayed retirement credits continue to provide an incentive for some workers to defer the start of benefits. As noted above, up until they reach age 70, workers receive an increase in the benefit amount for each month they wait to start receiving benefits.

[26] People younger than 65 are eligible for Medicare if they meet certain conditions: workers who have end stage renal disease, and Social Security or Railroad Retirement disability beneficiaries after a 2-year waiting period. Because the program does not cover all medical expenses or the cost of most long-term care, many Medicare beneficiaries supplement their Medicare coverage with other types of insurance, such as private Medicare supplemental plans.

[27] A person may purchase continued health insurance coverage after leaving his or her employer, under the Consolidated Omnibus Budget Reconciliation Act of 1985 (COBRA) and the Health Insurance Portability and Accountability Act (HIPAA). With COBRA, continuation of coverage is generally available for a period of at least 18 months. Such coverage can be prohibitively expensive, as the retiree may be required to cover the entire premium. Once COBRA or other continuation coverage has been exhausted, HIPAA may enable a person to purchase individual coverage without regard to pre-existing medical conditions.

[28] Individuals who have health insurance through a spouse or other family members may not face the same incentives.

[29] TIAA-CREF Institute, *The Retiree Health Care Challenge* (Prepared by Hewitt Associates, November 2006).

[30] Thomas Buchmueller, Richard W. Johnson, and Anthony T. Lo Sasso, "Trends in Retiree Health Insurance, 1997-2003," *Health Affairs*, vol. 25, no. 6 (2006) 1507–1516.

[31] Richard W. Johnson and Rudolph G. Penner, "Will Health Care Costs Erode Retirement Security?" *Issue in Brief, No. 23* (Boston, Mass: Center for Retirement Research at Boston College, October 2004).

[32] In addition, since workers contact SSA to apply for Medicare, some who had not already done so may choose to apply for Social Security benefits at the same time.

[33] Tax-qualified pensions receive preferential tax treatment in exchange for satisfying certain requirements established in the Internal Revenue Code (employers receive a current deduction on contributions they make to qualified plans within certain limits). Under current law, there are a number of requirements that private pension plans must satisfy, including contribution, benefit, and vesting requirements. Qualified plans include, for example, 40 1(k), 403(b), 457, and qualified employee annuity plans.

[34] Or the 5th anniversary of plan entry if a participant entered within 5 years of NRA.

[35] On May 22, 2007, the Treasury Department issued final regulations under the Internal Revenue Code, permitting distributions to be made from a pension plan upon the attainment of the plan's NRA, but stating that the plan cannot set an NRA that is earlier than the typical retirement age for the industry in which the covered workforce is employed. The regulations provide a safe harbor of age 62 or above (age 50 or above when substantially all the participants in the plan are public safety employees). See "Distributions From a Pension Plan Upon Attainment of Normal Retirement Age," 72 Fed. Reg. 28604 (May 22, 2007).

[36] In 2003, an estimated three-quarters of workers with private sector DB plans, had plans providing early retirement at age 55 or earlier. U.S. Bureau of Labor Statistics, *National Compensation Survey: Employee Benefits in Private Industry in the United States, 2003*, Bulletin 2577, October 2005.

[37] Exceptions to this rule apply in cases where a plan participant continues to work for an employer that maintains a plan allowing distributions to begin by April 1 of the calendar year after the year in which the worker retires.

[38] In these cases distributions may be lump sums or other payments. In addition, an employee may receive distributions from a multiemployer or union plan as long as the employee no longer works for any of the participating employers.

[39] This must be in the form of a series of substantially equal periodic payments and must be for the participant's life or life expectancy or the participant's and his or her spouse's joint life expectancy. Other exceptions to the tax penalty for claiming before 59½ include rollovers to IRAs or other pensions, and cases of total and permanent disability, and death.

[40] Internal Revenue Service, *Pension and Annuity Income*, Publication 575, cat. no. 15142B, 2006, 31.

[41] A cash balance plan, a type of hybrid plan, is legally classified as a DB plan because participants' benefits are determined by a benefit formula. However, cash balance plans have certain features, such as hypothetical "individual accounts," that make it resemble a DC plan. However, changes in the value of investments do not directly affect the benefits available to participants.

[42] Both DB and DC pension holders face risks. For example, workers with a 401(k) plan face the risk that the value of their account may decline during the additional year of work even if the balance is invested entirely in bonds. In addition to the risk of default, the value of bonds falls when interest rates rise. Should a worker with a 401(k) choose to purchase a fixed annuity, they also face a risk that the amount of the annuity they receive may decline over the year. The annual income from a fixed immediate annuity generally declines when interest rates decline. Both DB and DC plan holders typically face a risk that an increase in inflation will diminish the purchasing power of their pension over time. Instead of purchasing an annuity providing a flat benefit, a DC pension holder could purchase annuities that provide an increase by a set rate, such as 3 percent per year, to compensate for anticipated inflation, but the initial amount of the annuity payments would be lower. Annuities that are fully adjusted for inflation are not widely available in the U.S. In contrast, DB pension holders face some risk that their employer may not be able to fulfill its pension commitment. In DB plans, investment risks rest with the employer or plan sponsor and benefits are, within limits, insured by the Pension Benefit Guaranty Corporation (PBGC). For discussion of the PBGC's role in insuring DB pensions see GAO, *Answers to Key Questions about Private Pensions Plans*, GAO-02-745-SP (Washington, D.C.: Sept. 18, 2002) and GAO, *Private Pensions: The Pension Benefit Guaranty Corporation and Long-Term Budgetary Challenges*, GAO-05-772T (Washington, D.C.: June 9, 2005).

[43] Abbigail J. Chiodo and Michael T. Owyang, "Putting Off Retirement: The Rise of the 401(k)" *National Economic Trends* (St. Louis, Missouri: Federal Reserve Bank of St Louis, March 2002).

[44] In 2003 an estimated 23 percent of private sector workers with DB pensions had plans that were also integrated plans, i.e. they take into account Social Security benefits received by workers.

[45] According to the 2003 National Compensation Survey, an estimated 14 percent of private sector workers participating in a DB plan have an age of 60 or less or no age requirement, and another 9 percent have a retirement age of 62. An estimated 20 percent of those with DB plans face maximum benefits provisions that cap the number of years of service in the benefit formula. Researchers studying pensions held by older workers concluded that most of those participating in DB plans faced decreasing lifetime benefits for additional years of work beginning about age 60. These estimates of negative accruals were based on analysis using a 3 percent real discount rate. See Leora Friedberg and Anthony Webb, "Retirement and the Evolution of Pension Structure," *NBER Working Paper No. 9999* (Cambridge, Mass.: National Bureau of Economic Research, September 2003).

[46] 72 Fed. Reg. 28604 (May 22, 2007); see also the Pension Protection Act of 2006, Pub. L. No. 109-280, § 905, providing for distributions to employees who have reached age 62 and have not separated from employment.

[47] Because of the recent changes in the Social Security earnings test, people at or above their full retirement age can also receive full social security benefits together with their paycheck and pensions.

[48] Although tax law generally permits non-hardship in-service distributions from qualified DC plans without tax penalty beginning at age 59½, plan administrators have the option to make them available or not. A 2006 survey of plans by the Profit Sharing/401(k) Council of America indicated that a majority of responding plans made them available and nearly three quarters of them did so for participants over age 59½.

[49] Eligibility for reduced retired worker benefits begins the first full calendar month in which eligible workers are age 62. Benefits for that month are paid during the following month. If, for example, a worker's 62nd birthday is January 5, his or her first month of eligibility will be February, and he or she will receive the first check in March.

[50] These descriptive statistics are for HRS respondents born 1931 to 1941 who had worked at least 10 years by the time they reached age 62. Some workers leave retirement and return to the work force.

[51] Mark Duggan, Perry Singleton, and Jae Song, "Aching to Retire? The Rise in the Full Retirement Age and Its Impact on the Disability Rolls," *Working Paper #11811* (Cambridge, Mass.: National Bureau of Economic Research, December 2005).

[52] This analysis focused on men; results for women were not provided.

[53] Generally workers are eligible to draw benefits at age 62 and 1 month. However, workers born on the first or second day of the month are eligible at 62 and 0 months. Recent analysis by Social Security researchers identified similar declines at age 62 following the rise in the full retirement age. Jae G. Song and Joyce Manchester, "Have People Delayed Claiming Retirement Benefits? Responses to Changes in Social Security Rules," Paper prepared for the International Social Security Association Research Conference, March 2007, Warsaw (Washington, D.C.: Social Security Administration, Division of Economic Research: December 2006).

[54] Employee Benefit Research Institute and Mathew Greenwald & Associates, Inc., "2007 Retirement Confidence Survey Fact Sheet: Attitudes About Social Security and Medicare," Employee Benefit Research Institute, April 2007, 2.

[55] For people who reached their full retirement age in 2000 or later, the age at which they start drawing benefits may also have been affected by the elimination of the earnings test, as described below.

[56] The estimated proportion of workers taking benefits at the full retirement age has, however, declined somewhat from 17 percent to 13 percent for workers born in 1935 and 1940 respectively.

[57] The proportion of 66 year-olds in the workforce increased from 34 percent in 2000 to 38 in 2004. The proportion of 67 year-olds increased from 35 to 39 percent. By assessing the proportion of 66 and 67 year-olds in the workforce between 2000 and 2004, we are limiting the number of birth year cohorts we can examine because not all of the birth cohorts had reached these ages between 2000 and 2004. For example, only four and three of the 10 birth cohorts in the HRS had reached the ages of 66 and 67 respectively, in 2000.

[58] Jae G. Song and Joyce Manchester, "New Evidence on Earnings and Benefit Claims Following Changes in the Retirement Earnings Test in 2000," *Journal of Public Economics* vol. 91, nos. 3-4, April 2007.

[59] Leora Friedberg and Anthony Webb, "Persistence in Labor Supply and the Response to the Social Security Earnings Test," *Working Paper 2006-27* (Boston, Mass.: Center for Retirement Research at Boston College, December 2006).

[60] Steven J. Haider and David S. Loughran, "The Effect of the Social Security Earnings Test on Male Labor Supply: New Evidence from Survey and Administrative Data" (Forthcoming, Journal of Human Resources, 2007).

[61] Pierre-Carl Michaud and Arthur Van Soest, "How did the Elimination of the Earnings Test above the Normal Retirement Age affect Retirement Expectations?" *RAND Working Paper 478* (RAND Corporation, January 2007).

[62] Friedberg and Webb (2006) found an increase among those in the 60th – 80th percentiles. Song and Manchester (2007) found an increase among those in the 50th – 80th percentiles.

[63] To analyze the relative likelihood of retiring we used a subset of HRS workers who were either in the labor force or partially retired at the beginning of the study in 1992. See appendix I for complete description of our sample selection criteria.

[64] For convenience we use the terms "more likely" or "less likely" to refer to adjusted odds ratios above or below 1, respectively. See appendix I for details.

[65] The income measure in our analysis was limited to the respondent's earnings (including wages, salary, and bonuses from employment or self-employment), but not his or her spouse's income. This income measure excludes other types of income such as interest, dividends, and rent.

[66] We did not find a statistically significant relationship between DB pensions and women's retirement age.

[67] In the earlier years of the HRS, respondents were asked if they had any type of health insurance coverage obtained through their or their spouses' or partners' employer, former employer or union. If they indicated having such coverage, they were asked whether the health insurance plan was available to people who retire. In later years of the study respondents were asked about whether they had employer-sponsored retiree health insurance until the age of 65.

[68] David M. Linsenmeier, "Do Retiree Health Benefits Cause Early Retirement?" *Working Paper 22* (Princeton, NJ: Princeton University Center for Health and Wellness, November 2002). In this study, the author used the same dataset and birth year cohorts that we are using in our analysis. But he used the first five waves of the data set and respondents were included in the analysis if they were working and had health insurance at the beginning of the study period.

[69] Employee Benefit Research Institute and Matthew Greenwald Associates Inc., *Health Confidence Survey* (2003).

[70] Our analysis may underestimate the effect of health limitations on early retirement. As detailed in appendix I, the sample used in our regression had a greater proportion of those in better health than the nationally representative sample from which it was drawn.

[71] We studied the type of pension held by either the respondent or the spouse from employment during the study period. Our analysis did not include information about pensions from previous employment. We compared the likelihood of retiring before age 62 for those that had a DB plan with the likelihood for those without a DB plan. Those with a DB plan may have also had a DC plan. Those without a DB plan may have had a DC plan

or no pension plan. Similarly, in our analysis of DC plans, we grouped respondents with both DB and DC plans along with those who reported having only a DC plan.

[72] We recognize that some physically demanding jobs, such as firefighters and police officers, often offer DB plans. The final model for men less than 62 also included a variable indicating if the respondent's health limited their ability to work. Our model does not attempt to explain the causality of the retirement decision, but is intended to note associations with the retirement decision, in this case both health limitations and DB plans are associated with the decision to retire, among other factors.

[73] DC pensions may not have been as important to the older members of our sample, as 401(k) plans began in the early 1980s. The oldest members of our sample were in their early fifties at this time and did not have much time to accumulate a large balance in such accounts.

[74] Alicia H. Munnell, Kevin E. Cahill, and Natalia A. Jivan, "How has the Shift to 401(K)s Affected the Retirement Age?" *Issue Brief No. 13* (Boston, Mass.: Center for Retirement Research at Boston College, September 2003).

[75] Friedberg and Webb.

[76] The HRS is sponsored by the National Institute of Aging (grant number NIA U01AG009740) and is conducted by the University of Michigan.

[77] There are five cohorts in the HRS: the AHEAD cohort, those born before 1924; the Children of the Depression cohort, those born 1924-1930; the original HRS cohort born between 1931 and 1941, the War Baby cohort, those born between 1942-1947; and the Early Baby Boomer Cohort, those born 1948-1953. The original HRS cohort respondents entered the study in 1992 and are interviewed every 2 years.

[78] Respondents in the workforce in 1992 were those who worked full-time, worked part-time or were unemployed (not working, but seeking work). In addition for our analysis of full retirement we included respondents classified as partially retired.

[79] We excluded these groups in part in order to be able to analyze the timing of workers' retirements in relation to their pre-retirement characteristics.

[80] The HRS is a sample of the non institutionalized (community-based) population in the contiguous United States.

[81] While the larger HRS data set does have links to restricted SSA earnings data and some pension information from employers, we were not able to utilize these sources of information.

[82] Wan He, Victoria Velkoff, and Kimberly DeBarros, *65+ in the U.S.: 2005*, *Current Population Reports, P23-209* (Washington, D.C.: U.S. Census Bureau, December 2005).

[83] GAO-06-80, 41-43.

[84] This includes the respondent's earnings (including wages, salary, and bonuses from employment or self-employment), but not their spouse's income. It excludes other types of income such as interest, dividends, and rent.

[85] This data set is a 1 percent sample of SSA beneficiaries that has information on earnings and the claiming of Social Security benefits.

[86] In 1996, legislation was passed which raised the earnings test threshold.

[87] The NBDS is a sample of Social Security beneficiaries who first received Old Age, Survivors, and Disability Insurance benefits between mid-1980 and mid-1981, who were interviewed by SSA in 1982 and 1991. The BEPUF is nationally representative of Social Security beneficiaries who were entitled to these benefits in 2004.

[88] Paul Fronstin, "The Impact of the Erosion of Retiree Health Benefits on Workers and Retirees," *Issue Brief No. 279* (Washington, D.C.: Employee Benefit Research Institute, March 2005).

[89] Our analysis of income was limited to a respondent's earned income, including wages, salaries, and bonuses from employment or self-employment. It excluded their spouse's income and unearned income such as interest, dividends, and rent.

In: When to Retire: Issues in Working and Saving for a Secure...   ISBN: 978-1-60876-982-7
Editor: Maurice R. Davenworth   © 2010 Nova Science Publishers, Inc.

Chapter 3

THE RETIREMENT SAVINGS TAX CREDIT: A FACT SHEET

Patrick Purcell

SUMMARY

The Economic Growth and Tax Relief Reconciliation Act of 2001 (P.L. 107-16) authorized a non-refundable tax credit of up to $1,000 for eligible individuals who contribute to an IRA or an employer-sponsored retirement plan. The credit was first available in 2002, and as enacted in 2001, it would have expired after the 2006 tax year. The Pension Protection Act of 2006 (P.L. 109-280) made the retirement savings tax credit permanent. Beginning in 2007, the eligible income brackets were indexed to inflation. The maximum credit is 50% of retirement contributions up to $2,000. The credit can reduce the amount of taxes owed, but the tax credit itself is non-refundable. The maximum credit is lesser of $1,000 or tax that the individual would have owed without the credit. Eligibility is based on the taxpayer's adjusted gross income. Taxpayers under age 18 who are full-time students are not eligible for credit.

The Economic Growth and Tax Relief Reconciliation Act of 2001 (P.L. 107-16) authorized a tax credit to encourage low- and moderate-income families and individuals to save for retirement.[1] Eligible taxpayers who contribute to an individual retirement account (IRA) or to an employer-sponsored plan that is qualified under §401, §403 or §457 of the tax code can receive a non-refundable tax credit of up to $1,000. This credit is in addition to the tax deduction for contributing to a traditional IRA or to an employer- sponsored retirement plan. In determining the amount of the credit, neither the amount of any refundable tax credits for which the taxpayer is eligible nor the adoption credit are taken into consideration. The retirement savings credit was first available in 2002, and as enacted in 2001, it would have expired after the 2006 tax year. Section 812 of the Pension Protection Act of 2006 (PPA, P.L. 109-280) made the retirement savings tax credit permanent. Section 833 of the PPA provided that for years after 2006, the eligible income brackets will be indexed to inflation in increments of $500.

Taxpayers claim the credit on their federal income tax returns. Taxpayers who contribute up to $2,000 (for all plans combined) to a traditional IRA, a Roth IRA, or an employer-sponsored retirement plan receive a credit that reduces the amount of income tax they owe. The maximum credit is the lesser of $1,000 or the amount of tax that would have been owed without the credit.

The amount of the credit declines as income increases. In 2008, for individuals with adjusted gross incomes (AGI) under $16,000 and married couples with incomes under $32,000, the credit is 50% of contributions up to $2,000 for a maximum credit of $1,000. (See Table 1.)

Because the credit is based on AGI, it increases the net benefit of contributing to a retirement plan. For example, a married couple filing jointly with income of $32,000 who contribute $2,000 to a §401(k) plan would reduce their taxable income to $30,000 and qualify for a $1,000 tax credit. The net effect is that the $2,000 contribution to the 401(k) plan costs them only $1,000.

Table 1. Credit Amounts for the Savers' Credit in 2008

Filing Status and Adjusted Gross Income			Amount of Credit
Single	Head of Household	Married, Filing Jointly	
$1 to $16,000	$1 to $24,000	$1 to $32,000	50% of contribution up to $2,000 ($1,000 maximum credit)
$16,001 to $17,250	$24,000 to $25,875	$32,001 to $34,500	20% of contribution up to $2,000 ($400 maximum credit)
$17,251 to $26,500	$25,876 to $39,750	$34,501 to $53,000	10% of contribution up to $2,000 ($200 maximum credit)
More than $26,500	More than $39,750	More than $53,000	Zero

The credit is not available to taxpayers under age 18 or to full-time students. If a worker or spouse receives a pre-retirement distribution from a retirement plan (such as a hardship withdrawal), any credit taken in that same year and in the two subsequent years will be reduced by the amount of the distribution. For example, if an individual took a $1,000 hardship withdrawal in 2005 and qualified for a $500 credit for that year, $500 of the hardship withdrawal would offset the $500 credit in 2005. The remaining $500 of the hardship withdrawal would offset any credits (up to $500) in 2006 and 2007. Because it is non-refundable, some families may not benefit from the retirement savings tax credit because they have no net income tax liability. Also, the credit may not be large enough to provide a savings incentive for families with incomes near the upper limits. For families in the highest income bracket that qualifies for the credit, the maximum credit is $200 for a contribution of $2,000. On the other hand, families that increase their saving to claim the retirement savings credit and who are eligible for the earned income tax credit (EITC) may increase the amount of the EITC for which they qualify.

Data from the IRS indicate that the retirement savings tax credit was claimed on about 5.3 million tax returns — 4% of all tax returns — filed each year from 2002 through 2005. The average annual credit was $190. The average retirement plan contribution on which the credit was claimed was $1,200. Thus, the average credit was equal to about 16% of the average amount contributed to retirement plans by taxpayers who claimed the retirement savings credit.

End Notes

[1] The retirement savings tax credit is authorized in the Internal Revenue Code at 26 U.S.C., §25B.

In: When to Retire: Issues in Working and Saving for a Secure...   ISBN: 978-1-60876-982-7
Editor: Maurice R. Davenworth   © 2010 Nova Science Publishers, Inc.

Chapter 4

THE WORKER, RETIREE, AND EMPLOYER RECOVERY ACT OF 2008: AN OVERVIEW

Jennifer Staman

SUMMARY

In December of 2008, Congress unanimously enacted the Worker, Retiree, and Employer Recovery Act of 2008 (WRERA) (P.L. 110-455), which makes several technical corrections to the Pension Protection Act of 2006 (P.L. 109-280) and contains provisions designed to help pension plans and plan participants weather the current economic downturn. This report highlights the provisions of WRERA relating to the economic crisis, such as the temporary waiver of required minimum distributions and provisions that temporarily relax certain pension plan funding requirements. This report also discusses certain technical corrections to the Pension Protection Act made by WRERA, and certain other notable provisions of the Act affecting retirement plans and benefits.

There has been a great deal of concern over the effect of the current economic downturn on retirement plans. One company recently reported that at the end of 2008, the "chaos" in the financial markets led to a $409 billion deficit in defined benefit pension plan funding for the plans of S&P 1500 companies.[1] The report indicated that this deficit will negatively affect corporate earnings in 2009.[2] Due in part to the large investment losses in pension plans and other retirement accounts, in December of 2008, Congress unanimously enacted H.R. 7327, the Worker, Retiree, and Employer Recovery Act of 2008 ("WRERA" or "the Act"). While several provisions of WRERA make technical corrections to the Pension Protection Act of 2006 ("PPA"),[3] the Act also provides some temporary relief from certain requirements that may be difficult for pension plans to meet due to current economic conditions. This report provides an overview of some of the key provisions of WRERA, in particular, the provisions relating to the funding of single and multiemployer plans, the temporary waiver for required minimum distributions, as well as certain technical corrections and other provisions that affect the two primary types of pension plans, defined benefit and defined contribution plans, as well as individual retirement accounts and annuities (IRAs).[4]

WRERA's Provisions Relating to the Economic Crisis

Title II of WRERA contains provisions designed to protect both individuals and retirement plans from the potentially large losses of plan amounts due to the decline of the stock market and the current economic climate. These provisions include a temporary waiver of the required minimum distributions, and temporary relief from funding rules created by the PPA that apply to single and multi-employer plans.[5] In essence, these provisions permit a delay in taking required distributions and meeting pension funding obligations, in an effort to give retirement plans and accounts more time for economic conditions to improve and for the losses in investments to be recovered.

Temporary Waiver of Minimum Distribution Rules

Under section 401(a)(9) of the Internal Revenue Code, employer-sponsored retirement plans, such as 401(k), 403(b) and 457 plans, and individual retirement accounts and annuities ("IRAs") must make certain annual required minimum distributions in order to maintain their "qualified" (i.e., tax-favorable) status.[6] The theory behind these required distributions is to ensure that tax- deferred retirement accounts that have been established to provide income during retirement are not used as permanent tax shelters or as vehicles for transmitting wealth to heirs. For employer- sponsored plans, required minimum distributions to participants must start no later than April 1 of the year after the year in which the participant either attains age 70½,or retires, whichever is later.[7] For traditional IRAs, required minimum distributions must commence by April 1 following the year the IRA owner reaches age 70½. Alternative minimum distribution requirements apply to beneficiaries in the event that the participant dies before the entire amount in the participant's account is distributed.[8] Failure to make a required distribution results in an excise tax equal to 50 percent of the required minimum distribution amount that was not distributed for the year, which is imposed on the participant or beneficiary.[9]

Following the decline in the stock market, there was concern about individuals taking these required distributions when there has not been enough time to recover losses.[10] Section 201 of WRERA suspends the minimum distribution requirements, both initial and annual required distributions, for defined contribution arrangements, including IRAs, for calendar year 2009.[11] Thus, plan participants and beneficiaries are allowed, but are not required, to take required minimum distributions for 2009. However, it should be noted that the required distributions for 2008, or for years after 2009, are not waived by the new law.

Amendment of the Funding Transition Rule for Single-Employer Plans

The Internal Revenue Code sets out certain minimum funding standards that apply to defined benefit plans.[12] The funding standards for single-employer plans were completely revamped by the PPA, which created more stringent standards than under prior law. When fully phased in, the new funding requirements established by the PPA will generally require plan assets to be equal to 100 percent of plan liabilities on a present value basis. Under these standards, when the value of a plan's assets is less than the plan's "funding target,"[13] a plan's minimum required contribution for a plan year is comprised of the plan's "target normal cost," (i.e., the present value of the benefits expected to be accrued or earned during the year, minus certain plan expenses), plus a "shortfall amortization base," an amount which is established if the plan has a funding shortfall.[14] However, under a special exemption, if the value of the plan's assets is equal to or greater than the funding target, then the shortfall amortization amount will be zero.[15] The PPA also created a transition rule, under which a shortfall amortization base does not have to be established if, for plan years beginning in 2008 and ending in 2010, the plan's assets are equal to a certain percentage of the plan's funding target for that year. The percentage of the funding target is 92 percent for 2008, 94 percent for 2009, and 96 percent for 2010.[16] In other words, the PPA, through this transition rule, gave pension plans a three year period to ease into the new plan funding requirements, in which plans could gradually increase the value of the plan assets, thus relieving them from the burden of having to contribute a large part of the funding shortfall in one year.

The PPA placed a limitation on the transition rule, under which the rule will not apply with respect to any plan year after 2008 unless the shortfall amortization base was zero (e.g., the plan failed to meet the transition rule, or be 92 percent funded in 2008). Section 202 of WRERA allows plans to follow the transition rule even if the plan's shortfall amortization base was not zero in the preceding year.[17] Thus, a plan that was not 92 percent funded in 2008 would only be required to be 94 percent funded in 2009, instead of 100 percent.[18] This provision gives plans some additional time to be 100 percent funded, a requirement that may have become more difficult to fulfill because of the decline in the financial markets and the resulting loss of value of plan assets.

Temporary Modification on Freezing Benefit Accruals

As provided by the PPA, underfunded single-employer defined benefit plans may be subject to certain restrictions on benefits and benefit accruals.[19] Under one of these restrictions, if a plan's "adjusted funding target attainment percentage" (AFTAP)[20] is less than 60 percent (i.e., generally speaking, if a plan is less than 60 percent funded) for a plan year, a plan must stop providing future benefit accruals.[21] Section 203 of WRERA provides that for the first plan year beginning during the period of October 1, 2008 through September 30, 2009, this restriction on benefit accruals is determined using the AFTAP from the preceding year, instead of the current year, *if* the AFTAP for the preceding year is greater. Thus, this provision allows a plan to look to the previous year's funding levels in order to determine whether there must be a restriction of benefit accruals. For plans that have lost a lot in the value of plan assets, looking to the AFTAP for the previous year may allow some plans to continue providing future benefit accruals that would otherwise have to cease them. However, plans that have higher funding levels for the current year will not be affected by this provision.

**Table 1. General Characteristics of Plans in Endangered or Critical Status under
Internal Revenue Code Section 432**

	Endangered Status	**Critical Status**
Criteria	Less than 80% funded, *or*	Less than 65% funded, and the sum of the fair market value of the plan assets plus the reasonably anticipated contributions to the plan (for the current plan year and the next 6 than the value of the benefits expected to be paid (plus administrative expenses), *or*
	Has an accumulated funding deficiency for the plan year, or is projected to have a deficiency within the next 6 years, taking into account any extension of amortization periods approved by the Treasury Secretary	
	("seriously endangered" plans meet both criteria)	Has an accumulated funding deficiency for the current plan year, not taking into account any amortization extension period, or the plan is projected to have a deficiency for any of the next 3 years, or 4 years if the plan is less than 65% funded, *or*
		(1) The normal cost for the plan year, plus interest for the current plan year on the amount of unfunded benefit liabilities under the plan, exceeds the present value of the reasonably anticipated contributions for the current plan year, (2) the present value of nonforfeitable benefits of inactive participants is greater than the present value of nonforfeitable benefits of active participants, *and* (3) the plan has an accumulated funding deficiency for the current plan year, or is projected to have a deficiency for any of the next 4 years (not taking into account amortization period extensions), *or*
		Sum of the fair market value of plan assets plus the present value of the reasonably anticipated contributions for the current plan year and each of next 4 years is less than the present value of all benefits projected to be payable under the plan during the current plan year and each of the next four years (plus administrative expenses).
Required Actions	Adoption of a **funding improvement plan**, which includes options for a plan to attain a certain increase in the plan's	Adoption of a **rehabilitation plan**, which includes options to enable the plan to cease being in critical status

Table 1. (Continued)

	Endangered Status	Critical Status
	funding percentage, while avoiding accumulated funding deficiencies over a funding improvement period. The funding improvement period is, in general, 10 years for endangered plans, and 15 years for seriously endangered plans.	by the end of the rehabilitation period, generally 10 years. The rehabilitation plan may also include reductions in plan expenditures, future benefit accruals, or increases in contributions.
		Imposition of a surcharge on employers, under which employers are obligated to pay 5% of the contribution otherwise required to be made. In the case of succeeding plan years in which the plan is in critical status, the surcharge is 10% of the contributions otherwise required.
Penalties under Internal Revenue Code Section 4971(g)	Employers failing to make a contribution as required under a funding improvement plan may be subject to an excise tax equal to the amount of the required contribution.	Employers failing to make a contribution as required under a rehabilitation plan may be subject to an excise tax equal to the amount of the required contribution.
	Seriously endangered plans failing to meet benchmarks laid out by the funding improvement plan by the end of the funding improvement period are treated as having an accumulated funding deficiency in an amount equal to the greater of the amount of the contributions necessary to meet such benchmarks, or the amount of the plan's existing accumulated funding deficiency.	Plans in critical status failing to meet rehabilitation plan requirements are treated as having an accumulated funding deficiency in an amount equal to the greater of the amount of the contributions necessary to meet such requirements, or the amount of the plan's existing accumulated funding deficiency.
		Multiemployer plans that fail to adopt a rehabilitation plan within a specified time period may be subject to an excise tax which is the greater of 5% of the accumulated funding deficiency, or $1,100 for each day during the taxable year between the date when the rehabilitation plan was required to be adopted, and the date it was adopted. This tax must be paid by each plan sponsor.

Temporary Delay of Designation of Endangered or Critical Status for Multiemployer Plans

Under section 432 of the Internal Revenue Code as created by the PPA, multiemployer plans failing to meet certain funding levels may be subject to certain additional funding obligations and benefit restrictions. These additional requirements depend on whether the plan is in "endangered" or "critical" status. A multiemployer plan is considered to be endangered if it is less than 80 percent funded *or* if the plan has an accumulated funding deficiency[22] for the plan year, or is projected to have a deficiency within the next six years. A plan that is less than 80 percent funded *and* is projected to have an accumulated funding deficiency is considered to be "seriously endangered." Endangered plans must adopt a funding improvement plan, which contains options for a plan to attain a certain increase in the plan's funding percentage, while avoiding accumulated funding deficiencies.[23] A multiemployer plan is considered to be in critical status if, for example, the plan is less than 65 percent funded and the sum of the fair market value of plan assets, plus the present value of reasonably anticipated employer and employee contributions for the current plan year and each of the next six plan years is less than the present value of all benefits projected to be payable under the plan during the current plan year and each of the next six years (plus administrative expenses).[24] Plans in critical status must develop a rehabilitation plan containing options to enable the plan to cease being in critical status by the end of the rehabilitation period, generally 10 years. The rehabilitation plan may include reductions in plan expenditures and future benefit accruals. Employers may also have to pay a surcharge in addition to other plan contributions.[25]

Each year, a plan's actuary must certify whether or not the plan is in endangered or critical status. Under section 204 of WRERA a sponsor of a multiemployer defined benefit pension plan may elect for the status of the plan year that begins during the period between October 1, 2008 and September 30, 2009, to be the same as the plan's certified status for the previous year. Accordingly, if a plan was not in endangered or critical status for the prior year, the sponsor may elect to retain this status and may avoid additional plan funding requirements. A plan that was in endangered or critical status during the preceding year does not have to update its funding improvement plan, rehabilitation plan, or schedule information until the plan year following the year that the plan's status remained the same. However, for plans that are in critical status, the Act clarifies that the freezing of the certification status does not relieve the plan from certain requirements.[26]

Temporary Extension of the Funding Improvement and Rehabilitation Periods for Multiemployer Pension Plans in Critical and Endangered Status

Section 432 of the Internal Revenue Code provides that a multiemployer plan that is in endangered or critical status must meet certain additional funding requirements. In general, endangered plans must adopt a funding improvement plan, and critical plans must adopt a rehabilitation plan.[27] Under both a funding improvement and a rehabilitation plan, there is a 10-year period under which a plan must meet a certain funding percentage. Seriously endangered plans have 15 years to improve their funding percentage. Section 205 of WRERA provides that a plan sponsor of a plan in endangered or critical status may elect, for a plan year beginning in 2008 or 2009, to extend the funding improvement period or the rehabilitation period by three years, to 13 years instead of 10 years. Plans in seriously endangered status have a funding improvement period of 18 years, rather than 15 years. The provision gives plans more time to meet their funding obligations. An election must be made by the plan in order to take advantage of this relaxed funding requirement.

TECHNICAL CORRECTIONS TO THE PENSION PROTECTION ACT OF 2006

WRERA made several technical corrections to the Pension Protection Act of 2006 (PPA). Some of the corrections are effective as if they were enacted as part of the PPA, while other provisions are to be applied prospectively. The technical corrections include the following:

Rollovers to Non-Spouse Beneficiaries

In general, distributions from retirement plans or accounts are subject to tax in the year they are distributed. Prior to the PPA, in the event that a participant died, distributions from the retirement plan of a participant could transfer (or "rollover") into a surviving spouse's IRA tax-free.[28] This rollover scheme was not available to non-spouse beneficiaries. Under section 402(c)(11) of the Internal Revenue Code, as created by the PPA, certain tax-qualified plans (e.g., a 401(k)) could offer a direct rollover of a distribution to a nonspouse beneficiary (e.g., a sibling, parent, or a domestic partner). The direct rollover must be made to an individual retirement account or annuity (IRA) established on behalf of the designated beneficiary that will be treated as an inherited IRA.[29] As a result, the rollover amounts would not be included in the beneficiary's income in the year of the rollover.

The Internal Revenue Service had previously taken the position that section 402(c)(11) permitted, but did not require, plans to provide this type of rollover option.[30] Section 108(f) of the WRERA clarifies that distributions to a nonspouse beneficiary's inherited IRA are to be considered "eligible rollover distributions,"[31] and plans are thus required to allow these beneficiaries to make these direct rollovers.[32] Plans must also provide direct rollover notices in order to maintain plan qualification.[33] This provision is effective for plan years beginning on January 1, 2010.

Missing Participants Program

In general, an employer that chooses to terminate a fully funded defined benefit plan must comply with certain requirements with regard to participants or beneficiaries whom the plan administrator cannot locate after a diligent search.[34] For these individuals, a plan administrator may either purchase an annuity from an insurer or transfer the missing participant's benefits to the PBGC. Prior to the PPA, the missing participant requirements only applied to single-employer plans. The PPA amended these requirements to apply to multiemployer plans, defined contribution plans, and other plans that do not have termination insurance through the PBGC. Section 104(e) of WRERA specifies that the missing participant requirements apply to plans that at no time provided for employer contributions.[35] WRERA also narrows the missing participant requirements to defined contribution plans (and other pension plans not covered by PBGC's termination insurance) that are qualified plans. The requirements of this section take effect as if they were included in the PPA.

Lump-Sum Payments for Underfunded Plans

Under the funding rules created by the PPA, single-employer defined benefit plans that fall below certain funding levels are subject to several additional requirements. One of these requirements prevents plans that have a funding percentage of less than 60 percent from making "prohibited payments," (i.e., certain accelerated forms of distribution, such as a lump sum payment) to plan participants. Current law also specifies that if the present value of a participant's vested benefit exceeds $5,000, the benefit may not be immediately distributed without the participant's consent.[36]Accordingly, if the vested benefit is less than or equal to $5,000 this consent requirement does not apply.[37] Section 101 of WRERA amends the definition of "prohibited payment" to exclude benefits which may be distributed without the consent of the participant.[38] As a result, lump sum payments of $5,000 or less may be paid by an underfunded plan that is otherwise precluded from paying larger lump sum distributions. This amendment applies to plan years beginning in 2008.

Disclosure Requirements for Distress/Involuntary Terminations

Under ERISA, pension plans must meet extensive notice and reporting requirements that disclose information about the plan to participants and beneficiaries as well as government agencies. Among these disclosures is a requirement that a terminating single-employer defined benefit plan provide "affected parties"[39] with certain information required to be submitted to the Pension Benefit Guaranty Corporation (PBGC).[40] Section 105 of WRERA clarifies that in order for a plan to terminate in a distress termination, a plan administrator must not only provide affected parties with information that the administrator had to disclose to the PBGC along with the written notice of intent to terminate, but also certain information that was provided to the PBGC after the notice was given.[41] This information may include a certification by an enrolled actuary regarding the amount of the current value of the assets of the plan, the actuarial present value of the benefit liabilities under the plan, and whether the plan's assets are sufficient to pay benefit liabilities.[42]

Further, in an involuntary termination, certain confidentiality provisions exist that prevent the plan administrator or sponsor from providing information about the termination in a form which includes any information that may be associated with, or identify affected parties. Section 105 of WRERA extends this confidentiality protection disclosure of this information by the PBGC.

SELECTED OTHER PROVISIONS OF WRERA

Other notable provisions included in WRERA are the following:

Rollover of Amounts Received in Airline Carrier Bankruptcy to Roth IRAs

Roth IRAs, a type of individual retirement arrangement, are a popular retirement savings vehicle.[43] While contributions to a Roth IRA are not deductible, qualified distributions[44] from a Roth IRA are not included in an individual's gross income. Roth IRAs are subject to certain contribution limitations, however, these limitations do not apply to qualified rollover contributions.[45] Section 125 of the WRERA permits a "qualified airline employee"[46] who receives an "airline payment amount"[47] to transfer any portion of this amount to a Roth IRA as a qualified rollover contribution. This transfer must occur within 180 days of receipt of the amount (or, if later, within 180 days of the enactment of WRERA). Thus, if such amounts are transferred to the former employee's Roth IRA, the employee may benefit, as qualified distributions from Roth IRAs are tax free. This section also provides that certain income limitations placed upon Roth IRA qualified rollover contributions should not apply to this transfer.[48]

Determination of Plan Assets to Account for Expected Earnings

In order to determine the minimum required contribution that must be made to a single-employer defined benefit plan, and the extent (if any) to which a plan is underfunded, the value of plan assets must be determined. For purposes of the minimum funding rules, the value of the plan's assets is, in general, the fair market value of the assets.[49] However, the Internal Revenue Code, as amended by the PPA, permits plans to calculate the value of the assets by averaging fair market values, but only if (1) the averaging method is permitted under regulations, (2) the calculation is not over a period of more than 24 months, and (3) the averaged amount cannot result in a determination that is at any time less than 90 percent or more than 110 percent of fair market value.[50] This averaging method may be more beneficial for plan sponsors in an economic downturn, as an averaging approach can produce lower asset values when asset values are rising, and higher asset values when asset values are decreasing.[51] Section 121 of WRERA provides that plans using the averaging method must adjust such averaging to account not only for the amount of contributions and distributions to the plan, but also for expected investment earnings, subject to a cap.[52] It has been noted that this provision could result in smaller underfunded amounts and, therefore, smaller required contributions.[53]

Plan Asset Valuation for Airline Plans

The PPA created certain relaxed funding requirements for defined benefit plans maintained by a commercial airline or an airline catering service. Under the PPA, plan sponsors of these plans could elect to amortize unfunded plan liabilities over an extended period of 10 years, or may instead follow special rules that permit these plan sponsors to amortize unfunded liabilities over 17 years. Plan sponsors selecting the 17-year amortization period, referred to by the Act as an "alternative funding schedule," had to comply with certain benefit accrual requirements, which included freezing some of the benefits offered under the plan and eliminating others.[54] In determining the minimum required contribution to the plan each year for purposes of these special rules, the PPA provided that the value of plan assets generally is the fair market value of the assets. Section 126 of WRERA provides that plans following the alternative funding schedule may determine the value of plan assets in the same manner as other single-employer plans. Thus, plans can use a fair market value determination, or they may use the averaging method as laid out in Section 430(g)(3) of the Internal Revenue Code.[55]

End Notes

[1] See Michael W. Wyand, *Funding Deficit of $409 Billion is Due to Financial Market 'Chaos,' Mercer Says*, BNA Pension and Benefits Daily (Jan. 8, 2009).

[2] *Id.*

[3] P.L. 109-280, 120 Stat 780 (Aug. 17, 2006).

[4] A defined benefit plan is a pension plan under which an employee is promised a specified future benefit, traditionally an annuity beginning at retirement. In a defined benefit plan, the employer bears the investment risk and is responsible for any shortfalls. 29 U.S.C. § 1002(35). A defined contribution plan is a pension plan in which the contributions are specified, but not the benefits. A defined contribution plan (also called "an individual account" plan) provides an individual account for each participant that accrues benefits based solely on the amount contributed to the account and any income, expenses, and investment gains or losses to the account. See 29 U.S.C. § 1002(34).

[5] A multiemployer plan is a collectively bargained plan maintained by several employers—usually within the same industry—and a labor union. Multiemployer defined benefit plans are subject to funding requirements that differ from those for single-employer plans. For a general discussion of the funding requirements for single and multi-employer plans, seeCRS Report RL34443, *Summary of the Employee Retirement Income Security Act (ERISA)*, by Patrick Purcell and Jennifer Staman.

[6] It should be noted that this section focuses on required minimum distributions for defined contribution plans. While defined benefit plans are also subject to minimum required distribution rules, these rules will not be discussed in this memorandum.

[7] 26 U.S.C. § 401(a)(9). An exception to this rule applies if the employee is a 5 percent owner of the employer. These owners must receive a distribution the year after the owner turns $70^{1}/2$, subject to exceptions. 26 U.S.C. § 401(a)(9)(C)(ii).

[8] See 26 U.S.C. §401(a)(9)(B). It is important to note that Roth IRAs are not subject to the required minimum distribution requirements during the IRA owner's lifetime. However, beneficiaries of Roth IRAs are subject to required minimum distribution rules that apply to traditional IRAs.

[9] 26 U.S.C. § 4974.

[10] The amount of required minimum distributions are calculated using the account balance of the end of the previous year. If, following this calculation, there is a great decline in the value of the plan, the distribution may be disproportionately large compared the lower level of plan amount. For a plan participant who does not immediately need this money from his or her account, it would benefit the participant to keep this money in the retirement account on a tax-deferred basis.

[11] 26 U.S.C. § 401(a)(9)(H).

[12] 26 U.S.C. § 430 *et. seq.* Pension plan funding requirements may also be found in the Employee Retirement Income Security Act (ERISA). See 29 U.S.C. § 1001-1461.

[13] In essence, a plan's funding target is the plan's liabilities. It is defined by the PPA as the present value of all benefits accrued or earned under the plan as of the beginning of the plan year. 26 U.S.C. § 430(d)(1). The funding target is different for plans which in "at-risk status"(*i.e.*, in general, has more severe underfunding). See 26 U.S.C. § 430(i).

[14] Minimum required contribution also includes a waiver amortization charge, an amount based on the portion of the minimum funding requirement, if any, that is waived by the Secretary and not satisfied by employer contributions. See 26 U.S.C. § 412(c)(3).

[15] 26 U.S.C. § 430(c)(5)(A).

[16] 26 U.S.C. § 430(c)(5)(B). Certain plans are precluded from the transition rule. See 26 U.S.C. § 430(c)(5)(B)(iv).

[17] 29 U.S.C. § 1083(c)(5); 26 U.S.C. § 430(c)(5).

[18] See Joint Committee on Taxation, *Technical Explanation of H.R. 7327, the Worker, Retiree, and Employer Recovery Act of 2008*, JCX-85-08 (Dec. 11, 2008) at 28.

[19] 29 U.S.C. § 1056; 26 U.S.C. § 436.

[20] In essence, a plan's AFTAP is the ratio of the value of a plan's assets to the plan's funding target, adjusted by the amount of the plan's purchases of annuities for certain employees. 26 U.S.C. § 436(j)(2).

[21] This restriction does not apply to a plan for the first five years of the plan, or if the employer makes an additional contribution to the plan that brings the funding level up to 60 percent. See 26 U.S.C. 436(e)(2); 26 U.S.C. 436(g).

[22] Subject to an exception, an "accumulated funding deficiency" is defined as the amount, determined as of the end of the plan year, equal to the excess (if any) of the total charges to the funding standard account (an account all multiemployer plans are required to have) of the plan for all plan years ... over the total credits to such account for such years." See 26 U.S.C. § 431(a).

[23] 26 U.S.C. § 432(b)(1).

[24] See 26 U.S.C. § 432(b)(2) for other ways in which a plan may be considered in critical status.

[25] 26 U.S.C. § 432(e).

[26] For example, plans in critical status will still be subject to an excise tax if there is a failure to make certain plan contributions.

[27] See notes 22-25 *supra* and accompanying text.

[28] See 26 U.S.C. § 402(c)(9).

[29] It should be noted that a nonspouse beneficiary may also acquire an IRA (in a trustee to trustee transfer) due to an IRA owner's death as an "inherited" IRA, under which the beneficiary may not make contributions, or rollover amounts into or out of the IRA. See 26 U.S.C. § 408(d)(3)(C).

[30] *See, e.g.,* Notice 2007-7, 2007-5 I.R.B. 395 (Jan. 29, 2007).

[31] An eligible rollover distribution is any distribution to the plan participant or IRA owner, but does not include certain periodic distributions, required minimum distributions, or hardship distributions. 26 U.S.C. § 402(c)(4).

[32] 26 U.S.C. § 402(c)(11)(A).

[33] 26 U.S.C. §402(f).

[34] 29 U.S.C. § 4050(a)(1).

[35] 26 U.S.C. § 4050(d)(4)(A)(ii).

[36] 26 U.S.C. §411(a)(11).

[37] Joint Committee on Taxation, *supra* note 18, at 3.

[38] 29 U.S.C. § 1056(g)(3)(E); 26 U.S.C. § 436(d)(5).

[39] An affected party means, with respect to a plan, each plan participant, beneficiary (either of a deceased participant or alternate payee under a qualified domestic relations order), an employee organization, and the PBGC. An affected party may designate (in writing) for another person to receive any notice required to be provided to the affected party. 29 U.S.C. § 4001(21).

[40] For more information the PBGC's role in single employer plan terminations, see CRS Report RS22624, *The Pension Benefit Guaranty Corporation and Single-Employer Plan Terminations*, by Jennifer Staman and Erika Lunder.

[41] Joint Committee on Taxation, *supra* note 18, at 7.

[42] 29 U.S.C. § 1341(c)(2).

[43] For a general discussion of Roth IRAs, see CRS Report RL30255, *Individual Retirement Accounts (IRAs): Issues and Proposed Expansion*, coordinated by Thomas L. Hungerford and Jane G. Gravelle, and CRS Report RL31770, *Individual Retirement Accounts and 401(k) Plans: Early Withdrawals and Required Distributions*, by Patrick Purcell.

[44] Qualified distributions are any payment or distribution—(i) made on or after the date on which the individual attains age 59 1/2 , (ii) made to a beneficiary (or to the estate of the individual) on or after the death of the individual, (iii) attributable to the individual's being disabled (within the meaning of section 72(m)(7) [26 U.S.C. § 72(m)(7)]), or (iv) which is a qualified special purpose distribution. 26 U.S.C. § 408A(d)(2).

[45] A "qualified rollover contribution" may be made to a Roth IRA from another Roth IRA, as well as from a traditional IRA, or from an "eligible retirement plan," such as a 401(k), 403(b), or 457 plan if certain requirements are met. See 26 U.S.C. § 408A(e).

[46] A "qualified airline employee" is defined in section 125 of WRERA as an employee or former employee of a commercial passenger airline carrier who was a participant in the carrier's qualified defined benefit plan that was terminated or became subject to certain relaxed funding requirements as set forth in section 402(b) of the Pension Protection Act of 2006.

[47] An "airline payment amount" is defined by WRERA as "money or other property which is payable by a commercial passenger airline carrier to a qualified airline employee– (i) under the approval of an order of a federal bankruptcy court in a case filed after September 11, 2001, and before January 1, 2007, and (ii) in respect of the qualified airline employee's interest in a bankruptcy claim against the carrier, any note of the carrier (or amount paid in lieu of a note being issued), or any other fixed obligation of the carrier to pay a lump sum amount." An airline payment amount does not include any amount payable on the basis of the carrier's future earnings or profits.

[48] Under 26 U.S.C. § 408A(c)(3)(B), a taxpayer is not allowed to make a qualified rollover contribution to a Roth IRA from an eligible retirement plan other than a Roth IRA during any taxable year if, for that taxable year, (i) the taxpayer's adjusted gross income exceeds $ 100,000, or (ii) the taxpayer is a married individual filing a separate return.

[49] 26 U.S.C. § 430(g)(3)(A).

[50] 26 U.S.C. § 430(g)(3)(B).

[51] See Lynn A. Cook, Minimum Funding: What if Technical Corrections Passes? Or Doesn't?, BNA Tax &Accounting, Insights and Commentary, *available at* http://www.bnatax.com/tm/insights_cook.htm.

[52] 26 U.S.C. § 430(g)(3)(B); 29 U.S.C. § 1083(g)(3)(B).

[53] *See* Andrea L. Ben-Yosef, *President Signs Pension Funding Relief and Technical Corrections Bill (H.R. 7327)*, BNA Pension and Benefits Daily (Dec. 24, 2008).

[54] Section 402 of the PPA.

[55] See notes 49-53 *supra* and accompanying text.

In: When to Retire: Issues in Working and Saving for a Secure...   ISBN: 978-1-60876-982-7
Editor: Maurice R. Davenworth   © 2010 Nova Science Publishers, Inc.

Chapter 5

WORKING FOR RETIREMENT SECURITY

Social Security Advisory Board

EXECUTIVE SUMMARY

Longer life spans and other demographic changes are making it increasingly expensive to finance an adequate retirement income. One way to reduce this burden is for older workers to participate longer in the workforce. Policy makers should consider ways to remove barriers to continued work at older ages with the objective of improving the economic security of American workers in their retirement years.

Over the past 50 years, Americans have enjoyed steadily increasing life spans, and they have also been retiring earlier. The combined effect of these two trends is that the average American worker today can now be expected to spend 50 percent more time in retirement than a similar worker 50 years ago. Experts project life spans will continue to increase.

As a result, the amount of income that must be put aside to fund workers' retirement must grow. Funding retirement is becoming more expensive for individual workers and for our public retirement systems, and the expense is growing to the point where it is putting strains on the ability of workers and society to bear it. Under our retirement systems that depend on workers and/or firms putting aside earnings during the working years to fund retirement income, the period of accumulation is getting shorter while the payout period is getting longer. Under our Social Security system, which uses the contributions of today's workers to pay today's retirees, the declining number of workers relative to retirees raises costs directly.

Although the need to set aside income has grown, many workers have not been accumulating enough savings in their personal or retirement accounts. Rapidly rising health care costs also consume a growing share of earnings and retirement incomes. Experts project these costs will continue to rise faster than national income. Social Security benefits, the major source of income in retirement for most workers, are on track to replace a smaller share of pre-retirement income (about 4 percent less) as the normal retirement age rises to 67, owing to reforms enacted in 1983. Most individuals choose to receive the earliest yet smallest

Social Security benefit available to them. The long-term financing imbalances in Social Security remain an unresolved issue.

For some share of our population, economic security in retirement is at risk. The problem is greater for widows and single women, who on average live longer than men, and tend to accumulate fewer savings and earn lower Social Security benefits.

In the past, this Advisory Board has recommended that policy makers address the long-term financial health of our Social Security system, and we have drawn attention to the predictable but growing threats to retirement security. In this report, the Board adds its voice to a growing consensus that one effective way to shore up retirement security in the future is to find ways to extend individual working careers when possible.

Continuing to work and/or postponing retirement benefits can significantly increase the resources available to individuals in retirement. Every additional year spent working provides income, reduces the need to draw down one's assets, provides an additional opportunity to save, and allows already accumulated savings to grow. This can be especially important for those approaching retirement with inadequate savings and for those who will experience longer than average lifetimes.

More Americans choose to begin receiving Social Security benefits at the earliest age of eligibility than at any other age. But for each year they delay taking benefits, they can significantly increase their monthly benefit for the rest of their lives. This choice can be critical for economic security at older ages.

At the same time, delaying retirement also has the potential to enhance economic security for those covered by employer-sponsored retirement plans. In most traditional defined benefit plans and in cash balance plans today, benefit accruals continue for many workers at advanced ages. In defined contribution plans, extending work has two beneficial effects: (1) it extends the period over which contributions are made; and (2) it shortens the period where accumulated savings are relied on for retirement income.

Having a greater share of older Americans continuing to work will also provide additional tax revenue to improve the financial condition of the Social Security system as well as state and federal government budgets. Extending individual working lives should ameliorate the projected decline in national labor force growth and add to national income.

We recommend that older workers should be given information about the personal advantages of remaining employed for a longer period of their lifetimes to the extent they are able. We also recommend that individuals be encouraged strongly to consider under what circumstances it would be advantageous for them to delay the age they choose to begin receiving Social Security benefits.

We recommend that the Social Security Administration continue to provide the most accurate and objective information possible to help the public make appropriate choices about when to claim benefits. The agency should review all communication with the public to ensure it is not inadvertently encouraging people to claim at the earliest date possible.

There are already signs that older workers are beginning to reverse a decades-long trend toward earlier retirement, perhaps responding to the pressures described above. In addition, fewer people are applying for Social Security benefits at the earliest possible age. Some recent survey data suggest that those nearing the usual retirement ages desire and intend to work to older ages.

A substantial share of older Americans, however, will not be able to work longer because of ill health, disability, or a lack of employment opportunities. And even for those who wish to work longer, important barriers to remaining employed still exist. Our current patchwork of laws and regulations should be changed to do a better job of helping those who can work a few years longer and secure a better standard of living in retirement.

We believe there are opportunities to reform policies and regulations that affect Social Security, public and private pensions, health care, and tax and labor laws that can assist workers to stay in the workforce longer and reward their efforts adequately.

We recommend that public policy should be geared toward removing barriers and improving incentives to continued employment at older age. A set of coordinated and coherent policies should encourage and support those who want to extend their working lives, while providing adequate support for those who are unable to do so.

We reiterate that our nation's systems of providing economic security to those who cannot work should be maintained and improved. Nothing in this report should be seen to contradict this strong belief.

Raising awareness of the benefits of longer working lives and supporting the choices of those who desire to do so will require more than just a more coherent set of policies:

We encourage employers to evaluate how older workers can continue to contribute in the workplace and, to the extent it is economically feasible, to adopt policies and practices that can accommodate a greater share of those who desire to extend their working lives. Older workers and their advocates, for their part, should consider the requirements they will have to meet so that continued employment benefits employer and employees alike.

In addition, individuals, institutions and public policies should recognize the importance of making lifelong investments that enhance a worker's ability to remain productive at older ages and adapt to the changing needs of the economy. Adequate preparation for retirement is a life-long endeavor.

INTRODUCTION

The Social Security Advisory Board's primary statutory responsibility is to analyze how the Social Security system, supported by other public and private systems, can most effectively assure economic security for those in retirement or who are disabled.

In our 2005 report, *Retirement Security: The Unfolding of a Predictable Surprise*, we described the major economic and demographic forces that will present the greatest challenges to economic security in retirement in the 21st century:

- longer life spans
- a declining ratio of workers to retirees
- a somewhat less generous Social Security system
- a private pension system that depends increasingly on employees to make active decisions about how much to contribute to retirement savings and how to invest

- health care costs that are growing faster than incomes and the economy as a whole
- globalization and economic changes that are shifting ways of doing business and changing employer-employee relationships.

We emphasized the need to meet those challenges through public policies to achieve sustainable Social Security and employer pension systems and to constrain health care costs. We also encouraged individuals to make responsible and informed choices about adequate saving, maintaining healthy lifestyles and considering how and when to retire.

In this report, we continue to focus on the need to assure adequate income in retirement by addressing two critical decision points: (1) when to withdraw from the workforce and (2) when to begin receiving Social Security benefits. Because of longer life spans, retirement is becoming increasingly expensive for individuals and families to fund. As our nation ages, and each worker must support a larger number of retirees, the cost of Social Security will increase. Working longer can help address both of these issues.

The Board is keenly aware that the decision to retire or withdraw from the workforce is not always voluntary, and that encouraging longer careers will not be practical for some portion of the population. Many older Americans are unable to work by virtue of their own health, or because of the need to take care of members of their family, or because of the unavailability of adequate economic opportunities. In addition, the willingness of older Americans to continue working depends heavily on the demand for their services and the state of the national economy.

Nothing in this report, therefore, should be seen to contradict our strong belief that our nation's systems of providing economic security to those who cannot work should be maintained and improved. Nonetheless, we believe there are substantial benefits to individuals and to the nation of extending the working lives of most Americans. The benefits may well be most important for those who have had a lifetime of low earnings, who may not have ever participated in a private pension plan, or who for whatever reason are most in need of the "floor of protection" that Social Security was designed to provide.

This report is organized as follows:

Section I describes our concerns about the current workforce and retirement conditions: retirement is becoming more expensive as we live longer, and low savings, escalating health care costs, the rising Social Security retirement age and early claiming all make it harder to achieve economic security in retirement.

Section II describes the advantages to both individuals and the nation of having a larger share of older workers remaining in the workforce.

Section III explains that while older workers are already beginning to delay retirement, there remain policies and practices that make working longer more difficult.

Section IV discusses a series of principles to guide policy makers in devising ways to improve the ability of those who are able to extend their working lives to do so.

I. RISING COST OF RETIREMENT

Retirement in the United States is becoming more expensive. Our Social Security system costs will rise as the proportion of the population in retirement rises. As life expectancies continue to increase, individuals will need to accumulate more resources during their working years to fund a longer-than-expected retirement. Low savings rates, insufficient pension balances, rapidly escalating health care costs, and the increase in the Social Security full retirement age to 67 will present challenges for workers and families who wish to maintain a decent standard of living as they withdraw from the workforce.

Our Social Security System Is Becoming More Expensive

The long-term financial shortfalls in the Social Security system are well known. This Board has written several reports detailing the causes of the impending and inevitable rise in the cost of benefits relative to payroll tax revenue. We have urged policy makers to address these long-term health of Social Security sooner rather than later.

The cause of the rising cost of Social Security is straightforward: our population is steadily growing older. Birth rates fell in the 1960s and have since remained at about those levels. Americans are, on average, living longer lives than at any time in our history. In 1960, only 9 percent of the population was age 65 or over. By 2000, that had risen to 12 percent. By 2030, 19 percent of the population will be age 65 or over. As the very large baby boom generation enters its retirement years, the share of the population that is no longer in the workforce rises dramatically.

Because the contributions of today's workers are used to pay the Social Security benefits of today's retirees, as the proportion of the population receiving benefits increases, the cost of the system increases.[1] **Figure 1** illustrates that over the next 25 years our society will shift from having about one retiree for every three workers to having about one retiree for every two workers. As a result, the cost of our Social Security system will increase by 25 percent.

Most discussions of how we choose to face these rising costs of Social Security lead to the inevitable conclusion that additional revenues will have to be raised, and/or benefits will have to be reduced. The additional costs will be borne by workers or retirees. In this context, the importance of encouraging a larger fraction of the population to stay in the workforce at older ages is clear. Increasing the share of the population that is working and reducing the share that is drawing benefits will reduce the burden of rising costs.

Preparing for Retirement Is Becoming More Expensive for Individuals

The forces that are making the nation's Social Security system more expensive are also making it more expensive for families and individuals to accumulate adequate resources to fund their own retirements.

First, individual life spans are getting longer. According to the Social Security Administration, a 65-year-old man was expected to live to age 78 in 1960, age 82 in 2000 and is projected to live to 85 in 2040. A 65-year-old woman was expected to live even longer: to

82 in 1960, 85 in 2000 and is projected to live to 87 by the year 2040. There will also be a substantial increase in those reaching very advanced ages. About one in four of today's 65-year-olds can be expected to live to age 90, and one in ten will live to age 95. While there is some disagreement among demographic experts, many believe the extension of life spans will occur even faster.[2]

Second, even as Americans have been living longer, they have been retiring earlier. The median age of withdrawing from the workforce has fallen about five years for men and seven years for women over the past 50 years. While recent evidence suggests a slowing of that decline and notable increases in employment rates among older cohorts, those who do retire at age 62 will, on average, spend approximately one-third of their adult lifetime in retirement.

The combined effect of these two trends – living longer and retiring earlier – is that the average American worker today can expect to spend 50 percent more time in retirement than a similar worker did just 50 years ago. **Table 1** illustrates these trends. In 1955 a typical working man would leave the workforce at 67 and expect to live in retirement about 12 more years until age 79.[3] Today, a typical working man retires at age 62 and lives about 19 more years in retirement, to age 81.

Clearly, to maintain a similar standard of living, saving for a longer and longer period of retirement requires setting aside a greater share of income during one's working life. Solely as a function of living longer, attaining retirement security becomes more expensive.[4] The costs are increasing no matter what the format of retirement savings or retirement plan. This is true for workers who fund retirement out of private savings, a 401(k) or an Individual Retirement Account (IRA). The costs are also borne by employers who make contributions to their workers' 401(k) account or fund defined benefit pension plans.

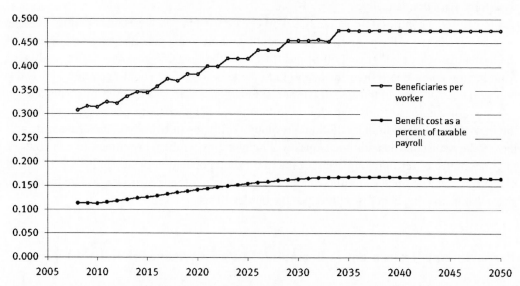

Source: The 2008 Annual Report of the Board of Trustees of the Federal Old-age and Survivors Insurance and Federal Disability Insurance Trust Funds.

Figure 1. Projected ratio of Social Security beneficiaries to workers: 2008-2050

Table 1. Median Age at Withdrawal from the Workforce and Expected Years of Life Remaining in Retirement by Gender for Selected Periods

Period	Median age at Retirement		Remaining life expectancy as of the median age of retirement	
	Men	Women	Men	Women
1950-1955	66.9	67.6	12.0	13.6
1965-1970	64.2	64.2	13.5	16.7
1980-1985	62.8	62.7	16.0	20.5
1985-1990	62.6	62.8	16.3	20.3
1990-1995	62.4	62.3	17.2	21.3
1995-2000	62.0	61.4	18.0	22.0
2000-2005	61.6	60.5	19.0	23.1

Source: Murray Gendell, "Older Workers: Increasing Their Labor Force Participation and Hours of Work," *Monthly Labor Review*, January 2008.

Below is a simplified example of how longer life spans and earlier retirements lead to pension costs that are about 50 to 100 percent more than 50 years ago.

Illustrating the higher cost of longer retirement:

This numerical exercise demonstrates that the cost of saving for retirement increases as the lifetime devoted to working gets shorter and the time spent in retirement, in part due to a longer life span, gets longer.

Consider two workers, Jacob and Emily whose only source of income in retirement is their own savings. Jacob exhibits patterns of work and retirement that would have been common in the early 1960s. He starts work at age 21 and retires on his 65th birthday. He will spend the remaining 13 years of his life (through age 77) in retirement. Emily exhibits patterns of work that are common in the first decade of the 21st century. She also starts work at age 21 but retires on her 62nd birthday, and then spends the remaining 21 years of her life (through age 82) in retirement.

We assume both start work earning $30,000 a year and get 4 percent annual pay raises. They earn a 6.5 percent annual return on their savings throughout their lifetime and their goal is to save enough so that they could withdraw in each year of retirement an amount that would replace 40 percent of their final year's salary.[5]

Jacob would have to set aside 4.78 percent of annual pay throughout his career to meet his retirement income goal. Emily, who has a shorter working life and longer retirement, needs to set aside 7.01 percent of annual pay throughout her career to meet her retirement income goal. Emily must save 47 percent more than Jacob, as a percentage of her pay, to meet the same retirement income goal.

For comparison consider a third worker, Hannah, who is similar to Emily in regard to her retirement income goals, retirement age and life expectancy, but because she spent more time in school, only begins working at age 25. All assumptions for the purposes of the calculation are the same as described above except her starting salary is higher, $35,000, in recognition of her higher education level. Hannah, who has an even shorter working life than Emily but just as long a period of retirement, must set aside 8.23 percent of her annual pay to *meet her retirement income goal. That amounts to 72 percent more than Jacob needs to save, and 17 percent more than Emily, as a percentage of annual pay.*

It should be noted that this example is for illustrative purposes only and it not meant to be prescriptive. In the real world, the future is subject to considerable uncertainty in the expected ability to work a full lifetime without interruption, in the ability to achieve a desired rate of return on investments, and in the ability to estimate one's own longevity. A real world worker, who was concerned about outliving his or her assets, might consider saving an even higher percentage of annual pay, or he or she may be able to purchase at retirement an insurance product with a guaranteed stream of income, known as an annuity. Social Security benefits are such a valuable part of retirement security because it provides insurance against the inability to work, against outliving one's assets in retirement, and also against the increased cost of living through inflation.

Additional Factors Make Accumulating Adequate Retirement Savings More Challenging

Even as the need to set aside income rises, there are other forces that will, for some, put economic security in retirement at risk. Many workers have not been accumulating enough savings in their personal or retirement accounts. Rapidly rising health care costs will consume a growing share of earnings and retirement incomes. Experts project these costs will continue to rise faster than national income. Social Security benefits, the major source of income in retirement for most workers, is on track to replace a smaller share of pre-retirement income as the retirement age rises to 67. Many individuals choose to receive the earliest yet smallest Social Security benefit available to them. Below we examine each one of these forces separately.

Savings

As Figure 2 illustrates, the household savings rate in the U.S. has fallen dramatically from a peak in the early 1980s to record lows today.[6] Along with declines in the financial savings rate, households have accumulated more debt, leading to an even greater decline in the total net savings rate. Although the household wealth of the baby boom is greater than previous generations, at least until the recent massive declines in the values of homes and the stock market, it is unclear whether those levels of wealth will be sufficient to support the retirement income expectations of future retirees. Recent survey data from the Employee Benefit Research Institute indicate that only about 70 percent of Americans report having saved money for retirement and a slightly smaller share are currently saving money.[7]

Retirement Plan Balances

About half of all full time workers participate in a retirement plan, and over the past 25 years there has been a dramatic shift from defined benefit (DB) plans to defined contribution (DC) plans. In 1980, 62 percent of those with any retirement plan had only a defined benefit pension, while 16 percent had only a defined contribution plans, and 22 percent had both. By

2005, that share had largely reversed – 63 percent are enrolled only in a DC plan and 10 percent only have a traditional defined benefit plan, while 27 percent have both.[8]

For many households, in addition to their home, the dominant form of saving for retirement is their 401(k) plan. While these tax deferred plans can be a very effective vehicle to accumulate adequate assets for retirement, current workers do not universally participate, and many contribute a lower percentage of their pre-tax earnings than they are allowed. In fact, some do not even contribute up to the amount that is matched by their employer.[9] As recent events in the financial markets have shown, the value of assets in retirement plans can decline quite dramatically, which can affect the timing of and adequacy of income in retirement.[10] Average balances in 401(k)s in 2006 were $121,000, but the median balance was just slightly more than half that at $66,650. As would be expected, average accumulated 401(k) assets increase with age, salary and job tenure with the same employer.[11]

Although average or median accumulations are important in explaining how private retirement savings plans are being used by workers, they mask the extent to which some people are using these vehicles effectively and others are not. Earlier we noted that a worker needed to save 8.2 percent of pay starting at age 25 if he or she wanted to retire by age 62 with accumulated savings that would replace 40 percent of pre-retirement salary during the retirement period. Under the assumptions we used there, such a worker would accumulate about three times pay in his or her retirement savings account by age 50 and about five times pay by age 62.

A recent study of actual savings behavior in a sample of private 401(k) plans found that few workers were saving at rates sufficient to reach these goals. The analysis in this study focused on workers between the ages of 50 and 64 who had been with their current employer for at least 20 years and were covered by a 401(k) plan. Among plan participants in the plans studied, 8.8 percent had no funds at all and 26.2 percent, including those with zero balances, had less than one-half their current annual pay. A total of 39.6 percent of participants had accumulated less than their annual pay. Only 36.5 percent had more than two times pay in their 401(k) accounts and only 9 percent had accumulated four times current pay.[12]

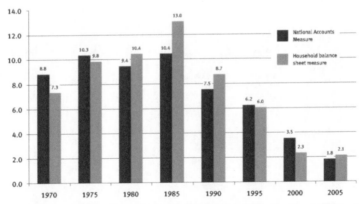

Source: McKinsey Global Institute, *Talkin' 'bout My Generation: The Economic Impact of Aging U.S. Baby Boomers*, June 2008.

Figure 2. Household savings rate 1970-2005 (percent of disposable income; 5-year trailing moving average)

Health Care Costs

The cost of health care is rising rapidly for workers and retirees, even more rapidly than pension costs, and constitutes a major challenge to economic security in retirement. Estimates of the annual growth of health care spending over the next ten years is about 7 percent, considerably faster than the currently projected growth of national income (including inflation), of about 5 percent, according to the *2008 Annual Report of the Board of Trustees of the Federal Old-age and Survivors Insurance and Federal Disability Insurance Trust Funds.*

For workers who are already not setting aside more of their income to fund their retirement, rapidly rising out-of-pocket health care costs and/or insurance premiums will put even more of a strain on their budgets. Some will undoubtedly save less to be able to afford the current cost of their health care. For those with employer sponsored health insurance, the average employee contribution to premiums for family coverage has increased from $1,542 in 1999 to $3,354 in 2008, an increase of 117 percent.[13] Those who are self-insured or without coverage at all face a similar cost increase from a higher base.

For retirees, health care expenditures are also expected to consume an ever increasing share of their incomes. In 2007, the average annual Medicare out-of-pocket expense for an individual amounted to $3,800 ($316 a month) with expected growth of 5-6 percent per year. Spending can vary significantly around this average, for example, based on a person's health habits or chronic illnesses. A recent study estimates that a couple retiring in 2010 would need to have an account worth about $206,000 to provide a stream of income over their lifetime that would cover their out-of-pocket health care costs.[14] Another way to appreciate the impact of rising health care cost in retirement is to compare the growth of the average Social Security benefit and average out-of- pocket costs for Medicare Parts B & D. In 2010, total out-of-pocket costs will comprise about one-quarter of the average Social Security benefit. By 2080 that will rise to about two-thirds.[15]

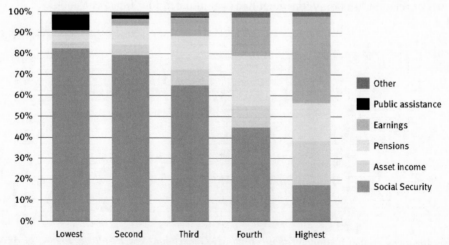

Source: U.S. Census Bureau, "Current Population Survey," Annual Social and Economic Supplement, 2007.

Figure 3. Sources of income for people age 65 and over, by income quintile, 2006

The costs are rising at the same time that fewer private employers are offering retiree health benefits, and even when these benefits are still offered, retirees face rising premiums, higher out-of-pocket expenses and more stringent eligibility requirements. Among employers with over 500 employees, the share offering health insurance to early retirees has fallen from 46 percent to 29 percent from 1993 to 2006, while the share offering them to Medicare-eligible retirees has fallen from 40 percent to 19 percent over that same period. Most active workers will never be eligible for employer- provided health insurance in retirement.[16]

An unanticipated episode of serious illness can create significant financial liabilities. And even the need to prepare for anticipated costs, for example for long-term care at advanced ages, tend to be underestimated. As Americans live to advanced ages, the need to plan for long-term care will grow as well.

Social Security

Social Security covers over 90 percent of all paid employment, and it has become the single most important source of income for most retirees. **Figure 3** illustrates that payments from Social Security, consistent with the program's **progressive design, are most important** for those with the lowest incomes. Social Security benefits are also more important for those at advanced ages as the share of income from other sources declines. Currently, benefits provide about 50 percent of income for the average beneficiary ages 62-64, about 62 percent for those ages 70-74, and 74 percent for those over age 80. More than four in ten beneficiaries over age 80 rely on Social Security for 90 percent of their total income, and just over one in four rely on it for 100 percent of their income.[17]

The amount of pre-retirement income Social Security benefits replace is falling. Under changes already enacted into law in 1983, the full retirement age gradually rose from 65 to 66, and starting in 2017 will incrementally rise to age 67 by 2022. Under the Social Security system, the raising of the full retirement age results in a relatively smaller benefit at any given age. A decade ago a person could retire at 62 and receive 80 percent of the benefit they would have been eligible for at full retirement age. In another decade, a person retiring at 62 will receive 70 percent of the benefit they would have been eligible for at full retirement age.

Workers covered by Social Security are eligible to receive benefits as early as age 62. Social Security reduces monthly benefits for those who claim earlier than the full retirement age and raises them for those who delay claiming after the full retirement age up until age 70. From the perspective of the Social Security program's finances, paying lower benefits for a longer period of time or higher benefits for a shorter period of time results in the same program costs. For any individual, the choice has a direct effect on the level of their inflation-protected Social Security benefits for the rest of their lives, and potentially the lifetimes of their spouses or survivors.

As Figure 4 illustrates, more people take their benefits at the earliest age they are eligible, 62, than at any other age. By choosing the smallest monthly benefit available to them for the rest of their lives, they are effectively reducing the value of the insurance Social Security provides against inadequate income later in life. To choose to begin receiving benefits at an age where one is still capable of working is to choose to receive less income protection at ages when other sources of income may not be available.

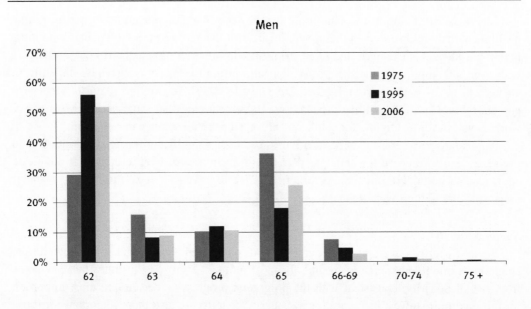

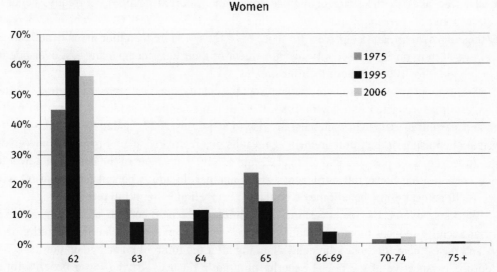

Source: Social Security Administration, *Annual Statistical Supplement to the Social Security Bulletin*, 2007.

Figure 4. Age distribution of those claiming retirement benefits in 1975, 1995, 2006

Are Americans Adequately Prepared for Retirement?

Various researchers using various methods have tried to address the question of whether the future generations will have adequate income in retirement. There is a wide range of conclusions, but most acknowledge that some share of the population – from as little as one out of six to as many as two out of three – is unlikely to have sufficient financial assets or streams of pension income sufficient to achieve a standard of living comparable to when they were working.[18] Because of recent large and widespread declines in the value of financial assets, the percentage of those nearing retirement that fall into this category today has likely increased.

The risk of inadequate retirement income appears to be greater for those with lower lifetime earnings, for younger cohorts and single persons.[19] Because of their different patterns of employment and earnings, women tend to accumulate fewer assets for retirement than men. They also live, on average, several years longer. Single women are far more at risk than married women because married women, in addition to their own accumulated assets, can inherit their spouse's wealth.

We do not attempt to resolve in this report which of these studies is most accurate in this report, but instead emphasize that the range of estimates is cause for concern and justifies considering ways to help individuals extend their working lives. As the next section will show, working longer can still improve retirement security whether individuals have made sufficient preparations or not.

II. MANAGING THE COST OF RETIREMENT

As funding retirement becomes more costly there are many responses we can take as a nation and as individuals. Finding ways to boost saving, improve retirement plan participation and coverage, reduce health care costs, and put Social Security on a sustainable footing would all be positive developments.

We believe that one effective strategy workers can use to manage the cost of retirement is to remain in the workforce longer. By working longer, one extends the period their retirement savings can accumulate and reduces the period of payout. We also believe many individuals and couples can better insure themselves against lower standards of living at older ages by delaying when they choose to take Social Security benefits. Waiting to take Social Security benefits can produce a higher stream of income for the rest of one's life.

There are also wider benefits to society. If a higher share of the population is working relative to those who are retired, the cost of our Social Security system will be lower, government budgets should improve and labor force growth will improve. We discuss each of these advantages below.

Impact on Individual Well-Being

Put simply, working longer and claiming retirement benefits later accomplishes three things: (1) it increases lifetime resources, (2) it shortens the period that must be financed from savings, and (3) it provides more guaranteed lifetime income.

Working Longer
Continuing to work provides a household with more lifetime earnings than if they stop working. In addition to wages, those workers who have health or disability insurance through their employer, or who receive employer contributions to their retirement plan, will continue to benefit from these forms of compensation, or could receive larger pension benefits.

Continuing to work lengthens the time to accumulate retirement income as additional contributions to savings can be made out of current earnings. Any accumulated balances will have additional time to grow.[20] Even those who have sufficient savings to continue at their current standard of living can benefit from accumulating larger savings balances as protection against unforeseen or emergency expenses. If health care costs continue to rise unabated, it may take more income to afford non-health care consumption.

Continuing to work shortens the draw down period from one's accumulated assets.[21] As was discussed in the previous section, funding a shorter retirement is less costly.

Delaying Social Security benefits

Independent of the decision to stop working, individuals can improve their economic security in retirement by waiting longer to claim their Social Security benefits.

Delaying claiming of Social Security will increase a person's monthly benefit amount for life. For example, as **Figure 5** illustrates, a person who is eligible today to receive a monthly benefit of $1,000 at age 66, would receive only $750 per month (or 25 percent less) if benefits are claimed at the earliest possible age of 62. Waiting until age 70 would increase monthly benefits by 32 percent to $1,320.[22]

Claiming Social Security benefits at either the full retirement age or later is valuable because the monthly sum provides a stream of inflation-protected income over the rest of one's lifetime. Thus delaying claiming provides a higher level of insurance against insufficient income at advanced ages. Although no one has perfect foresight about how long they or their spouse may live, many people underestimate the amount of time they spend in retirement and overestimate how long their assets will last. A 62-year-old man in the year 2008 is expected to live another 19 years, while a 62-year-old woman can be expected to live for 22 years. It should be noted that half of the people will live longer than their "expected" life span.

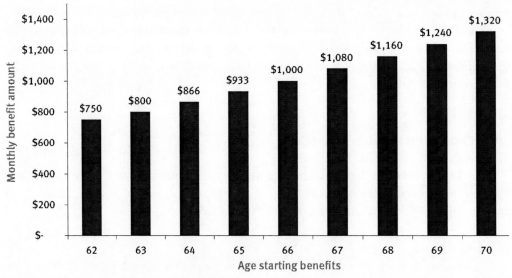

Source: Social Security Administration, 2008.

Figure 5. Monthly benefits increase with starting age
assuming eligibility for a benefit of $1,000 at the current full retirement age of 66

While strategies for maximizing Social Security income over one's lifetime can be complicated and depend on many circumstances, new research suggests that it can be advantageous for most individuals and couples to delay claiming Social Security benefits.[23] Couples, in particular should consider how much the future benefits of the longer living spouse can be increased if the higher earning spouse delays the age at which they begin to receive their benefits.[24]

Estimates of the Financial Impact of Working Longer

Those who continue to work and who claim benefits later can reduce the cost of saving for retirement, or can enjoy a higher standard of living when they stop working. Simulations conducted by researchers at the Urban Institute calculate that working an additional year and delaying Social Security by one year increases retirement income in each year of retirement by almost 10 percent. Working an additional five years can boost annual retirement income by more than 50 percent. The effect is greatest for those with lower lifetime income. Those in the bottom 20 percent of lifetime income could increase their annual retirement income by almost 16 percent after one year, and almost 100 percent if they were able to work five more years.[25]

Estimates by the Congressional Budget Office (CBO) arrive at a similar conclusion. They calculated what a typical married couple with the median household income would need to accumulate in savings to produce a stream of income that would replace 80 percent of their pre-retirement after-tax income.[26] If they both retire at 62 they would need to accumulate about $510,000 in assets in addition to Social Security. If they retire at age 66, they would need only $298,000 in accumulated assets and receive almost 40 percent more in annual Social Security payments. The CBO calculations show similar gains across all income groups and for single persons as well as couples.

Individual circumstances may be different, but across a wide range of scenarios, working longer and delaying the start of Social Security benefits can increase the stream of income available in retirement, and reduce the amount of assets that need to be accumulated by a given age. Those who accumulate more assets through pensions, personal saving or 401(k)s will be better off in retirement than those who accumulate less. But these results also suggest that working longer can help those who failed to save adequately for retirement.

There may well be additional non-financial benefits for individuals who continue to work at older ages. According to some researchers, work promotes social integration and social support, contributes significantly to a sense of personal identity, and may in fact promote physical health.[27]

Impact on Social Security finances

Increasing labor force participation by older workers has a modest but positive affect on the long-term finances of Social Security.

We begin by noting that there is no effect on Social Security finances if everyone claims their Social Security benefits one year later, but does not also work an additional year. The increase in monthly benefits from delaying an extra year is roughly offset by the shorter payout period.

By contrast, if everyone delays benefits and works an additional year, according to simulations done by the Urban Institute, Social Security's long term financial deficit in 2045 would be 2 percent smaller. If everyone worked five more years, the deficit in 2045 would be reduced by about 30 percent.[28] In general, having more people working increases the total payroll tax receipts but does little to increase benefit costs. The net effect depends in part on who works longer and at what wages, but under most scenarios overall financial impact would be positive.

Impact on Federal Budget/General Revenues

In a similar fashion increasing the employment rates of older Americans would increase federal and state income tax revenue in addition to payroll taxes.

According to the Urban Institute projections, if everyone worked an additional year, by 2045, federal and state taxes (including income and payroll taxes) would be higher by an amount that is equivalent to 28 percent of the projected Social Security Trust Fund deficit. If everyone worked five additional years, the additional total tax revenues in 2045 would be 59 percent larger than the projected Social Security deficit in that year.[29]

As the U.S. population ages the cost of public programs for retirees will claim a significantly larger share of federal budget resources. The growth in those programs, particularly Medicare and Medicaid, could make other government programs more difficult to fund. The greater the contributions to general revenues from additional labor force participation by older workers, however, the less necessary it will be to increase taxes, cut programs or increase borrowing to deal with the demands on the budget.

Impact on Labor Force Growth and GDP

Because of demographic trends discussed earlier, the working age population in the U.S. is expected to grow more slowly than in the past. According to the Social Security Trustees annual labor force growth is declining from about 2.5 percent during the late 1960s and 1970s, to just over 1 percent during the current decade, to less than 0.5 percent by 2020.

Slower growth in the labor force unless accompanied by faster growth in labor productivity will lead to slower economic growth. The Social Security Trustees project that annual real economic growth between 2020 and 2080 will average only 2.1 percent a year, compared to 3.1 percent growth average over the past 40 years.

The major factors influencing future labor force growth are demographic and behavioral. Positive workforce growth depends on larger numbers of workers entering the workforce in any given period than the number withdrawing for retirement or other purposes. The pool of new workers entering the workforce is largely determined by a combination of young people reaching working age and new potential workers coming to the country from elsewhere around the world.

The size of future cohorts of workers will depend both on birth rates and the net rate of immigration. If birth rates were to rise, it would still take about two decades to affect the size of the workforce because added newborns today would not be entering the workforce until they reached their late teens or early twenties. Increased immigration of working age adults has a more immediate impact on labor force growth. While more immigration would help to ameliorate some of the issues being raised here, the current political environment does not suggest that this a solution that policymakers will likely pursue as they consider the policy options open to them.

Another way to stimulate workforce growth rates is to change behavior patterns among the population groups able to work. Over much of the last half of the 20th century, for example, the labor force in the United States grew considerably because an increasing percentage of women of working age chose to work outside the home. At the same time, the growth in the U.S. labor force was dampened because many workers chose to retire at earlier ages than prior generations. Labor force participation rates of women are such today that there is little potential to increase aggregate labor force levels by encouraging more prime-age women into the labor market. But there are many able-bodied people in their 50s and 60s, who have been retiring but could instead choose to extend their working lives and have a significant effect on the size of the labor force going forward.

III. INFLUENCES ON A CHANGING RETIREMENT LANDSCAPE

The concept of leaving the labor force simply because one reaches an arbitrary age is a fairly recent phenomenon. Historically, it was quite common for people to remain in the labor force as long as they were physically able to do so because they simply did not have enough income to retire. Even as recently as the late 1940s nearly half of the men aged 65 and over were still in the labor force compared to only about one in five today. For most of the 20th century, economic and policy developments that have improved retirement income security have allowed workers to devote a larger portion of their lives to an increasingly attractive period of retirement. The steady growth of household income during one's working years allowed for the accumulation of personal savings, while public and private pensions systems arose to provide secure streams of income during retirement.[30]

The expectation that workers could retire with economic security sometime in their early 60s has become an important accomplishment of national policy as well as a measure of national prosperity. But economic and demographic forces continue to evolve with important implications for how and when workers can and should expect to retire. This section describes how today's workers are adapting to this changing landscape: how some workers are already making the decision to continue working longer and how policies and practices affect the ability of workers to improve their economic security in retirement.

Changing Patterns in Labor Force Participation

For most of the 20th century, men have retired at earlier and earlier ages as they have become increasingly able to afford leaving the workforce. However, over the past 15 years this trend seems to have leveled off and even reversed for men over age 60 (see **Figure 6**). In the 30 years from 1955 to 1985 the labor force participation rates of men aged 60-64 fell 33 percent before leveling off. Since 1994 the rate has increased about 12 percent. Those most likely to work at older ages are more educated, in better health, and have higher incomes.

The working lives of women have followed a different pattern than the working lives of men, as **Figure 7** illustrates. Over the past 40 years, more and more women at all ages have entered the labor force and for the most part are staying to older ages. The labor force participation of women aged 60 to 64 increased 15 percent from 1955 to 1985; between 1985 and 1993 the rate continued to rise but a slower rate of about 10 percent. The rate began to accelerate in 1994, rising to over 25 percent. Women are more likely to stay attached to work for longer periods than in previous generations where women tended not to work outside of the household or moved in and out of work. In addition, women over age 55 are currently much more likely than men of a similar age to work part-time.

It seems quite likely that this trend toward working longer may continue. In a recent survey by the McKinsey Global Institute about 40 percent of baby boomers said they expected to work longer during what they might have previously thought of as their retirement years. Of those about one-third said they would do so to stay engaged in the world of work, because they enjoyed the job, the interactions with others, or the chance to make positive change. About two-thirds expected to work longer for financial reasons, to maintain benefits, maintain their lifestyle, or to meet expenses.[31] The desire to maintain employer-based benefits, in particular health insurance, is a major decision factor for some workers when they are weighing their retirement options.[32]

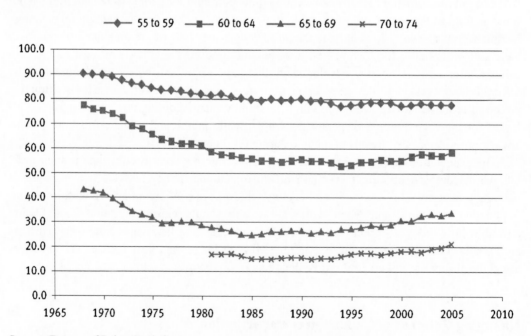

Source: Bureau of Labor Statistics.

Figure 6. Labor force participation rates of men by age group: 1968-2005

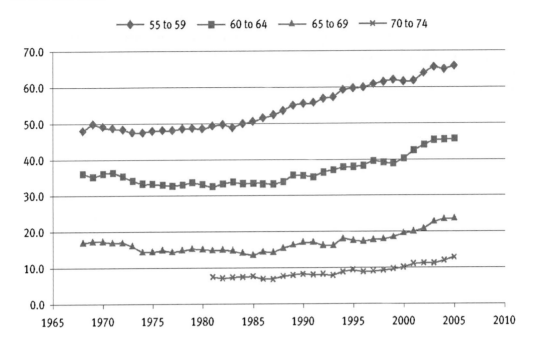

Source: Bureau of Labor Statistics.

Figure 7. Labor force participation rates of women by age group: 1968-2005

Possible Reasons for the Increase in Labor Force Participation

The reasons for the more recent patterns of increased labor force participation by older workers are varied. For some, this is a response to the rising cost of retirement and changing structure of incentives in public and private retirement plans. Social Security rule changes have raised the full retirement age and increased the rewards that come with working and claiming benefits after reaching the full retirement age. Private employer-sponsored retirement plans have undergone a dramatic shift away from defined benefit plans and toward defined contribution plans that are generally portable, accrue gradually and do not have a target retirement age. And for some workers, the need to maintain health insurance coverage that is tied to employment has led to decisions to delay retirement.[33]

Recent Trends in Claiming Social Security Benefits

As workers delay their withdrawal from the workforce, they are also choosing to delay slightly the age at which they take their Social Security benefits.[34] In 1995, over 45 percent of men aged 62 to 64 were receiving Social Security retirement benefits. By 2006 only about 38 percent of men aged 62 to 64 were receiving retirement benefits.[35] The age at which both men and women have been claiming retirement benefits has been rising for many of the same reasons that may explain why they are remaining in the workforce longer. Recent changes in Social Security rules, namely the increase in the full retirement age[36] and the elimination of the retirement earnings test after the full retirement age,[37] have had some effect on benefit claiming. The tendency to elect benefits at the earliest age is diminishing.[38] The incremental addition to benefits for delaying claiming benefits beyond the full retirement age until age 70, known as "delayed retirement credits" has grown more generous providing an additional incentive to postpone taking benefits.

Wide-Range of "Retirement" Ages May be Sending Mixed Signals

For each individual the decision about how and when to retire is a very complex issue that requires an assessment of available retirement income and assets, personal and family health status, as well as such factors as job satisfaction, and availability of desirable work opportunities. There are many areas of federal law and regulations that affect mature workers, and navigating the myriad retirement options and rules can be quite challenging for many potential retirees. The nation's well-intentioned patchwork of laws and regulations designed to meet the needs of workers in a wide range of circumstances sends a variety of often confusing signals about when is the "right" time to retire. Depending on which type of program or plan is involved, the "retirement age" can range from as early as age 55 to as late as age 70.

Workers with sufficient covered employment are first eligible for reduced Social Security benefits at age 62. The "full" retirement age for Social Security has traditionally been 65, but has increased from age 65 to 66 at the beginning of this decade, and in the next decade will gradually increase to age 67 for workers born in 1960 and later. The maximum benefit is available to those who claim at age 70.[39] Medicare eligibility begins at age 65, and it has not changed since its inception, despite increases in longevity and increases to Social Security's full retirement age.

Tax and pension regulations define a wide range of retirement ages. IRS rules require that the "normal retirement age" in a defined benefit tax- qualified pension plan not exceed age 65.[40] Normal retirement ages vary across firms but participants in defined benefit pension plans may be eligible for benefits at earlier ages provided they leave employment of the plan sponsor.[41] State and local retirement plans frequently base eligibility on years of service rather than on age and, as a result, it is not unusual for employees to qualify for an unreduced benefit before age 60. Tax rules permit withdrawals without penalty from both defined benefit and defined contribution plans as well as IRAs as early as age 59½. If distributions are provided as an annuity, there is no tax penalty even at earlier ages. IRS rules also require minimum payouts by age 70½.

What effect this range of retirement eligibility ages has on the decisions of workers to retire is unclear. But some researchers believe that the age at which public and private rules define the earliest eligibility for retirement does play an important role in setting social expectations about what is normal or acceptable.[42]

Understanding the Messages about Claiming Retirement Benefits

When to claim Social Security retirement benefits is a very important decision in the lives of most workers and should be made within the context of an individual's unique circumstances. The Social Security Administration has developed a variety of public information tools designed to present the salient issues relevant to that decision. Many of these communication vehicles, however, unintentionally send unclear messages about the relationship between the claiming of benefits and withdrawing from the workforce – between taking "retirement benefits" and actually "retiring" from work. The agency inadvertently frames the benefit election choice in a manner that treats these very different and separate decisions as if they were inextricably linked, and as a result may send mixed signals to potential retirees about how continuing to work affects their benefits. The Advisory Board recognizes and is encouraged by recent efforts of the Social Security Administration to review its public information vehicles and clarify its procedures and communication strategies.

Pension Plans and the Effect on Retirement Decisions

Pension plans, whether public or private, form the foundation for retirement security in the United States for many workers. Their relative generosity has been instrumental in assuring retirement security for several generations. However, we have entered an era where the expected income from pensions is, for many private sector workers, shrinking or disappearing and this realization may result in changing expectations relative to the length of time they spend in active employment. Moreover, the features of these plans can influence an employee's decision to stop working, as well as the employer's decision to encourage older workers to stay at work.

Recent changes in federal law have created a more favorable employment environment that could aid in the retention of older workers. While workers still need to understand their particular pension plan rules and how those rules may affect their retirement timing, the option of working longer and continuing to contribute to a pension plan deserves consideration. As we have discussed earlier, working and contributing for a longer period can have a positive financial impact on an individual's overall income stream in retirement.

Defined Benefit Plans

Traditional defined benefit (DB) pension plans provide retirement benefits based on a specific period of participation and contribution. While the age of eligibility may vary, each plan carries a definition of normal retirement age; and the benefits typically accrue based on salary and/or years of service. For each year spent working after reaching the plan's retirement age, in some plans, the employee often foregoes a year of pension benefits without adding appreciably to the amount of the pension.

Social Security provides an extremely valuable income stream that protects retirees against outliving their assets and the increasing cost-of-living. For most retirees it is the single largest source of income throughout retirement. Somewhat different than traditional defined benefit plans, Social Security benefits accrue rapidly with years of work up to some point, and then the rate of accrual diminishes up to 35 years of coverage. After that, it drops to almost nothing for many workers.

Specifically, Social Security benefits are calculated based on the average of a worker's highest 35 years of earnings.[43] To qualify for benefits, workers must have at least ten years of covered earnings in order to qualify for benefits. For a worker with only ten years of covered earnings at retirement, the earnings are still averaged over a 35-year period. The redistributive feature of Social Security means a typical worker earns about half of his or her lifetime benefits in the first ten years of covered employment. Beyond that, each year of earnings for an individual with fewer than 35 years of earnings increases lifetime average earnings but at a declining rate, since it replaces a zero in the 35-year average. As average lifetime earnings increase, the Social Security benefit continues to grow. But an individual who has already worked 35 years will not increase their average lifetime earnings or benefit much, if at all, with a 36th year of covered earnings but will continue to pay the payroll tax.[44] There is little additional financial payoff from Social Security in continuing to work after 35 years.

Defined Contribution Plans

In contrast to defined benefit plans, benefits in a defined contribution (DC) plan, such as a 401(k), continue to increase with age because the pension balance can increase as long employees continue to make contributions and assets are allowed to earn interest or grow. Employer contributions are typically based on a percentage of salary matched to the employee's contribution up to some limit. Defined contribution plans require participants to assume the risks associated with the value of their investments, and must develop a strategy to avoid outliving their accumulated assets on retirement. Research shows that in part due to the absence of age-related incentives, workers in defined benefit plans retire as much as two years earlier, on average, than those in defined contribution plans.[45] In addition, research suggests that those who experience significant income loss in their DC plans, such as during the major downturn in the stock market after 2000, are less likely to retire.[46]

Cash Balance Plans

Cash balance plans are defined benefit plans that promise a benefit based on an account balance that grows annually, typically by a stated percentage of the employee's compensation and a rate of interest accumulation. Balances continue to accumulate with the number of years in the plan, like a defined contribution plan, thereby providing an incentive to work longer. Unlike a DC plan, the investment risk is borne solely by the employer, and the employer is required to offer the benefits in the form of a life annuity.

Recent Changes in Pension and Tax Law

Recent changes in pension and tax law have improved the ability of employers to provide incentives to employees to extend their working lives. Pension statutes and regulations traditionally have prohibited individuals from working for the same employer while receiving retirement benefits, unless they have reached the plan's normal retirement age.[47] *The Pension Protection Act of 2006*, however, now permits employers to pay in-service benefits to employees age 62 and over. In addition, this law provides for the automatic enrollment of employees in a firm's 401(k) plan. This shift in emphasis from optional enrollment to an automatic one will likely result in significantly higher plan participation rates. As workers become more involved in their retirement plans and begin to appreciate the ease of this savings method, they are more likely to strive to maximize their balances, which for some will mean working longer.[48]

Policies May Adversely Affect Options

Medicare

Health care, as an employment and a retirement security issue, is one of the most pressing concerns for all Americans. For mature workers under age 65 who are covered under an employer-based health care, the decision to stay at work is often motivated by this access to health insurance. However, the link to the work place may become less important for some once they reach 65, the age at which Medicare coverage begins.

Nearly all retirees have Medicare as their primary source of health insurance.[49] Medicare pays for acute care and requires that beneficiaries pay part of the cost of their health care. This leaves about half of the expenses to be covered by other sources. As a result, most Medicare enrollees have some type of supplemental insurance, either through an employer's retiree health plan or private insurance that covers the gap in coverage; in the case of low-income workers, Medicaid may cover the additional expenses. In any case, Medicare is the primary payer and the supplemental insurance covers the shortfall.

However, for individuals aged 65 and over who are working and are covered by an employer–sponsored health insurance plan, Medicare becomes a "secondary payer." Thus, any health insurance claims that arise must be paid first by the employer's plan; then any remaining uncovered services may be paid for by Medicare, provided the services are covered under Medicare.[50] The purpose of the policy is to allow Medicare to target its limited resources at those who do not have another source of coverage.

Some researchers are concerned that the policy may have the unintended effect of making it harder to keep older workers in the workforce.[51] There are two alternative ways of looking at the issue. From an employer's perspective, older employees appear to be relatively more expensive because costs which might have been borne primarily by Medicare are now the employer's responsibility.[52] From an employee's perspective, potential take-home pay is less because they must take a significant share of their compensation in the form of health benefits, even though they are entitled to primary coverage through Medicare. Whether understood as an increased cost to employers or a decrease in an employee's take-home pay, the secondary payer policy may lessen employer demand for older workers, or employees may become less inclined to continue working much past 65.

Retirement: Does It Have to be "All-or-Nothing"?

As workers begin to approach their later years and think about retirement, many choose to stop working entirely. But for others, a transition phase from full time work into something less, but still short of complete withdrawal from the labor force, has tremendous appeal. Phased retirement, often defined as continuing to work for the same employer while gradually reducing the hours of work, presents a unique opportunity for employees and employers. As the nation faces the retirement wave of the baby boomers it is critical for employers to manage this exodus of knowledge and expertise; facilitating an employee's ability to retire in a more staged fashion is one option.

A variety of approaches to phased retirement such as job sharing, reduced work schedules, and rehiring retired employees on a part-time basis, can be used under the current pension laws. However, the extent to which current laws and policies discourage phased retirement arrangements, or render them not financially feasible, may encourage some to retire earlier than they would prefer. The structure of some traditional defined benefit plans could make phased retirement financially untenable if working at reduced hours affects an employee's benefit calculation. If, for example, pension benefits are based on a worker's final salary, moving to part-time status at the end of a career could result in significantly lower benefits. Furthermore, current tax rules and the *Employee Retirement Income Security Act* (ERISA) requirements that make it difficult for employers to establish equitable phased retirement plans present a potential barrier to change.[53]

Health and Opportunity Shape Older Workers' Decisions

The long trend during the past century toward earlier retirement has been, in many respects, the very positive result of higher incomes during the working phase of life and the increasing attractiveness of leisure opportunities.[54] Some older individuals are financially prepared for retirement and will be able to sustain their lifestyle through the many years ahead. For some mature workers the decision to work longer is not merely a financial decision; working beyond the earliest point of retirement eligibility may have no appeal, even if it means improving their standard of living in retirement. The more powerful influence on the decision to withdraw from work may be one's own health status or that of family members, or it may be their assessment of the availability or attractiveness of alternative employment.

Health

Americans are living longer and are healthier than ever before. For most, these two factors can have a positive influence on whether they choose to work longer. Yet, there are individuals who may wish to continue working but are unable to for health reasons. For those in poor health, applying for Social Security disability benefits or electing early retirement benefits may be the appropriate or only choice.

About one in four workers age 51 to 55 develops serious health problems by age 62 that limit their ability to work.[55] Although the incidence of Social Security disability is projected to remain stable or fall slightly in the population as a whole,[56] the incidence of disability rises rapidly after age 50. In 2006, for example, the incidence of Social Security disability awards for men aged 50-54 was .89 percent, and for men aged 60-64 the rate was just over 1.7 percent. Current estimates are that 15-20 percent of those in their early 60s will not physically be able to work longer, at least not in jobs they are qualified for and that are available to them.[57] The population of those too unhealthy or disabled to work is concentrated among those who have held physically demanding jobs and those whose health has interfered with their work careers throughout their lives. These latter groups, including those who receive

Social Security disability benefits, are also less likely to have been able to save adequately for their retirement.

Job Opportunities

The desire and the ability to work at older ages are often muted by the lack of available opportunities. One in five workers age 51 to 55 is laid off from their job by age 62.[58] Although older workers are no more likely to be laid off than their younger counterparts, they may have significantly more difficulty finding new jobs if necessary. The ability of older workers to remain employed or to find a job may also be more dependent on local labor market conditions than for younger, more mobile workers.[59] Older workers may also be less willing to re-locate to find work. In the nation's rural, frontier and tribal communities, there may be few jobs available for anyone.

Some older workers may find that their skills have become obsolete or do not match those needed by employers. Older workers may not be willing or able to make additional investments in their own education or training since the return on that investment may be uncertain or last only briefly. It is not clear that there are adequate or effective training opportunities available for older workers.

The decision to look for a job or invest in acquiring new skills might also be affected by pessimistic perceptions about the willingness of employers to hire older workers. Awareness of laws forbidding age discrimination in hiring may mitigate that perception. Older workers may also be more sensitive to the conditions of work and the willingness of employers to accommodate flexible work arrangements. They may be unwilling to work if they cannot work part-time, or if their pay is significantly less, or if a job is too physically demanding.

Employer's Demand for Older Workers

If continuing to work is to be an effective antidote to less secure retirements for older Americans, then employers will have to be willing to employ older workers. The attitudes of employers toward their current employees who wish to extend their careers, and toward older job applicants looking for a new job or coming back to work after a period of retirement can be a significant boon or a significant barrier to older workers. From an objective standpoint one would expect firms to hire workers regardless of age if it makes economic sense.

Older workers are often more expensive. Those with longer job tenure or seniority or with greater experience tend to have higher wages or salaries. Fringe benefits for older employees also tend to be more costly.[60] Because health insurance claim costs are higher for older workers on average, employers with a greater share of older workers may face higher premiums.[61] The cost of hiring older workers under traditional defined benefits plans can be higher than for younger new employees.[62] The net costs of training tend to be higher for older workers relative to younger workers, because there is less time for the employer to recover the costs of the investment.

The important questions are: do older workers have characteristics that make them valuable to employers despite their higher costs, and do employers accurately perceive their value. Older workers may, in fact, be more productive than their younger counterparts; many employers report that this is in fact their belief.[63] Older workers may have firm–specific knowledge or experience that is hard to replace. Survey data suggests that older workers are perceived as being more loyal, more reliable, more experienced and as having a stronger work ethic than younger workers.[64]

Age Discrimination

The Age Discrimination in Employment Act (ADEA) prohibits age based discrimination in hiring, firing, layoffs, compensation and working conditions for workers age 40 and over in firms with over 20 employees. Similarly, age discrimination laws are vigorously enforced in the states, and legal action to address discrimination typically is brought first at the state level.

By some accounts, age discrimination is less prevalent today than in the past, although some studies report complaints that some employers treat older workers less fairly than younger workers, and that they are more likely to be laid off.[65] In fiscal year 2006, 14,000 claims were filed with the Equal Employment Opportunity Commission under ADEA. Research on the effects of the ADEA suggests the law has prevented companies from unfairly dismissing older workers. There is some concern, however, that companies may have been inhibited from hiring older workers in the first place for fear of making themselves more vulnerable to future suits. In fact, proving discrimination in hiring may be more difficult than doing so in the case of termination.

IV. GUIDING PRINCIPLES FOR FUTURE POLICY CONSIDERATIONS

The decision to retire, clearly a life changing event, can be a difficult one to make no matter how well prepared an individual may be. Ideally, older Americans should be able to enjoy a level of retirement income that allows them to maintain an appropriate standard of living, and retire with "dignity after years of contribution to the economy."[66] Clearly, individual savings and investment strategies play a major role, as do employer pensions and Social Security retirement benefits. No one can predict the future; workers who intend to extend their working lives may find those plans interrupted by disability, deterioration of their own health or by that of a spouse or close family member or by the development of unexpected changes in the labor market. The challenge is assuring that the nation's laws and policies facilitate adequate retirement income, while not harming the income security of those who cannot work in their later years.

Adequate preparation for a secure retirement should begin early in life, thus the policies and practices that affect that preparation should be available throughout a worker's lifetime not just as they approach retirement age. Investments in financial as well as human capital – education, training, health maintenance – should allow workers to attain the flexibility when making choices about work and retirement.

The issues raised in this report require serious consideration by policy makers. To that end, the Board echoes the call in recent reports of the Government Accountability Office and of the Organization for Economic Cooperation and Development (OECD) for a comprehensive government- wide strategy for dealing with the implications of an aging population and an aging workforce and would urge policy makers to study the approaches that other countries are using to encourage longer working lives (see Appendix II).

As a Board we recommend that policy makers should address the issue of enabling longer working lives. Rather than prescribe specific policies, however, we suggest several principles that should guide consideration of any future reforms.

- A primary objective of encouraging workers to remain in the labor force longer is to help people secure an adequate income in retirement at a time when that goal is becoming more and more challenging. The nation's retirement security policies should support and reward additional years of work. Policy makers should look closely at removing barriers that stand in the way of a worker's choice to stay in the workforce longer, or an employer's desire to accommodate older workers.
- Policy approaches should be consistent and coordinated in order to minimize unintended consequences. Too often we have seen cases where a well-intentioned policy change has resulted in negative outcomes for some parts of the population. Specifically, policies to encourage later retirement need to be coordinated with policies that address workers with the most difficulty remaining at work whether because of a lack of opportunities, insufficient skills, or medical condition. In late 2006, the Board issued a major report, *A Disability System for the 21st Century*, that addresses the need to strengthen our system of providing economic security to those who cannot or can no longer work because of disability. We encourage policy makers to consider the ideas in that report as they address the continuum of circumstances over the life course affecting the ability of Americans to work.
- Proposed policies should be designed using the sophisticated, rigorous and comprehensive modeling tools now available. Such tools should be used to simulate the likely effects of several policies at once and estimate their costs, including not just narrow programmatic measures, but broader budgetary and economic measures.
- Policies should be coordinated across a broad range of policy domains and contexts. At present there is no single federal agency responsible for coordinating such efforts. Moreover, legislative jurisdiction is spread across numerous Congressional committees, making it difficult to develop formal national policy goals for the desired level of labor force participation of older workers. The Federal Taskforce on the Aging of the American Workforce, coordinated by the Department of Labor's Employment and Training Administration was convened in 2006 to address this lack of coordination. Their policy recommendations, however, did not touch on major areas of policy including Social Security rules.
- Policies that change expectations about how long working careers should be or that change the balance of incentives between work and retirement should be fair. They should give workers sufficiently advanced notice that changing behavior is warranted, but also provide enough impetus for the kind of changes in behavior that will increase the economic security of workers and retirees alike. Any reform proposals must be transparent to the public and the implications of those proposals clearly understood. For example, mechanisms that adjust retirement ages or link pension returns to longevity provide policy makers with flexibility, but such changes may not be well understood by the public.

- Not all policies need to be targeted specifically at older workers. Older workers' needs are diverse and often coincide with the needs of younger workers, as well as people with disabilities. Policies that affect all workers such as universal design for more accessible work sites, more flexible work schedules, telecommuting, etc., can also have important benefits for older workers.

The nation's first major effort to deal with economic security in retirement, the Social Security Act of 1935, arose during a time of great economic hardship and uncertainty. Over time, as the nation's wealth grew, the system of social insurance that supports retirement security including Disability Insurance, Medicare, Medicaid, and SSI, as well as the employment-based private programs, and private savings have greatly improved the standards of living of those in retirement as well as provided an important level of security.

Almost 75 years after the founding of Social Security, our nation faces a different kind of challenge: longer life spans and relatively low birth rates mean our population will undergo an unprecedented degree of aging. This fundamental demographic shift in our population will challenge many of our assumptions about how we allocate income between workers and retirees, between the periods in our own lives when we are working and when we are retired. Devoting some additional share of our longer lifetimes to working is one way to meet this challenge. Employers and workers will have to adjust their expectations and make appropriate adjustments to the new realities of our evolving workforce. Policy makers can and should find ways to support that transition.

This Advisory Board has in the recent past addressed the need to look comprehensively at retirement security, to address the long-term financing shortfalls in Social Security, and to design a disability system for a new century. Even as policy makers turn their attention to these issues, we know that challenges to retirement security will continue. None is more pressing today than the rapidly rising cost of health care. Therefore, a crucial part of this process must be to educate and raise awareness about what is necessary to achieve economic security in retirement, not only among policy makers, professionals and researchers, but also among the general public.

APPENDIX 1. SUMMARY OF A PUBLIC FORUM ON POLICIES TO HELP EXTEND THE WORKING LIFE OF OLDER AMERICANS HELD FRIDAY, JANUARY 18, 2008

In January of 2008, the Social Security Advisory Board and the University of Illinois Center for Business and Public Policy sponsored a public forum to facilitate discussion of public policies and workplace practices to help older workers extend their working lives. Nine experts from academia, think tanks, federal, state and international governmental organizations, and representatives of private employers and organized labor were invited as speakers to share their ideas and perspectives. Over 100 guests representing policy makers, federal government agencies, advocacy groups, and independent research organizations were in attendance and participated in the discussion.

This appendix summarizes the main points of each of the presenters, highlighting the nature of the issues involved and proposed policy options to address them. The ideas of the speakers do not reflect any endorsement by the Advisory Board. All the papers and presentation materials from that public forum are available to the public on the Advisory Board's website.

Forum Presenters

Alicia Munnell, Drucker Professor of Management Sciences and Director of the Center for Retirement Research, Boston College

Professor Munnell observed that the retirement system is contracting and that a substantial portion of the population will not have as much income in retirement as they would want to maintain their standard of living. She suggested that "most people should work longer and claim their Social Security benefits later." She made three policy recommendations. First, the Social Security Administration should develop educational materials including an informational guide to help older workers and their families decide when to claim retirement benefits. Second, some administrative hurdles should be placed in front of those who are prone to apply for benefits at the earliest age, for example, by requiring spousal approval. Third, raise the earliest eligibility age for Social Security retirement benefits, currently age 62, in a way that would protect the most vulnerable.

Presentation slides: http://www.ssab.gov/documents/Slides-1MunnellPDF.pdf

Paper: http://www.ssab.gov/documents/Paper1MunnellSSABForum1-18-08.pdf

John Shoven, Schwab Professor of Economics, Stanford University and Director of the Stanford Institute for Economic Policy Research

Professor Shoven explained that because Americans are living longer but still retiring relatively early, they must prepare for considerably longer retirements than in the past. He said that a 65-yearold man in the year 2000, a 70-year-old woman in the year 2000 and a 59-year-old man in 1970 all had about the same mortality risks. He noted that several aspects of current retirement policy impose relatively high implicit taxes on older workers and recommended several policy reforms to remove barriers for longer careers. First, increase to 40 from 35, the number of years of earnings used to calculate a workers retirement benefits. Second, calculate lifetime monthly earnings in the Social Security benefit using only the months a person actually works and then prorating the benefit amount. Third, eliminate payroll taxes for those who already have 40 years worth of earnings. He stated that these changes could be done in a way that keeps the average benefit constant. A final policy option he recommended would be to change Medicare from being the secondary payer to the primary payer for those workers eligible for Medicare, and also enrolled in an employer sponsored health plan.

Presentation slides: http://www.ssab.gov/documents/Slides-2ShovenPDF.pdf

Paper: http://www.ssab.gov/documents/Paper2ShovenSSABForum1-18-08.pdf

Eugene Steuerle, Senior Fellow, Urban Institute (currently Vice-President Peter G. Peterson Foundation)

Dr. Steuerle made the observation that working more at older ages has broader implications than the impact on Social Security since it would increase national income, personal income, government tax revenues and as a result would reduces pressure on other workers to support all other government programs. He suggested several ways to encourage more work at older ages. First, change the "announcement effect" of Social Security that tells people they are "old" at age 62. Second, improve the transparency of Social Security benefits, by changing the confusing presentation of "actuarial adjustments," removing the "earnings test," and changing the presentation of replacement rates to adequately reflect relative income at older ages. Third, reducing implicit taxes on work at older ages due to the Social Security benefit formula, for example by eliminating payroll taxes after the retirement age, and removing the Medicare as secondary payer rule. Fourth, he described ways to "backload" benefits, by changing the lifetime benefit package so you receive more benefits at older ages and less at younger ages.

Presentation slides: http://www.ssab.gov/documents/Slides-3SteuerlePDF.pdf

John Martin, Director, Employment, Labor and Social Affairs, Organization for Economic Cooperation and Development

Mr. Martin made two recommendations. The first was to link pension benefits to life expectancy. He noted that 13 of the 16 OECD countries, as part of their pension reform packages, had introduced measures that would automatically link future pensions to changes in life expectancy. His second recommendation was to increase incentives for older unemployed workers to find jobs. He suggested that one way to do this was through introducing some form of wage insurance. For a displaced worker who accepts a job at a lower wage, as is often the case with re-employed older workers, wage insurance would provide an earnings supplement to make up part of the gap in earnings in the new job, compared to the previous job.

Paper: http://www.ssab.gov/documents/Paper6MartinSSABForum1-18-08.pdf

Keith Brainard, Research Director, National Association of State Retirement Administrators

Mr. Brainard noted that more than 16 million workers—about 12 percent of the nation's workforce—are employed by state or local governments. Ninety-eight percent of those employees have access to an employer-sponsored retirement plan, and 90 percent of them have some form of traditional pension or defined benefit plan as their primary retirement benefit. He described several approaches that state legislatures have approved to allow retiring participants to return to work after they have met normal retirement eligibility, but without forfeiting their pension benefit. He noted, however, that some such programs do not clearly mesh with federal tax laws or age discrimination and employment act laws.

Paper: http://www.ssab.gov/documents/Paper4BrainardSSABForum1-18-08.pdf

Thomas Dowd, Administrator, Office of Policy Development and Research, Employment and Training Administration, U.S. Department of Labor

Mr. Dowd described the work of a federal government interagency task force that the Department of Labor convened in 2006 to focus on the aging of the American workforce and the impacts of this demographic change on American society. The task force identified the following strategies: inventory the legal and regulatory barriers and disincentives to employment of older workers; coordinate research and demonstration agendas across federal agencies; develop a blueprint for awareness and outreach activities for older workers;

facilitate self-employment for older workers; promote flexible work arrangements; make available to states tools and technical assistance to support the employment of older workers; and make available to older workers education resources on retirement and financial literacy.

Report of the Taskforce on the Aging of the American Workforce, February 2008: http://www.doleta.gov/reports/FINAL_Taskforce_Report_2_27_08.pdf

Cynthia Donohoe, Vice President, Benefits, BAE Systems, Inc.

Ms. Donohoe discussed her company's initiatives to retain experienced workers through a phased retirement program. After describing the flexible work schedules and options that her company provides, she discussed some practices that can encourage employees to take advantage of those options. One was to provide information to employees to show both the financial gains and the health advantages associated with longer employment. Another was to help employees find the options to extend their careers that best fit their situations. She also mentioned the need to educate managers to make them aware of alternatives for their employees. Finally, she noted that employee engagement is important. Employees have to feel that what they are doing is important and valued.

Presentation slides: http://www.ssab.gov/documents/Slides-8MahoneyslidesPDF.pdf

Kevin Mahoney, Associate Director, Human Capital Leadership and Merit System Accountability Division, U.S. Office of Personnel Management

Mr. Mahoney described U.S. Office of Personnel Management's (OPM) efforts to deal with the coming retirement wave in the federal workforce. Strategies include advertising to help attract potential employees and restructuring of the hiring process to make it faster and more user-friendly. OPM has also suggested legislation, which has sponsors in both the House and the Senate, that would allow retirees to return to work on a part-time basis without adversely affecting their pension annuity.

Presentation slides: http://www.ssab.gov/documents/Slides-8MahoneyslidesPDF.pdf

Gerald Shea, Assistant to the President for Governmental Affairs, AFL-CIO

Mr. Shea stated that in order to keep people at work, they need good jobs, including decent wages, health care coverage, and some way to provide savings for retirement. He said that we cannot change the terms of the global economy, but we can help our country adjust to it through both private initiatives and public policy. One route that the AFL-CIO has taken toward developing good jobs is by creating, with employers and on its own, career-advancement programs. Such programs encourage workers to transition to a different skill set through higher education. He said that the educational system has not provided people with the reading and math skills they need for apprenticeship programs. As a result, there is a need to create a skill-building system that allows people to get into productive career paths toward good jobs.

Presentation slides: http://www.ssab.gov/documents/Slides-9SheaPDF.pdf

APPENDIX II. WHAT SOME OTHER COUNTRIES ARE DOING

Many other advanced industrial countries in Europe and Asia are faced with the same economic challenges of rapidly aging populations and long trends toward earlier retirement. Compared to the United States, Japan and most countries in Europe are experiencing significantly more rapid population aging as their life expectancies' improve faster and birth rates have fallen further. While about one in five Americans are projected to be over 65 by 2050, about one in three will be over 65 in countries such as Japan, Korea, Italy and Spain. Labor force growth in many of the 30 developed countries that are part of the Organization for Economic Co-operation and Development (OECD) is expected to halt or even fall.[67] In most of these countries, the public pension programs are also more generous and incentives for early retirement are greater than in the United States. Effective retirement rates in about two-thirds of OECD countries, however, are lower than in the United States.

But just as the challenge of their aging workforces appear more severe than in the U.S., their efforts to reform public retirement systems and encourage workers to delay retirement and remain employed longer have been more aggressive.

Recent reforms of public pension systems in OECD countries have reduced incentives for early retirement:[68]

- Twelve counties have reduced pension generosity for workers retiring at a given age with a given contribution history.
- Six have enacted other measures that reduce overall replacement rates.
- Eleven have increased the rewards and penalties involved with timing of retirement. Seven countries are increasing pension eligibility ages for both men and women, and five others are increasing ages for women.

Thirteen OECD countries now automatically link future retirement benefits to changes in life expectancy.[69] Two-thirds of the major retirement-income reforms in OECD countries since 1990 have linked benefits and life expectancy in a variety of ways. In the late 1990s, five countries began to use defined contribution plans as a substitute for some or all of their public pensions; two others mandated contributions to private pensions in addition to their public plans. Three countries replaced their defined- benefit public plans with notional accounts. These notional accounts are financed on a pay-as-you-go basis, but they imitate defined-contribution plans by calculating benefits in a way similar to annuities, using life expectancy as a factor. Three countries have linked their defined-benefit public plans to life expectancy by introducing automatic reductions of benefit levels as life expectancy increases. And two countries have linked to either the pension eligibility age or the number of years of contributions needed to qualify for a full pension.[70]

OECD countries have also been reviewing other programs that may be alternative routes to leaving the workforce prematurely, such as long-term sickness and disability benefits and unemployment benefits, although changes in these programs have been more limited than those in pension programs. Canada and the Netherlands, for example, have reduced the number of new disability beneficiaries between 50 and 64 years of age. And Australia and the Netherlands have increased job-search requirements for unemployed older workers.[71]

OECD countries have also recognized the need to change employer attitudes and practices. Most OECD countries have enacted age-discrimination legislation and some have also undertaken public information campaigns to improve employer attitudes toward older workers. The United Kingdom, for example, began its Age Positive information campaign in 1999 to promote the benefits of age diversity in the workplace. The Netherlands has employed a cooperative effort of government, employers, and labor unions to improve attitudes toward older workers.[72]

The expense of older workers' wages relative to their productivity may discourage employers from hiring or retaining them. OECD countries have taken a variety of approaches to this problem. Korea has encouraged the use of a "peak wage" system that would give greater employment security to older workers in exchange for downward flexibility in wages. Policies in some other countries have had a less direct effect. Moving from a system that sets wages based on seniority to one that uses individual performance, as has been done in Sweden's public sector, has the effect of increasing wage flexibility.[73] Several other countries have taken a more direct approach, offering wage subsidies or exemption from social insurance taxes for employers if they hire unemployed older workers.[74]

Some OECD countries have also taken measures to improve the employability of older workers by promoting training, providing employment assistance, and improving working conditions. In the late 1990s, Norway introduced a Competence Reform to meet growing demands for workplace skills. One of the target groups was older workers who did not have access to education when they were young. The effectiveness of training in returning unemployed workers to employment is difficult to evaluate, and there has been a range of outcomes of programs in various countries.[75]

Several OECD countries have been trying employment assistance programs targeted at older workers. The New Deal 50 Plus program in the United Kingdom, for example, provides participants with their own personal advisor at a job center to help with the job search and arrange for training to improve employability. In the Netherlands, specialized companies have been hired to provide workforce re-integration services to jobseekers over 50. Korea and Japan have established special offices to support older jobseekers. Canada, Australia, and the Czech Republic have also been experimenting with new approaches to provide employment services to older workers.[76]

Some countries are also undertaking programs to encourage longer working lives through meeting older workers' needs through rehabilitation, training, and improvements in health and safety. Germany, for example, initiated a campaign called "30, 40, 50 plus – Working healthily as you get older." Finland has a program to help employees better manage health conditions in order to maintain employability. In Denmark, a worker whose work capacity has become limited can hold a "flexjob," receiving full-time pay while working only part-time or at a reduced pace, and the employer receives a subsidy for the reduced production. A number of efforts have also been undertaken to ease the transition from full-time to part-time work. In 2004, the United Kingdom changed its regulations on occupational pensions to allow workers to access pension benefits while continuing to work for the same employer on a part-time basis.[77]

SOCIAL SECURITY ADVISORY BOARD

Establishment of the Board

In 1994, when Congress passed Public Law 103-296 establishing the Social Security Administration as an independent agency, it also created an independent, bipartisan Advisory Board to advise the President, the Congress, and the Commissioner of Social Security on matters related to the Social Security and Supplemental Security Income programs. Under this legislation, appointments to the Board are made by the President, the Speaker of the House of Representatives, and the President pro tempore of the Senate.

Advisory Board members are appointed to staggered six year terms, made up as follows: three appointed by the President (no more than two from the same political party); and two each (no more than one from the same political party) by the Speaker of the House (in consultation with the Chairman and the Ranking Minority Member of the Committee on Ways and Means) and by the President pro tempore of the Senate (in consultation with the Chairman and Ranking Minority Member of the Committee on Finance). Presidential appointments are subject to Senate confirmation. The President designates one member of the Board to serve as Chairman for a four year term, coincident with the term of the President, or until the designation of a successor.

Sylvester J. Schieber, Chairman

Sylvester J. Schieber is a private consultant on retirement and health issues based in New Market, Maryland. He retired from Watson Wyatt Worldwide in September 2006 where he had served as Vice President/U.S. Director of Benefit Consulting and Director of Research and Information. From 1981 - 83, Dr. Schieber was the Director of Research at the Employee Benefit Research Institute. Earlier, he worked for the Social Security Administration as an economic analyst and as Deputy Director at the Office of Policy Analysis. Dr. Schieber is the author of numerous journal articles, policy analysis papers, and several books including: Retirement Income Opportunities in An Aging America: Coverage and Benefit Entitlement; Social Security: Perspectives on Preserving the System; and The Real Deal: The History and Future of Social Security. He served on the 1994 - 1996 Advisory Council on Social Security. He received his Ph.D. from the University of Notre Dame. First term of office: January 1998 to September 2003. Current term of office: October 2003 to September 2009. Appointed by the President in September 2006 to serve as Chairman of the Advisory Board from October 2006 to January 2009.

Dana K. Bilyeu

Dana K. Bilyeu is the Executive Officer of the Public Employees' Retirement System of Nevada. As the Executive Officer of the $21 billion pension trust she is responsible for all aspects of fund management including analysis of plan funding, investment oversight, operational and strategic planning, and fiduciary and governance issues. Mrs. Bilyeu is principally responsible for the relationship with the System's independent actuary and oversees the data reconciliation process for actuarial valuations of the System. In her capacity as the Executive Officer, Mrs. Bilyeu provides information and analysis to the Nevada Legislature in consideration of pension policy issues affecting state and local government. Prior to her appointment as the Executive Officer, Mrs. Bilyeu served for eight years as the System's Operations Officer, overseeing all aspects of benefit administration, including survivor, disability, and retirement benefit programs. Mrs. Bilyeu also was responsible for cost effectiveness measurement for all activities of the System. She was accountable for technology oversight as well as policy issues related to the public safety sector of public employment. Prior to her employment at the System, Mrs. Bilyeu was the System's legal counsel, representing the System in a variety of aspects from benefits litigation, contracts analysis, to Board governance. Mrs. Bilyeu is a member of the National Association of State Retirement Administrators, the National Council on Teacher Retirement, the National Conference of Public Employee Retirement Systems, and the National Association of Public Pension Attorneys. She also serves on the Public Employee Advisory Board for the International Foundation of Employee Benefit Plans. She received her Juris Doctor from California Western School of Law and her B.A. from the University of Arizona. Term of office: December 2006 to September 2010.

Jeffrey R. Brown

Jeffrey R. Brown is a professor in the Department of Finance at the University of Illinois at Urbana- Champaign. Prior to joining the Illinois faculty, Dr. Brown was an assistant professor of public policy at Harvard University's John F. Kennedy School of Government. During 2001-2002, he served as Senior Economist at the White House Council of Economic Advisers, where he focused primarily on Social Security, pension reform, and terrorism risk insurance. During 2001 he also served on the staff of the President's Commission to Strengthen Social Security. In January 2005, President Bush nominated Dr. Brown to become a member of the Social Security Advisory Board for a term ending September 2008. Professor Brown holds a Ph.D. in economics from the Massachusetts Institute of Technology, a Masters of Public Policy from Harvard University, and a B.A. from Miami University. He is a Research Associate of the National Bureau of Economic Research, a Research Fellow with the Employee Benefits Research Institute, and a Senior Fellow of the China Center for Insurance and Social Security Research. Professor Brown is a member of the American Economic Association, the American Risk and Insurance Association, the National Academy of Social Insurance, and the Risk Theory Society. Professor Brown has published extensively on public and private insurance markets, including publications in *The American Economic Review*, *The Journal of Political Economy*, *The Journal of Public Economics*, *The Journal of Monetary Economics*, *The Journal of Risk and Insurance*, *The National Tax Journal*, and numerous books. He is the recipient of the Lumina Award for Outstanding Research in Insurance and E-Commerce. Professor Brown is coauthor of the book, *The Role of Annuities in Financing Retirement* (MIT Press), and is co-founder and co-editor of *The Journal of Pension Economics and Finance*, published by Cambridge University Press. He has served as a consultant / expert panel member for the Executive Office of the President of the U.S., the

General Accounting Office, the U.S. Treasury, the World Bank, and several private firms. Prior to graduate school, he was a Brand Manager at the Procter & Gamble Company. Term of office: October 2006 to September 2008.

Dorcas R. Hardy

Dorcas R. Hardy is President of DRHardy & Associates, a government relations and public policy firm serving a diverse portfolio of clients. After her appointment by President Ronald Reagan as Assistant Secretary of Human Development Services, Ms. Hardy was appointed Commissioner of Social Security (1986 to 1989) and was appointed by President George W. Bush to chair the Policy Committee for the 2005 White House Conference on Aging. Ms. Hardy has launched and hosted her own primetime, weekly television program, "Financing Your Future," on Financial News Network and UPI Broadcasting, and "The Senior American," an NET political program for older Americans. She speaks and writes widely about domestic and international retirement financing issues and entitlement program reforms and is the co-author of *Social Insecurity: The Crisis in America's Social Security System and How to Plan Now for Your Own Financial Survival*, Random House, 1992. A former CEO of a rehabilitation technology firm, Ms. Hardy promotes redesign and modernization of the Social Security, Medicare, and disability insurance systems. Additionally, she has chaired a Task Force to rebuild vocational rehabilitation services for disabled veterans for the Department of Veterans Affairs. She received her B.A. from Connecticut College, her M.B.A. from Pepperdine University, and completed the Executive Program in Health Policy and Financial Management at Harvard University. Ms. Hardy is a Certified Senior Advisor and serves on the Board of Directors of Wright Investors Service Managed Funds, and First Coast Service Options of Florida. First term of office: April 2002 to September 2004. Current term of office: October 2004 to September 2010.

Marsha Rose Katz

Marsha Rose Katz is a Project Director at the University of Montana Rural Institute in Missoula, where her work has concentrated on assisting persons with disabilities to utilize Social Security work incentives to start their own businesses or engage in wage employment. Since coming to the Rural Institute in 1999, Ms. Katz has focused on providing training and technical assistance on both employment and SSI/SSDI to rural, frontier and tribal communities across the country. Previously, she worked for nearly 20 years in a disability rights community based organization, the Association for Community Advocacy (ACA), a local Arc in Ann Arbor, Michigan. She served as both Vice President of ACA, and Director of its Family Resource Center. It was at ACA that Ms. Katz began her nearly 30 years of individual and systems advocacy regarding programs administered by SSA, especially the SSI and SSDI programs. Ms. Katz has written numerous articles and created many widely distributed user- friendly general handouts on SSI and SSDI, the majority of which focus on the impact of work on benefits, and utilizing work incentives. She is the author of *Don't Look for Logic: An Advocate's Manual for Negotiating the SSI and SSDI Programs*, published by the Rural Institute. Her Bachelor's and Master's Degrees are from the University of Michigan. Ms. Katz's many years of experience as a trainer, technical advisor, and advocate have been guided and informed by her partnership with people with disabilities, from her husband, Bob Liston, to the people she assisted in her work with ACA and the Arc Michigan, her current work at the Rural Institute, and her longstanding participation in ADAPT, the nation's largest cross-disability, grassroots disability rights organization. Term of office: November 2006 to September 2012.

Barbara B. Kennelly

Barbara B. Kennelly became President and Chief Executive Officer of the National Committee to Preserve Social Security and Medicare in April 2002 after a distinguished 23-year career in elected public office. Mrs. Kennelly served 17 years in the United States House of Representatives representing the First District of Connecticut. During her congressional career, Mrs. Kennelly was the first woman elected to serve as the Vice Chair of the House Democratic Caucus. Mrs. Kennelly was also the first woman to serve on the House Committee on Intelligence and to chair one of its subcommittees. She was the first woman to serve as Chief Majority Whip, and the third woman in history to serve on the 200-year-old Ways and Means Committee. During the 105th Congress, she was the ranking member of the Subcommittee on Social Security. Prior to her election to Congress, Mrs. Kennelly was Secretary of State of Connecticut. After serving in Congress, Mrs. Kennelly was appointed to the position of Counselor to the Commissioner at the Social Security Administration. As Counselor, Mrs. Kennelly worked closely with the Commissioner of Social Security Kenneth S. Apfel, and members of Congress to inform and educate the American people on the choices they face to ensure the future solvency of Social Security. Mrs. Kennelly served on the Policy Committee for the 2005 White House Conference on Aging. Mrs. Kennelly received a B.A. in Economics from Trinity College, Washington, D.C. She earned a certificate from the Harvard Business School on completion of the Harvard-Radcliffe Program in Business Administration and a Master's Degree in Government from Trinity College, Hartford. Term of office: January 2006 to September 2011.

Mark J. Warshawsky

Mark J. Warshawsky is Director of Retirement Research at Watson Wyatt Worldwide, a global human capital consulting firm. He conducts and oversees research on employer-sponsored retirement programs and policies.

A frequent speaker to business and professional groups, Dr. Warshawsky is a recognized thought leader on pensions, social security, insurance and health care financing. He has written numerous articles published in leading professional journals, books and working papers, and has testified before Congress on pensions, annuities and other economic issues. In addition to being a member of the Social Security Advisory Board , he is also on the Advisory Board of the Pension Research Council of the Wharton School.

From 2004 to 2006, Dr. Warshawsky served as assistant secretary for economic policy at the U.S. Treasury Department. During his tenure, he played a key role in the development of the Administration's pension reform proposals, particularly pertaining to single-employer defined benefit plans, which were ultimately included in the Pension Protection Act (PPA) of 2006. He was also involved extensively in the formulation of Social Security reform proposals, and oversaw the Department's comprehensive 2005 study of the terror risk insurance program. In addition, Dr. Warshawsky led the efforts to update and enhance substantially the measures and disclosures in the Social Security and Medicare Trustees' Reports, as well as the setting of the macroeconomic forecasts which underlie the administration's budget submissions to Congress.

Dr. Warshawsky's research has been influential in the 2001-2 regulatory reform of minimum distribution requirements for qualified retirement plans, the increasing realization of the importance of financial protection against outliving one's financial resources in retirement, and a product innovation to integrate the immediate life annuity and longterm care insurance. For the latter research, he won a prize from the British Institute of Actuaries in 2001 for a professional article he co-authored. Favorable tax treatment for this integrated product was also included in PPA due to Dr. Warshawsky's advocacy.

Dr. Warshawsky has also held senior-level economic research positions at the Internal Revenue Service, the Federal Reserve Board in Washington, D.C. and TIAA-CREF, where he established the Paul A. Samuelson Prize and organized several research conferences. A native of Chicago, he received a Ph.D. in Economics from Harvard University and a B.A. with Highest Distinction from Northwestern University. Term of office: December 2006 to September 2012.

Members of the Staff

Katherine Thornton, Staff Director
Deborah Sullivan, Deputy Staff Director
Joel Feinleib
Beverly Rollins
George Schuette
Jean Von Ancken
David Warner

End Notes

[1] The cost of a pay as you go pension system can be expressed as [number of beneficiaries/ numbers of workers] x [average benefits/ average covered wages]. Under the U.S. Social Security system benefit formula, benefits increase with increases in the average wage, so the second term is rather stable. The major source of increased cost, therefore, is the significant increase in the ratio of retired beneficiaries to workers.

[2] Social Security Administration projections of life expectancy in 2040 assume reductions in the mortality rate of about 0.6 percent per year, yielding improvements in life expectancy of about 0.6 years per decade. The 2007 Technical Panel Report on Assumptions and Methods examined the range of expert projections and suggested improvements on the order of one year per decade are more reasonable. For evidence that eradication of smoking could dramatically improve life expectancy see Haidong Wang and Samuel Preston, *Forecasting U.S. Mortality Using Cohort Smoking Histories*. For a more pessimistic view of future improvements in life spans

see Bruce Carnes and Jay Olshansky, "A Realist View of Aging, Mortality and Future Longevity," *Population and Development Review*, 33(2), 2007. David M. Cutler, Edward L. Glaeser,

[3] In this discussion we refer to the "typical worker" as someone at the *median* age of retirement. Half of workers can expect to spend more time in retirement and half less.

[4] We assume for the sake of simplicity that the returns on savings and investments will remain similar to the long run historical averages.

[5] For simplicity, we assume savings are deposited at the end of the year and are compounded annually.

[6] For a discussion of how different data sources affect measurement of the private savings rate, see: Rudolph Penner, "Measuring Personal Saving: A Tale of American Profligacy," Urban Institute Brief Series, May 1, 2008.

[7] Ruth Helman, Jack VanDerhei, and Craig Copeland, "The 2008 Retirement Confidence Survey: Americans Much More Worried about Retirement, Health Costs a Big Concern," Employee Benefit Research Institute Issue Brief, April 2008.

[8] Employee Benefit Research Institute, based on U.S. Department of Labor, Form 5500 Summary Report. See http://www.ebri.org/ publications/benfaq/index.cfm?fa=retfaqt14a

[9] James Choi, John Beshears, David Laibson, and Brigitte C. Madrian, "The Importance of Default Options for Retirement Savings Outcomes: Evidence from the United States." In Stephen J. Kay and Tapen Sinha, eds., *Lessons from Pension Reform in the Americas*, pp. 59-87. Oxford: Oxford University Press, 2008.

[10] We note that this is also true for balances in employer sponsored defined benefit plans. In the case of the private DB plans, the financial risk is borne by the employer, because by law they must meet their benefit payment obligations. In the DC plan, as in private savings, the financial risks are borne by individuals who are responsible for their level of contribution and choice of investment portfolio.

[11] Employee Benefit Research Institute Issue Brief: "401(k) Plan Asset Allocation, Account Balances, and Loan Activity in 2006," August 2007.

[12] Sylvester J. Schieber, Pension Aspirations and Realizations: *A Perspective on Yesterday, Today and Tomorrow* (Washington, D.C.: Watson Wyatt Worldwide, 2007).

[13] Kaiser Family Foundation and Health Research and Education Trust, "Employer Health Benefits," *2008 Annual Survey*.

[14] Another way to put this is a couple would have to buy an annuity worth $206,000 today to fund the average out-of-pocket costs over the rest of their lives. See Alicia H. Munnell, Mauricio Soto, Anthony Webb, Francesca Golub-Sass, and Dan Muldoon, "Health Care Costs Drive Up the National Retirement Index," Center for Retirement Research at Boston College Issue in Brief, February 2008.

[15] *2008 Annual Report of The Boards Of Trustees of The Federal Hospital Insurance and Federal Supplementary Medical Insurance Trust Funds*, 2008.

[16] Provision of retiree health care benefits is declining for private employers, but remaining stable under public retirement systems such as for state and federal workers. See also Paul Fronstin and Stephen Blakely, "Is The Tipping Point in Health Benefits Near?" *Wall Street Journal*; and Paul Fronstin, "The Future of Employment-Based Health Benefits: Have Employers Reached a Tipping Point?" Employee Benefit Research Institute Issue Brief, December 2007.

[17] Social Security Administration, *Income of the Population 55 or Older*, 2004, released July 2008.

[18] At low end of estimates, less than 20 percent of near retirees had less wealth than their "optimal targets." See: John Karl Scholz, Ananth Seshadri and Surachai Khitatrakun, "Are Americans Saving "Optimally" for Retirement?" *Journal of Political Economy*, 2006. A McKinsey Global Institute report in 2008, reported that two-thirds of baby boomers will not be able to replace 80 percent of their pre- retirement earnings. Estimates by scholars from Boston College in the New National Retirement Risk Index are somewhere in the middle at about 40 percent.

[19] Center for Retirement Research at Boston College, "Retirements at Risk: A New National Retirement Risk Index," June 2006; and Alicia H. Munnell, Anthony Webb, and Francesca Golub-Sass, "Is There Really A Retirement Savings Crisis? An NRRI Analysis," Center for Retirement Research at Boston College, August 2007.

[20] On average over time the expectation is that investment returns will continue to grow the longer they remain invested. Saving should be a part of preparation for economic security as early in life as possible.

[21] Individuals who convert their savings, or pension balances into annuities, can insure themselves, for a price, against outliving their assets.

[22] These reduced or increased benefits apply for the rest of the claimant's life, although benefits are increased each year to keep up with inflation. If additional earnings are high enough to replace earlier earnings in the benefit calculation, additional work will increase benefits even further.

[23] James I. Mahaney and Peter C. Carlson, "Rethinking Social Security Claiming in a 401(k) World" in John Ameriks and Olivia S. Mitchell, Eds., *Recalibrating Retirement Spending and Saving*, September 2008. Alicia H. Munnell and Mauricio Soto, "Why Do Women Claim Social Security Benefits So Early?" Issue Brief, Center for Retirement Research at Boston College, October 2005. Steven A. Sass, Wei Sun, and Anthony

Webb, "When Should Married Men Claim Social Security Benefits?" Issue Brief, Center for Retirement Research at Boston College, March 2008.

[24] The odds of one or both members of a 65-year-old married couple living past age 90 are close to 60 percent.

[25] Barbara Butrica, Karen E. Smith, C. Eugene Steuerle, "Working for a Good Retirement," Urban Institute Retirement Project Discussion Paper, May 23, 2006.

[26] Congressional Budget Office Economic and Budget Issue Brief, "Retirement and the Need for Saving," May 12, 2004.

[27] See Richard Johnson, Urban Institute.

[28] Barbara Butrica, Karen E. Smith, C. Eugene Steuerle, "Working for a Good Retirement," Urban Institute Retirement Project Discussion Paper, May 23, 2006.

[29] We mention the increase in total taxes to measure the scale of revenue increase. Only payroll taxes are used to pay Social Security benefits.

[30] See Dora Costa, *The Evolution of Retirement: An American Economic History 1880-1990*, University of Chicago Press, 1998.

[31] McKinsey Global Institute, Talkin' 'Bout My Generation: The Economic Impact of Aging U.S. Baby Boomers, June, 2008.

[32] Gaobo Pang, Mark Warshawsky, and Ben Weitzer, *The Retirement Decision: Current Influences on the Timing of Retirement among Older Workers*, Watson Wyatt, February 2008.

[33] Friedberg, Leora, "The Recent Trend Towards Later Retirement," Center for Retirement Research at Boston College Issue Brief, March 2007; and Gaobo Pang, Mark Warshawsky, and Ben Weitzer, *The Retirement Decision: Current Influences on the Timing of Retirement among Older Workers*, Watson Wyatt, February 2008.

[34] Jae Song and Joyce Manchester, "Have People Delayed Claiming Retirement Benefits? Responses to Changes in Social Security Rules," *Social Security Bulletin*, Vol. 67, No. 2, 2007; also Muldoon and Kopcke, "Are People Claiming Social Security Benefits Later?" Center for Retirement Research at Boston College Issue Brief, June 2008.

[35] Congressional Research Service Report for Congress, *Older Workers: Employment and Retirement Trends*, September 15, 2008.

[36] The 1983 Amendments to the Social Security Act implemented a schedule of gradual increases in the full retirement age. For individuals born in 1937 or earlier, the full retirement age – or the age at which full retirement benefits are payable, remains at age 65. But for people born in 1938 and later, the full retirement age increases by 2-month intervals until it reaches age 67 for those born in 1960 or later. The amendments did not change the age for claiming reduced benefits at the earliest age of 62.

[37] The *Senior Citizen's Freedom to Work Act of 2000* eliminated the earnings test for individuals aged 65-69 who had elected to receive retirement benefits. Prior to this change, beneficiaries who had reached full retirement age and worked and earned above a certain threshold had their monthly benefits either reduced or withheld in its entirety.

[38] Jae Song and Joyce Manchester, "Have People Delayed Claiming Retirement Benefits? Responses to Changes in Social Security Rules," *Social Security Bulletin*, Vol. 67, No. 2, 2007.

[39] Incremental benefit increases, known as delayed retirement credits, were first made available in 1971 to those working until 1970, briefly raised to age 72 then returned to 70 in 1983.

[40] Or the 5th anniversary of plan entry if a participant enters within five years of the normal retirement age. GAO, *Retirement Decisions: Federal Policies Offer Mixed Signals About When to Retire*, July 2007.

[41] In about two-thirds of private employer plans the normal retirement age is set at 65; in about one-sixth of them, the age is 62, and in most of the remainder, age is set at 60 or 55. Bureau of Labor Statistics (BLS) National Compensation Survey: Employee Benefits in Private Industry in the United States, 2002–2003. Washington, DC: U.S. Department of Labor, 2005.

[42] See Eugene Steuerle presentation to Social Security Advisory Board Forum ,"Policies to Help Extend the Working Life of Older Americans," in Appendix I of this report. The volume *Social Security Programs and Retirement Around the World*, Volume I, Univers ity of Chicago Press, 1999 edited by Jonathan Gruber and David Wise shows that across countries, the age workers withdraw from the workforce responds to the official retirement age in national pension systems.

[43] The benefit calculation starts with the full record of a worker's lifetime annual earnings. Past earnings up to age 60 are indexed by the "Average Wage Index" to reflect increases in the standard of living over time. Earning after age 60 are inflated by growth in the Consumer Price Index. The top 35 years of indexed earnings, including if necessary years with 0 earnings, are chosen divided by 420 (12x35) to get the worker's Average Indexed Monthly Earnings (AIME). A progressive formula is applied to the AIME to yield the Primary Insurance Amount which is then decreased or increased based on the age of the claimant relative to their full retirement age. A person who continues to work while receiving benefits will have their benefits recalculated annually if additional earnings are large enough to replace one of the 35 highest.

[44] It is possible that the 36th year of working will replace an earlier, lower amount of earnings in the average, but earnings after age 60 are not indexed and are likely to make only a small difference.

[45] Leora Friedberg and Anthony Webb, "Retirement and the Evolution of Pension Structure," *Journal of Human Resources*, XL(2):281-308, 2005.

[46] Pang, Warshawsky and Weitzer, *The Retirement Decision: Current Influences on the Timing of Retirement among Older Workers*, Watson Wyatt, February 2008.

[47] Federal law allows workers to access defined contribution benefits at age 59½ regardless of employment status. Employers may only allow plan participants who have left the firm to withdraw benefits. (Johnson, Mermin, Steuerle, 2006, p.28.)

[48] It is also possible that employees who participate in their 401(k) plan from an early age, who contribute sufficiently and who earn returns on par with historical averages, may find they have accumulated enough savings to retire at earlier ages without needing to work longer.

[49] At age 65, enrollment in premium-free Medicare Part A (hospital insurance) and Part B (physician and medical services), which has a premium, is automatic; however, there is an "opt-out" provision for Part B. Under certain conditions, postponing enrollment in Part B can increase the monthly premium by 10 percent.

[50] By law employers must provide the same coverage to their older and younger employees and they cannot require older workers to contribute more to their own health plans than younger workers. They cannot provide only Medigap coverage, and they cannot provide cash in lieu of health insurance benefits to those over 65.

[51] Gopi Shah Goda, John B. Shoven, Sita Nataraj Slavov, "A Tax on Work for the Elderly: Medicare as a Secondary Payer," NBER Working Paper No. 13383, September 2007 estimates the implicit tax rate faced by workers age 65 and over who are eligible for Medicare and who have employer sponsored health insurance.

[52] Employers are prohibited from requiring older employees to contribute more to their own health plan than younger workers. In addition, age-discrimination rules limit the ability of employers to reduce salaries based solely on age. See Richard W. Johnson, Gordon Mermin, C. Eugene Steuerle, "Work Impediments at Older Ages," Urban Institute Retirement Project Discussion Paper, May 2006.

[53] Richard W. Johnson, Gordon Mermin, C. Eugene Steuerle, "Work Impediments at Older Ages," Urban Institute Retirement Project Discussion Paper, May 2006.

[54] Dora Costa, *The Evolution of Retirement: An American Economic History 1880-1990*, University of Chicago Press, 1998.

[55] Richard W. Johnson, Gordon Mermin, Dan Murphy, "The Impact of Late-Career Health and Employment Shocks on Social Security and Other Wealth," Urban Institute Discussion Paper Series, December 2007.

[56] *2008 Annual Report of the Board of Trustees of the Federal Old-Age and Survivors Insurance and Federal Disability Insurance Trust Funds*, 2008.

[57] See for example, John A. Turner, "Promoting Work: Implications of Raising Social Security's Early Retirement Age," Center for Retirement Research at Boston College, Issue in Brief, August 2007.

[58] Richard W. Johnson, Gordon B.T. Mermin, and Dan Murphy, "The Impact of Late-Career Health and Employment Shocks on Social Security and Other Wealth," Urban Institute Discussion Paper Series, December 2007.

[59] Leora Friedberg, Michael Owyang, and Anthony Webb, "Identi-fying Local Differences in Retirement Patterns," Center for Retire-ment Research at Boston College Working Paper, December 2008.

[60] Richard W. Johnson, Gordon Mermin, C. Eugene Steuerle, "Work Impediments at Older Ages," Urban Institute Retirement Project Discussion Paper, May 2006.

[61] Under law, employers cannot require older employees to contribute more to their own health plan than younger workers do. As health care cost continue to escalate faster than growth of the economy or inflation these costs may become more and more salient to employers.

[62] In a typical traditional DB plan new employees near the plan's retirement age will qualify for pension benefits that represent a significantly higher share of their wages than a much younger new employee. Federal law prohibits employers from requiring more than seven years of service to qualify for full benefits and more than 80 percent of DB plans require 5 years. We note, however, that increased vesting periods in DB plans may promote longevity in the workplace in ways DC plans do not.

[63] Munnell, Sass, and Soto, *Employer Attitudes Toward Older Workers: Survey Results*, 2006.

[64] *Ibid.*

[65] Scott Reynolds, Neil Ridley and Carl Van Horn, "A Work-filled Retirement: Workers' Changing Views on Employment and Leisure," *Worktrends* 8.1, 2005. http://www.heldrich.rutgers.edu/ uploadedFiles/Publications/WT16.pdf

[66] P.L., 89-73 Older Americans Act of 1965.

[67] The 30 OECD countries include 23 European countries, the United States, Canada and Mexico, Australia, New Zealand, Japan, South Korea.

[68] Organisation for Economic Co-Operation and Development, *Live Longer, Work Longer*, 2006, pp. 88-9; John Martin, "Some Suggestions for Reforms Based on OECD Countries' Experiences," p. 3.

[69] John Martin, *ibid.*

[70] *Ibid.*, pp. 5-6.

[71] OECD, pp. 96-7.

[72] OECD, pp. 104-07.

[73] In the United States, this policy would not likely pass muster of age discrimination laws as currently interpreted.

[74] *Ibid.*, pp. 111-12.

[75] *Ibid.*, 118-22.

[76] *Ibid.*, 123-30.

[77] *Ibid.*, 131-34.

CHAPTER SOURCES

The following chapters have been previously published:

Chapter 1 – This is an edited, excerpted and augmented edition of a United States Congressional Research Service publication, Report Order Code R40707, dated July 14, 2009.

Chapter 2 – This is an edited, excerpted and augmented edition of a United States Government Accountability Office (GAO), Report to Congressional Committees. Publication GAO-07-753, dated July 2007.

Chapter 3 – This is an edited, excerpted and augmented edition of a United States Congressional Research Service publication, Report Order Code RS21795, dated December 20, 2007.

Chapter 4 – This is an edited, excerpted and augmented edition of a United States Congressional Research Service publication, Report Order Code R40171, dated January 29, 2009.

Chapter 5 – This is an edited, excerpted and augmented edition of a Social Security Advisory Board publication, dated September 2008.

INDEX

T

U

V

W